ISBN :   978-1-7377854-0-8

SCARS & STRIPES

A Journey through the US Immigration System

This book is a work of non-fiction.

The events and situations are true.

SCARS & STRIPES

DEDICATION

This book is dedicated to my wife, Dianne, and to my children, Sarah and Michael, without whose strength, patience, tolerance, understanding and belief in family, the outcome of this journey would have been very different. To my nephew and godson, Sean, who never lost hope, and even in our darkest hours continued to suggest new avenues to explore. To members of the US Marine Corps who provided invaluable support and testimonials about the efficacy and impact of my work in saving lives on the battle-field. To Wilton and Catherine Connor, the backbone of our underground immigration railroad. You have all been incredible travel-companions. To our fathers, Nick Ennis and Bertie Stewart, who never saw us cross the finish-line, and to our mothers, Kay Ennis (87) and Jennifer Stewart (92) who did. To our daughter, Sarah – the real victim of this journey. And of course, to the millions of immigrants who don't have the advantages we enjoyed – a white skin, a tertiary education, the English language, financial resources, and access to a network of privileged American Citizens.

Bruce Stewart
Charlotte, North Carolina
September 2021

REVIEWS

"A total rollercoaster and a horror story. A jaw-dropper of a book."
Peter Terry – Actor & Playwright

"A must-read for anyone coming to America."
Juli Treadway-Lawson – Author : So You've Networked – Now What?

"Riveting account of one family's dramatic quest for the American Dream."
Peter Hegarty – British American Textile Manufacturing Executive

"A shocking tale of a family trying to navigate the US Immigration System the "right" way, and how that broken system sends them to hell and back."
Byrn Hinton – Immigrant American Chief Technology Officer

"Brutal and inhumane. At times I felt embarrassed to be an American."
Anonymous – Senior Officer US Marine Corps

CONTENTS

FOREWORD

Charlotte, North Carolina

My name is Bruce Stewart. I've enjoyed 33 years of marriage to Dianne, and we have two children – Sarah, a Master's degree graduate and Michael, a Mechanical Engineering graduate. I spent my childhood in the little seaside village of Hermanus, about 80 miles south-east of Cape Town, South Africa, with my parents Bertie and Jennifer, and my younger siblings, Ian, Fiona and Craig.

My Dad was the local pharmacist and my Mum was privileged to be a stay-at-home mom, house-maker, homework-helper, driver and peace-maker. I attended Rondebosch Boys High School in Cape Town, received a law degree from Stellenbosch University and then moved to Johannesburg to work for the Department of Justice in 1976, the Coca-Cola Company in 1978, Consol Packaging in 1984 and then my own company, Speed Reading International, in 1988 (a company I had started in 1976).

In 1988 I married Dianne and we were blessed with Sarah in 1989 and Michael in 1994.

In 2001 we set out to pursue our dream of living in America.

This is our story.

SCARS & STRIPES

PROLOGUE – THE IRISH CONNECTION

In 1951, I am born in South Africa. For inexplicable reasons at the time, my father registers my birth as an Irish foreign birth, since my grandfather was born in Ireland. This entitles me to Irish Citizenship and an Irish Passport. Some years later, my wife and children also acquire derivative Irish Citizenship and Irish Passports.

In 1988, after failed talks with Israeli Prime Minister Simon Perez, Hamas, the extremist Palestinian Sunni-Islamic fundamentalist organization, establishes Unit 101, headed by Mahmoud al-Mabhouh, whose function is to kidnap Israeli soldiers. Unit 101's operators include Mohammed Youssef al-Sharatha and Muhammad Nazim Nasser.

On February 16, 1989, Sergeant Avi Sasportas of the Israeli Special Forces unit, Maglan, gets into a vehicle carrying two Hamas militants disguised as Israeli Jewish ultra-orthodox men, who kill him shortly thereafter by shooting him in the face. On May 7, 1989, Avi Sasportas' body is found buried in a field near the site at which he had been abducted.

On May 3, 1989, Corporal Ilan Saadoun is given a leave of absence from the Israeli military. Saadoun makes his way back home, hitch-hiking from Latrun, and arrives at the Masmiya intersection. At

19:30 a white Subaru car with Israeli license plates stops at a hitch-hiking stop. Mahmoud and Muhammad are in the vehicle, disguised as Israeli Jewish ultra-orthodox men, and they invite the soldier to join them. Saadoun gets in the car. During the ride, the kidnappers struggle with Saadoun and shoot him in the head. The attackers bury Saadoun's body in the Palmachim scrap site.

For the next 20 years, Israel plans revenge for the murders, and issues a "Red Page" order - Mossad's code name for an order to kill someone - to "Caesarea", the elite unit of the Mossad, the Israeli intelligence agency assigned to the riskiest missions and to do work involving sabotage, espionage and assassinations. Each of these orders is jointly authorized by the Israeli prime minister and defense minister. "Red Pages" do not have to be executed right away. In fact, they have no expiration date and the orders remain valid until they are expressly cancelled.

Unlike other intelligence agencies, the Mossad cannot provide its agents with real passports corresponding to a false identity. Instead, the Mossad usually uses the passports of Israelis with dual citizenship or forged passports from other countries.

On January 20, 2010, Mahmoud al-Mabhouh, code-named "Plasma Screen", is drugged, electrocuted and suffocated in his hotel room, room 230 at the Al Bustan hotel in Dubai, U.A.E. According to a Hamas statement, Al-Mabhouh had been involved in the 1989 abduction and killing of two Israeli soldiers, Avi Sasportas and Ilan Saadoun, whose murders he celebrated by standing on one of the corpses. In a videotaped admission, two weeks before his death, and broadcast on Al-Jazeera in early February 2010, Al-Mabhouh admitted his involvement, saying he had disguised himself as an Orthodox Jew.

Investigations into the assassination of Al-Mabhouh reveal that eight Irish passports are used in the assassination, and all are forgeries, but based on information from valid passports. Irish citizens whose information had been used for the forged passports are issued with new passports. Dubai Police have Interpol issue red notices (arrest warrants) for Gael Folliard, Kevin Daveron, Ivy Brinton, Evan Dennings and Anna Shauna Clasby, all of whom allegedly entered Dubai on forged Irish passports.

The United States declines a request from the United Arab Emirates to assist in an investigation into the assassination of Al-Mabhouh, the Hamas commander. The US denies reports that it had received a request for assistance from Dubai, but a WikiLeaks cable proves otherwise - a cable sent from the embassy in Dubai, less than a month after the assassination, reveals that senior UAE officials asked the American ambassador and US Secretary of State Hillary Clinton, to urgently probe "cardholder details and related information for credit cards reportedly issued by a US bank to several suspects" in the murder.

The WikiLeaks cable not only proves that the request was indeed made, but that it was recorded in a secret State Department cable. By not accepting the request, the Obama administration harms the Dubai investigation efforts, and assists Israel instead.

Unfortunately, we know nothing of this…...

In 2002, American citizen Bradley Gifford Wilde joins the US State Department and is posted to the US Embassy in Kuala Lumpur, Malaysia.

Born in San Francisco, California, Wilde lived in Guam and the Panama Canal Zone before returning to the USA to earn a Bachelor's Degree in Political Science from Stanford University, a Juris Doctor from Cornell School of Law and an MBA from UCLA. After some years in the private sector, Wilde joins the State Department and takes a posting in Kuala Lumpur, Malaysia. In March 2003 he attends a meeting of the secretariat of the ASEAN Regional Forum Inter-Sessional Meeting on Counter-Terrorism and Transnational Crime in Sabah, Malaysia. This is understood to be pursuant to Wilde's unofficial role with Diplomatic Security Services, a recently created "spook" service.

Wilde's next posting is as American Consul in the US Embassy, Budapest, Hungary, and in 2007 Wilde becomes Deputy Chief of American Citizen Services of the US Embassy in Manilla, Philippines.

By 2010, Bradley Wilde, the apparent "spook" from Diplomatic Security Services, and believed by some to be a staunch hibernophobe, has become head of the Visa Section in the US Embassy in Ballsbridge, Dublin, Ireland.

The first breezes of the impending storm have arrived. The Stewarts have Irish passports. Israel needs access to Irish passports for its Caesarean assassins. And alleged hibernophobe, Bradley Wilde, becomes head of the visa section of the US Embassy in Ireland, now effectively in control of every Irish Passport passing through the embassy in Ballsbridge, Ireland.

Of course, we know nothing of this either. In later years, with my training courses to the US military and US intelligence agencies, I will emphasize that it's not so much a matter of knowing what you know, or even knowing what you don't know, but rather the invariably far-reaching consequences of not knowing what you don't know.

PART 1 : AMERICAN DREAM

Monday July 9, 2001

We have landed. It is 10pm and we have spent our first day in the USA as immigrants to this country.

Getting here was a long journey - more than six months of planning and research before we submitted our application for the coveted L-1 Intra-company transfer visa and another six months of planning and tying up the pieces in South Africa. We'd set up a branch of Speed Reading International in the USA some time previously and needed to spend time here in building this business. We successfully petitioned for L-1 intra-company executive / managerial transfer visas to enable us to take up executive transfers between our parent company in South Africa and the US subsidiary.

Speed Reading International's core training program is ExecuRead, a proprietary methodology for rapidly processing incoming written data, triaging this data for mission relevance, critically analyzing the data for potential risk-impact, and decision-making for appropriate action and response. In South Africa this training is in high demand by executives and managers in competitive industries and by financial analysts. Increased enquiries from the UK and USA prompted a decision to expand the business internationally.

The United States immigration system is a complex set of laws designed to regulate and control entry into the United States, regardless of whether you want to come here for a holiday or for business purposes. Originally called the Immigration and Naturalization Service, the INS was all about regulation and control, and to get into the USA you need one of literally dozens of visas, each of which is controlled by a complex set of regulations. A business-person wanting to enter the USA for business reasons would require a B-1 visa, a tourist, a B-2 visa and a student wanting to come here for study purposes, an F-1 visa. These are all non-immigrant non-employment visas – they are temporary in nature and do not entitle the bearer to stay in the USA permanently or to seek permanent residence or to take up employment in the USA.

Should you however wish to come to the USA to work, you need an employment-based visa, such as an H-1B visa if you have been offered skilled-worker employment, or an L-1 visa if you are being transferred between an overseas company and a branch in the USA. Within the category of L visas, we have the 7-year L-1A visa for intra-company transfers of executives and managers, and the 5-year L-1B visa for intra-company transfers of workers with specialized knowledge. Again, the H and L visas are non-immigrant visas -- they are temporary in nature and do not entitle the bearer to stay in the USA permanently or to seek permanent residence. Indeed, should the bearer of an H or L visa have a change of heart and wish to seek permanent residence in the USA, the visa status needs to be changed from non-immigrant status to immigrant status, through the filing of an I-140 Change of Status petition, and if this is approved, the filing of an I-485 petition for permanent residence is required.

Unlike the L visa, which is essentially a transfer of a senior manager or specialist within company operations, because the H-1B visa allows you to accept employment in the USA, your prospective employer has to show that the job cannot be filled from the US labor force. Similarly, most of the employment-based green cards also require evidence that the position could not be filled from the local labor work-force, before the skill can be imported. The bottom line therefor is that if you want to work in the USA, the first and biggest step is to successfully petition for an employment-based visa.

The Rolls Royce of employment based non-immigrant visas is the L-1A executive / managerial transfer visa. For two important reasons – firstly, there is no requirement to show that the job cannot be filled from the local US labor force, and secondly, the requirements for the L-1A visas are identical to the requirements for a possible I-140 petition to convert the visa from non-immigrant to immigrant status, the doorway to petitioning for permanent residence.

To qualify for our L-1A visas, we had to prove the following :

- *That Dianne and I HAD been employed as executives / managers of the South African company for at least a full year,*
- *That Dianne and I WILL be employed in executive / managerial positions within the US company,*
- *That there is a qualifying relationship between the South African and US companies.*

This was hardly insurmountable. I founded the South African business in 1979 and Dianne and I had jointly managed the company since 1988. Plus, as the joint owners of the South African entity, we will accordingly be the sole owners of the US affiliate entity.

That our L-1 visas are only valid for 1 year is, according to our immigration attorney, to give the USA an "out" if we prove unworthy of the USA or if our business fails and the USA is at risk of having to support us.

For insurance purposes, both Dianne and I petition, individually, for, and are granted, L-1A executive transfer visas. Although at double the cost, the principal benefits are two-fold :

1. Dianne will be permitted to work, and

2. in the event of something happening to me, she will not lose her status in the USA.

Under the prevailing law, without an L-1 visa, Dianne will only have a derivative L-2 visa which is granted to the spouse and children of the L-1 visa-holder. But if the L-1 visa-holder loses that visa, such as dying or becoming permanently incapacitated and unable to work, or even losing his or her employment with the petitioning company, the derivative visa-holders lose their status immediately and have to leave the country. With a separate petition and now being an L-1 visa-holder in her own right, Dianne's status will be independent of mine.

An important note here is that the legacy INS (now USCIS) has accepted the submitted evidence that BOTH Dianne and I

- *WERE employed in executive / managerial positions in the South African company, and*
- *WILL be employed in executive / managerial positions in the US company, and*
- *that a qualifying relationship EXISTS between the South African and US companies.*

If something can go wrong, it probably will.

As the final weeks in South Africa draw to a close, the little problems start – our 'unbelievable' buyer of everything, becomes no more than a "Walter Mitty", leaving us in the lurch at the last moment with everything unsold and very little funding for a project which consumes money at a prolific rate. Having wound down BSA, a public relations consultancy that Dianne and I started in 1989 just after we got married, the financial burden on Speed Reading International becomes even greater.

If that's not enough, at D-day minus two weeks, Michael goes to hospital, pale, sick and very weak, with some very disturbing blood analysis results. After a week in hospital and a bone marrow biopsy, we know that he does NOT have cancer, but are none the wiser as to what he does have. Three days later he is rushed back to hospital with a suspected testicular torsion, and after an abdominal operation to repair a congenital hydro-seal, we are at D-day minus two and very uncertain as to whether he will be fit enough to travel. Plan B is that Sarah and I will go ahead, with Michael and Dianne to follow later. On Saturday morning, the day of departure, the doctors pronounce Michael fit to travel as a partial invalid.

By this time, my work time-table is in disarray. When Pickfords Removals move into our home in Fourways, Johannesburg, and consign everything to either the airfreight shippers for immediate shipment, or to storage for later containerization, the family moves in with Dianne's sister and brother-in-law. This proves a hindrance to my efforts to finish off the office work and I move back into an empty house where I can be close to my office and unrestricted in the working hours I am keeping. I am surviving on cold-showers, coffee and cigarettes. Tempers start getting frayed on Thursday morning – the previous afternoon, Dianne had finished tidying up the Fourways house and had inadvertently packed my bath-towel : at 3am the following morning, after 2 hours sleep, I rush out of bed for a quick shower before heading for the airport and my flight to an out-of-town training course. After a piping hot shower followed by 60 seconds under the ice-cold (mid-winter) water to wake me up, I find no towel and not a sausage to get dry with. Getting bluer by the minute, I eventually find a soiled dish-cloth in the kitchen laundry basket and this has to suffice! Words are spoken later that day.

Saturday. D-day. Family and friends gather for the final farewells – not a good idea. The kids start howling first. Then the mothers add their tears and wailing to the melee, and finally few of the fathers can retain any serious degree of composure. Not good. Very cruel to all concerned. Next time – announce you are leaving on Monday and sneak off 3 days earlier!

At 5pm we are off to the airport – a bigger entourage than the President of the United States – 15 pieces of baggage filling 3 cars, plus those family and friends brave enough, silly enough and still with tears to shed. We arrive at Johannesburg International Airport and it's pandemonium – thousands of people crowding into an airport designed by a committee of architectural drop-outs, with numerous carefully designed bottle-necks all aimed at raising frustration levels and delaying that magical time when you can end the agony of tears, guilt and heart-break.

Finally in a fit of airport-rage, I totally lose my cool, announce that someone should burn the fucking place down and start all over again, and then proceed to tear down the barricades and clear a path for the melee of passengers and trolleys to get moving again. Not a word from the airport staff – I think that if any of them were to identify themselves, the other passengers will do to them what I have just done to their pretty but bloody useless barricades.

At check-in counter, we arrange a wheel-chair for Michael and prime him to be crestfallen and sore but brave and 'feeling ok'. Consigned to a wheel-chair (after all – he has a 3-inch incision in his stomach that is only 3 days old), we are whisked through emigration and passport control and head for the front of every queue (line, to my American friends). Nothing other than VIP treatment all the way, with dedicated porters to help Michael with his 15 pieces of baggage! Bugger First or Business Class – next time we fly, it's "C-Class"! We even get taken out to the plane in the special truck that hoists you up in the air and allows you to move out of the truck and straight into the plane without climbing stars. And what a big plane it is – over 70 meters long with 377 passengers and not an empty seat to spare.

Finally, at 8pm on Saturday we are on the plane – the 747-400 SAA/Delta special to Atlanta, reputed to be the longest almost-non-stop flight these days – something like 15 or 16 hours with a brief refueling and crew-change stopover at Sal Island off the coast of Dakar – a lovely half-way break with fresh air, a chance to stretch legs and have a smoke.

Then it's back on the plane for the second half of this very long 8700-mile (14000km) flight. For once we have absolutely no difficulty in sleeping in cattle-class seats – with so little sleep over the past 6 months, we sleep the sleep of the dead. And it's a long sleep too – we are flying East to West, and so the darkness of night continues for 15 hours or more, as we are flying away from the rising sun.

Little do we know that others, out in the deserts of Arabia, are planning their own trip to the USA. Neither do we have any inkling of how THAT trip will impact our own lives.

Finally at dawn, the sun is up and Oh! what a spectacular view. The Boeing 747-400 is floating, seemingly at the very edge of space – flying at over 560mph (900kph), those ultra-long, slender wings are almost like those of a glider – 220 feet (66.44 meters) from tip to tip. We are 38,000 feet (11,500 meters) above the surface of the earth and the temperature is a life-crushing -95° Fahrenheit (-70° Celsius). The sky is a painfully deep blue, and the cloud-formations are so far below us, it's hard to imagine that terra firma is even further down.

The awakening brings back the harsh reality of what we have done, and it's a sobering thought. While the hysteria of the previous day became, to some degree, a self-sustaining process, it appears inescapable that we have left a hole in the lives of a number of people, and while we are the richer for having known those people, we are all the poorer for having lost each other. And yet, in spite of the pain we have caused to so many people in making this move, it has become a mission so important to us that we will pay almost any price.

A prophetic thought on my part.

A sardonic chuckle on the part of father Fate.

Many raised the question – having achieved so much in South Africa in terms of success, friends and material possessions, why risk it all so late in life? The answer is simply this – we don't know why. All we know is that this is the logical next step in our lives. It's a gut thing. Oh yes, we have tried to rationalize it in terms of the South African situation – crime, education, security, currency – but if those were the reasons, we would be experiencing feelings of anger at being forced to leave. This is not the case – we are overjoyed that America has tested us, and found us worthy – given us the opportunity to experience a nation that half the world wants to emulate and the other half destroy. America is the standard by which everything is measured and we have a chance to be part of that.

We have tried to weigh the pros and cons – at 50, I should be thinking of retirement, not gambling everything on a new business in a new country. But then I am not 50 – that's just some screw-up on my birth certificate! I still have the energy (or at least most of it) that I had when I started this business in 1976, I have become wiser (I think!), smarter (I hope) and certainly more passionate about the subject. I don't really believe that failure is an option - I know that the rewards will justify the risk and I have a great team – if you want the world to know about something, tell it to Dianne!

Immigration is less about moving to another country than it's about learning another way of life.

Like so many immigrants before us, the first couple of months will be a roller-coaster of new experiences. Finding our feet and trying to cope with the avalanche of new information. Sadly, we know no-one in Charlotte, North Carolina, so cannot get advice about how things are done here. I guess there are some pitfalls out there.

Day 1. Sunday July 8, 2001

We arrive in Atlanta. Ouch! It's 95° F and about 98% humidity. As we are still flying "C - Class", Michael has loads of porters to push his wheel-chair and carry his 15 pieces of luggage. After customs and immigration, mere formalities -- we go straight to the front of the queue – you don't screw around with the "Amakrokakroka" (an endearing Zulu slang term for broken-people – not politically correct however!) -- we are about to hire our Buick from Alamo Car

Hire when the genius behind the counter sees the 15 pieces of luggage, 3 pulley-bags and Michael in the wheel-chair and suggests that we might want to consider something a little bigger than the Buick! We settle for a nice big Chevy Venture MPV, load it to the gunnels with our stuff and set off for the so-called 4-hour drive from Atlanta to Charlotte, little realizing that Sunday 8 July is the last day of the 4 July Independence Day long-weekend! We're learning our first lesson! It's a very long and tiring trip!

We arrive in Charlotte NC on Sunday evening, dump our stuff and crash, 27 hours after leaving Johannesburg airport. We are staying in a delightful corporate apartment, fully furnished, three bedrooms, two bathrooms, double-story, big lounge with all appliances. We'll be here for most of this week until we have the opportunity to buy or rent some furniture for our permanent apartment at Beacon Hill Lane – still being cleaned, painted, carpeted – four bedrooms, three bathrooms, lounge, dining, kitchen, attic and office/den for me.

We are having our small frustrations that not only make life interesting, but which are the start of our USA education process – we ordered a Chevy Blazer before we left South Africa and it is now supposed to be waiting for us at the local Charlotte Chevy Dealer. However, before we can collect our vehicle, we need to get our social security numbers and arrange for vehicle insurance. And Social Security numbers are applied for and granted via the internet. But I do not have internet access. To get internet access and to get vehicle insurance, I need a bank account in the USA. But to get a bank account I need a social security number. I feel a bit like a fox chasing its own tail.

Finally, I call Paul Westervelt, a new friend we made on our 2000 "look-see-decide" trip, and ask him to 'loan' me his internet user-name and password so I can start making some progress. Now we try to get legal. Once we move into the more permanent apartment which will be our home until we have enough cash-flow to buy a house, I will get a cable internet link-up – 24 hours a day online and very fast. Sounds almost surreal when compared to the mind-numbing speeds of dial-up in South Africa.

Doing a quick shop today – not a good idea to compare prices if paying with South African Rands at R8 to $1. How times have changed. Back in the seventies when I came to the USA with Coca-Cola, we were getting a Dollar-and-a-Quarter for every Rand.

Day 7. Saturday July 14, 2001

Buying anything in the USA on 'tick' (credit) is not as easy as it seems. Even more difficult than buying a house, is buying a car – because so many people pay the deposit and then sneak the car across the border into Mexico.

So we got smart … or so we thought! For immigrants moving to the USA, you can order your car before you arrive, and all of the paperwork is done in advance, including the financing, credit investigations, etc. To give you a chance to get all the paperwork together and the deal signed and sealed while you still have your South African life intact. This is all done by International Autosource in New York. We do a great deal (we think), order a Chevy Blazer 4x4 at a discounted price of $30,000 including all the extras, taxes and bells and whistles. A $3,000 deposit (paid in South Africa) and an interest rate of 5.9% over 3 years will leave us with a monthly repayment of only $830 (the number looks small enough to someone working with Rands!) and the car will be ready for collection from a Charlotte dealer anytime from 7 July, the day of our departure from South Africa. All looks OK, but we are soon to learn that South Africa does not hold exclusive rights to royal fuck-ups!

On Monday we call the dealer to arrange a time to collect our Blazer.

"What Blazer?" he asks.

"The Blazer delivered by International Autosource," we say.

"Don't know about this one", he says, "but we'll look into it."

On Tuesday we go to visit the dealer – you know, to help him find our car. After an hour or more there, and the temperature is over 100 degrees with energy-sapping humidity, we all agree that the car is not there. We phone New York and ask them to find out where the blazes my Blazer is.

"We'll get back to you," says New York.

So off we go to do some more shopping.

Then the call. (Important tip here – don't even think of moving to the USA unless you have a cell phone operational from the minute you arrive here!) New York advises that my Blazer has gone to California – some idiot in Detroit got confused between California and Carolina – but no problem, the Blazer will be here in about four weeks! But, if you REALLY need something very similar, we can do that for you in about two weeks!

Bugger the waiting, let's see what's on the dealer's lot and get something NOW. Back to the dealer.

"Have you got a Blazer for me," I ask.

"Sure do," he says, "but the Blazer is being discontinued and we have a few left with good discounts. We can do you a full-house Blazer for $27,000!" Strike one against International Autosource for trying to sell me a 'dud' at an inflated price! "Why not go for the TrailBlazer – bigger, better, more features and not much more costly – got a beauty right here in the lot?"

"Wow," we say, "what great service. OK, we'll take this one – you do the paperwork, we'll be back on Wednesday to finalize and collect the car."

On Wednesday we arrive, only to be told that they've sold my car and that a new one will arrive that afternoon. OK, what the heck - this is a bit like South African service, but with an American accent.

We'll go shopping again. Nice big auction of office furniture. We buy a whole bunch of stuff and off to U-Haul to hire a truck.

"Bad luck Mr Stewart – you don't have a driver's license."

"Nonsense," I say, "I have an International Driver's License."

"No," she says, "that's an International Driving PERMIT and not a license. Come back when you have a driver's license!"

"Well, can I rent a trailer from you?," I ask.

"Sure honey," she says, "just as soon as you find a car with a tow-hitch! And by the way, you cannot rent cars with tow-hitches in the USA."

So it's back to the dealer. "Where's my f----ing Trailblazer???"

"It will be here tomorrow – in the meantime, get your comprehensive insurance organized – you cannot drive away without insurance."

I call Allstate Insurance. "Howdy ma'am. I need full cover insurance for a Trailblazer."

"No sir, cannot help – you must have been driving for 6 months before you qualify for full coverage."

"Lady, I've been driving for 35 years!"

"Sorry Sir, if not in the USA, it doesn't qualify. Bad luck."

"Okay, so how does a new driver in this country get insurance?" I ask.

"I guess new drivers are covered by their parent's insurance. Perhaps you could ask your parents to add you to their policy?"

"They live in South Africa."

"Oh dear! That is a bit of a problem."

Back to the Chevy Dealer. "Ok guys, I'm getting pissed. It's almost a week and I'm no closer to a car than I was a week ago. Let's forget about everything else. Just assume that I walked in here with the following deal – I want a TrailBlazer by tomorrow (Friday) – and I want you to finance this car AND get me full-coverage insurance, all within 24 hours. Can you do this?"

"No sir, you have no credit rating in the USA."

"Okay" I say, "let's up the ante a bit – what if I put down $10k cash as a deposit?"

"Oh yes sir, 10 grand buys you a whole bunch of credit rating."

Done!

It's now Friday afternoon. Still no car. And still no progress report from the Chevy dealership. We're on our way home feeling somewhat demoralized. We need a car and I need to go and collect my stuff from the auctioneer. Suddenly a radio advert – Keffer Dodge – the biggest Dodge Dealer in Town - come and see the New Dodge Viper – a snip at $75K!

"Yeah Dad," shouts Michael, "let's go see a Viper."

So we go window-shopping at Keffer Dodge. We meet a nice young salesman who knows bugger-all about what he's selling, we all ogle the Viper, nod at the Intrepid Motorsport and then kick the tires of the Dodge Durango - a mean-looking 4x4 with a 5.7 liter V8 Magnum engine and 3 rows of seats. Does everything except make coffee.

"Interested?" he asks politely (this, by the way, is potentially his very first sale!).

"Well pal," I say, "I've been given a run-around by the palookas at Chevy and I'm a touched pissed with the world. It's 4pm on Friday afternoon and I've got 5 grand in my wallet as a cash deposit if you can put me behind the wheel of this Durango before 4pm tomorrow (Saturday)."

You've never seen a salesman work so fast. In under an hour, he is back with us, very apologetically asking whether we can increase the deposit slightly – "it's not that our finance people don't trust you – it's just that you've been in the USA for under a week, you're renting your apartment and all your furniture, you don't have a job or any other source of income and your company hasn't started trading yet, you have no credit score, and this makes them just a tiny bit cautious."

"No problem, how about 10 grand?"

"Oh, much better Sir!"

He's back in an hour. "Congratulations Mr Stewart. Your finance has been approved and we can have you in the car within the next hour or so."

"What's the deal," we ask.

"Only $600 a month over 5 years," he says.

"What's the interest rate?" I ask.

"They didn't tell me that," he says.

"Well go ask them!" He's back in a flash, but not before I do my sums. "It's only 11 percent," he says. That's an effective rate of 16.25%!

We stand up and start walking out. "No deal, we can get 5.9% from General Motors – unless you can sharpen your pencil, forget it. Let's sleep on it."

Saturday morning – Keffer Dodge calls. "Mr Stewart, the best we can do is 8.75%, your finance is approved, we've got full-coverage insurance and we'll throw in a tow-package. If you can get here by 11am, we'll have you driving out of Keffer Dodge in your new Durango by 1pm."

And here we are. Proud owners of a new Dodge Durango R/T at last. There's a moral here. Before trying this immigration thing, you need education far more than preparation – Dianne spent 3 weeks in South Africa preparing a file on our credit situation in South Africa – certificates of earnings, financial statements, letters from bankers and creditors, insurance records, an ITC report and a full international Dun & Bradstreet report – there was no need for any financial institution in the USA to need anything that was not contained in that file. Or so we think! The reality however is that the Dodge financing was based solely on the 30 percent deposit. The USA takes not the slightest interest in your overseas credit record. If it's not an American credit report, it's not a credit report! Pure and simple. There's even a Dun & Bradstreet International and a Dun & Bradstreet USA and I doubt they even know about one another in terms of sharing client information.

But we have our 'wheels' and Michael, with his 7-year-old flair for innocent questions and comments that lays us in the isles, asks whether a Keffer Dodge is like a 'Keffer Taxi' in South Africa??!! Yeah, I know. Not PC. But funny nonetheless. Years later, Dianne will be driving a Hyundai, purchased from Keffer, and with her personalized number plate "Budgie". We have some South African guests visiting us and cannot understand why they are looking at Dianne's Keffer Budgie tag and roaring with laughter. Then the penny drops! OMG! It's a fly thing. I'm not going to explain this. Just let it be!

On the home front, the kids have been incredible – they're spending 12 hours or more a day in the car, sitting, waiting for us to do all of those mundane things required to set up home – organizing social security cards, registering the kids for income tax, organizing telephones, electricity, and tons of shopping – crockery, cutlery, kitchen stuff, washing machine and tumble-dryer, microwave, furniture, etc. For the first time we're being exposed to a non-metric world, used only by the USA, Liberia and Burma, (for you Trivia folk!)

When we initially decided on this move, we had to sell the idea to our children and our families. And in doing so, we were really selling it to ourselves as well. We were creating an illusion. And reality is sometimes not as perfect as the illusion. We soon realize that to maintain confidence and enthusiasm levels, set-backs need to be down-played, minimized and then re-packaged as something totally expected. And while this was directed at the children, it also worked pretty well for Dianne and I.

We've not started any work as yet – we need to finalize setting up home and office and then I can start putting in some salt-mine time. We are still awaiting the airfreight – although we were told that the airfreight (all of the office equipment) would come on the same plane as us, or at most a day later, we subsequently find out that the airfreight takes 10 days to 2 weeks!! Bit of a pain as I cannot do much until it arrives.

All in all, a week into our new adventure, and it's as good or even better than we expected. But we're on a very steep learning curve and realize that very little is the same as it was back home.

Tuesday July 24, 2001

We've been in the USA for 16 days. We're settled into our new apartment and at the rate of R8 to the Dollar, are on a roller-coaster of expenditure and discovery of this complex and fascinating country. We still multiply by 8 because we're still spending the Rands we brought with us. The weather is still 85-degrees-plus, with very high humidity, so the air-conditioner runs pretty much non-stop.

We've filled the Durango for the second time at $1.50 a gallon for premium unleaded and learn another strange anomaly about the US

– a US Fluid Gallon is 3.8 liters or 4 quarts, while the British Imperial Gallon is 4.5 liters, equivalent to 10 pounds or 4.5 kilograms of distilled water.

We have still not received our airfreight, so I am still not working – apparently our airfreight has gone to Istanbul in Turkey. Yeah, explain that one to me. Just look at a map to see the relative positions of South Africa, Turkey and America!

We've had two telephone lines installed by Bell South, the local telephone company. The telephone people do not supply telephone units so we're off to buy some at Best Buy, the discount electronics store. Then when we try to telephone the shippers in Ohio, the phone service keeps telling us that our call cannot be connected at this time. I phone Bell South and ask why I cannot call Ohio.

"Well Sir, Ohio is another state. Who is your long-distance carrier?'" he asks.

I am tempted to say South African Airways, but I suspect this is not what he is looking for and ask him what he means.

"Well, the long-distance telephone service was de-regulated some years ago, and you have a choice of long-distance toll carriers."

"You mean the service we have in South Africa where we use Telkom to call next door or anywhere in the world, does not apply to the USA?"

"No Sir, with Bell South you have a service to make calls within the Carolinas – that's called Intralata. If you want to make calls outside the Carolinas, called Interlata, you need a long-distance carrier."

"Well, how many long-distance carriers are there?"

"About 60! "

"Can you recommend a suitable carrier?" I ask.

"No Sir, by law, Bell South may not recommend a carrier."

"Ok, can I ask you, who do YOU use at home?"

"Sorry sir, I cannot divulge that information either."

"OK then, help me out here – I am a dumb immigrant from South Africa, now in Charlotte. My car went to California, my luggage went to Turkey and I cannot make a phone call and the phone company won't tell me how to get connected. If you were in my shoes, what would you do?"

"Wow", he gasps, "first of all, I'm glad I'm NOT in your shoes, but I would go and read the Bell South phone-book – it has a wealth of information which should help you. Thank you for calling Bell South."

"WAIT!" I interrupt. "Where do I find a Bell South phone-book? When they connected me, they never gave me one?"

"There are three places you can get a phone-book. Here are the addresses ….."

A quick look at the map – they are on the other side of the city.

"Dad", the kids ask, "what's our big adventure for tomorrow?"

"We're going to find a phone-book!!!!"

"YEAH!!!!"

Of course, all too soon, this fun stuff will be replaced by a cell-phone, and land-lines will become all but obsolete. And parents and kids will be denied the pleasures of scouring the neighborhood for a phone-book which has also become obsolete.

Banking seems a lot easier. We are quite friendly with John Steadman, the president of the Scottish Bank here in Charlotte. A nice family boutique bank that has no glass wall between you and the teller, calls you by your first name, knows most of their customers by name and has soda, lollipops and popcorn dispensers in the banking hall for the customers and their kids. We open a personal account and four days later a box of five check-books (aka cheque-books) arrive in my mail-box.

Responding to an article in the local paper about the USA being so short of blood that they schedule two operations for the same time-slot, even though they only have sufficient blood for one of them, hoping that one patient won't leak at all, or that both patients will only leak a little bit, and being a serious blood donor myself (I have now donated some 54 pints), I tootle off to the local Charlotte blood bank to dump a pint.

"What blood-group are you," they ask.

"A-positive, low rhesus, high hemoglobin and CMV negative," I answer.

"Oh great, just what we need," they reply. "Where are you from?"

"South Africa."

"Sorry, come back in three years. Because of the Aids and Malaria risks in Africa, we don't take blood from Africa unless the donor has been out of Africa for an uninterrupted three years!"

The locals, I call them Charlatans, Di is more polite with Charlotteans, have yet to discover what that funny little sticky-out thing is on the side of the steering column. When you wiggle it only half your lights come on (and then they keep flashing) and since that is not enough to see where you are going, it makes a good place to hang your litter-bag. The silly buggers never indicate – just suddenly stop in either the left or right lane. Sometimes it's because of a traffic jam or because the fellow wants to turn left or right. As a result, the most common accident is bumper-bashing or a fender-bender. The only problem is that most cars are cell-phone-driven, soccer-mom-

and-kids-bearing SUVs (aka sports utility vehicles or 4x4s) and if one of these goes up your bum you are well and truly sorted out. Saw a brand-new Jeep Grand Cherokee with an F150 truck up its rear end. What a mess! I suppose it's a language issue. Americans call them "turn-signals" as in "I'm turning now". Civilized folk call them "indicators" as in "It is my intention to turn in a short while so you better get off my ass before I start slowing down."

Car insurance is not cheap. You must by law have liability insurance – that's 3rd party and balance of 3rd party. Insurance is also capped – in other words, you select your level of coverage. For example, I have vehicle insurance of $30k to cover the value of my Durango and then to cover 3rd party I have elected $30k per victim and $60k per accident. If I happen to nail a car full of people and they all get seriously hurt and claim a load of dollars from me, then my insurance will only pay $60k and I am in the can for the balance! I suppose this is why US insurance companies make a mint and the South African 3rd party guys are going down the toilet where the fuel levy buys you almost unlimited cover from a fund that has been raided by Government for years.

We've just come back from our big adventure of the day – exploring the city for a phone-book! Bell South gave us three addresses – all on the opposite side of town – very seedy and no trees. Hit No 1 : "Sorry Honey we're clean outa dem right now. Best you try North Graham". Only about 10 miles away in a totally different direction, an even seedier industrial area populated with a wide selection of fur-lined convertible 1970 Cadillacs, housing sound systems with subs that you can hear three blocks away, and cool dudes with more gold chains and bigger muscles than Mr T. We get a phone-book (yellow and white pages) and feel a lot safer – it's so thick and heavy you could brain a bison with it. Enthusiastically we turn to the front pages – remember, all this shit is about how to find a long-distance carrier so I can find my airfreight and get my shoes – the people at the bank now recognize me as the chap who has been wearing the same clothes and sandals since he opened his account two weeks ago! What do we find in the front pages of the bison-bashing Bell South book? Bugger-all, other than the message – "For long distance carriers, call your local Bell South office!" What did the seagull say just before it flew into the cliff? FaaaaaaaaaaaaaaaaaaaaCK!!

The Pickfords Debacle

In considering our move from Johannesburg, South Africa to Charlotte, North Carolina, possibly the most important feature, in our minds, is the selection and appointment of an international moving company to pack, store and ship our worldly possessions.

All too soon the word is out that we are moving, and the vultures are at the door, all bidding for our business with bigger and better promises.

We have two special requirements : firstly, that our personal goods and office supplies be airfreighted to the USA by a reputable agent (to enable us to start our business without delay) and secondly, a reputable company to store the contents of our home until we are settled in the USA and ready to buy a house and take shipment of our South African home contents.

Leading the field is Allied Pickfords, represented by Maylene Cape. Backed by the so-called reputation of Pickfords, she makes us two key selling offers – Pickfords will airfreight our office goods to us within a day or so of our flight to the USA, and Pickfords has a deal with International AutoSource whereby we are able to buy a car, while in South Africa, for delivery in the USA on our arrival, with all the necessary financing and paperwork being done in South Africa. A great selling proposal and we were hooked. It's Pickfords.

During the period 25 – 28 June, Pickfords packs and collects the contents of our Fourways home and collects the shipment for airfreight (most of which we have already packed). And does a stunning job! On Friday 6 July, I deliver the last couple of boxes for airfreighting to USA. I meet with Craig Sinclair, the Pickfords export coordinator and receive my first disappointment – notwithstanding Maylene Cape's promise that the airfreight will take only a couple of days, Craig Sinclair now advises that shipment will take 7 -10 days – he will do the final packing on Monday 8 July, ship on Tuesday 10 July and that we will only receive shipment by about 20 July.

A week after we arrive in the USA, I start making enquiries about our airfreight. Suddenly alarm bells started ringing – my emails to Pickfords in South Africa go unanswered and Allied Pickfords in Chicago, other than never answering their phones, prove to be most unhelpful. In addition, we hear that the airfreight is in Istanbul, Turkey, having been airfreighted on Turkish Airlines.

I then receive an email from Craig Sinclair, telling me that I must have misunderstood him about airfreighting on 10 July as he still has to pack the shipment. He advises that the shipment left South Africa on 20 July. What he was doing for 14 days between 6 July and 20 July, God only knows! (His staff packed a 40-foot container PLUS my airfreight in 4 days!) Perhaps my now-missing collection of fine Scotch Whiskey contributed to the speedy handling of my possessions …?

It is now 25 July and we are no closer to a solution. We do not know where our airfreight is and neither does Pickfords in South Africa or Allied Pickfords in the USA.

I have been sitting in the USA for 17 days waiting for the Pickfords miracle. The costs are mounting – I have already cancelled all advertising and marketing campaigns and cannot re-plan these until Pickfords finds out what has happened to my airfreight shipment. Is this another example of South African marketing bullshit – keep catching the customers and to hell with service? Would it be so difficult to keep in touch with the customer, with regular follow-ups – how did your trip go?, did everything turn out OK with International Auto Source?, anything we can help you with?, here is the status of your airfreight, if you need to find out anything about your shipment, please call this number and quote this tracking code!

The ball has now been given to Wanda Dodds at Pickfords, who has promised to investigate and get back to me. Let's see whether this story can possibly have a happy ending…

Day 33. Thursday August 9, 2001

We've been here 33 days and the bad news is that the airfreight has STILL not arrived, but the good news is that has apparently reached Charlotte. But we'll believe it when we actually set eyes on it. Our biggest concern is whether Pickfords has sent the correct stuff and not got our instructions all mixed up. The move from Fourways and Hermanus was so complicated as some items went into storage for the shipping-container, some items came with us on the flight out and the rest was meant to come via airfreight, as there was just too much to have taken with us as excess baggage. So, let's see if they managed to get that one right!

We're loving the local radio stations that give us so much more than the snippets of American news broadcast on stations in South Africa. Of course, back home, we, and I suppose the rest of the world, followed the Oval Office antics of President Clinton. Now in the States, we're getting American news round the clock. We're listening to a great talk radio station here called Newstalk Eleven Ten (1110 AM) and a hysterical program on Clinton having been given a $10 million advance on his new book, and listeners are asked to name the new book. Some suggestions include "My Life as the President - blow-by-blow!", …Di and I nearly crash the Durango, we are laughing so hard! Some years later I read that school-girls have no hesitation in giving the boys a "Lewinsky" to help them alleviate school stress. And that this service is proffered between classes in the stairwells and locker-rooms, often without much regard to privacy. After all, it's not sex. The President said so!

On Friday night we go "Uptown" (not downtown like in other US cities, but uptown, as the CBD is actually UP on a hill, and calling it downtown just isn't good enough for this particular city, or so say the locals. Some think it rather pretentious, but we sort of like the Uptown bit!!) So off we go "Uptown", to see "Raiders of the Lost

27

Ark" projected onto a vast empty wall on the side of one of the skyscrapers. We all sit in the square below with the movie above us. It's packed with families, oldies and children and it's like having a picnic in the center of the city. All pretty impressive. There we all are, enjoying a wonderful balmy evening with the full moon in a navy sky overhead, surrounded by the Bank of America 120-floor edifice, and some of the most awesome skyscrapers in the South. It's the event that's important, not the quality of the show. Everyone has already seen the movie anyhow, so it's more about the social outing than anything else. Most of the people around us end up chatting to everyone else and commenting and laughing at the movie, so it is by all accounts, a fun evening. We have a great couple behind us with their enormous Rottie (Rottweiler), that weighs about 180 pounds and desperately wants Michael's chicken burger, and their 6-month-old baby who is so well-behaved and never makes a peep. The best part about the evening? It's for FREE! Charlotte has these free evening events all the time and there is always a lot to choose from – Jazz, classical, outdoor theatre, concerts in the park. And of course, perfectly safe with cops all around for added personal security, all enjoying the event together.

The thing that amazes us constantly is receiving the mail at the door, hand delivered by the Mailman (or woman) each day (except Sunday) promptly at 12h30. You can even leave your outgoing mail for him/her to collect from the box when your mail is delivered. We get so excited opening the door each day at 12h30 to see what's arrived. It's like a present every day, only now it's mostly bills! The newspaper (The Charlotte Observer) also arrives every morning at 7am wrapped in a plastic bag, without fail, seven days a week.

Day 34. Friday August 10, 2001

We receive a call from the Charlotte agent to say that our airfreight has arrived at their offices. They get here 30 minutes later and a friend and I unload the entire 56 large boxes of stuff all packed in two enormous air containers. It's all very exciting to see all our goodies. However, Dianne's solid-silver Flute is missing, as is the box of cables needed to connect the office computers, printers &

peripherals. Not quite sure what has happened to them – either they were left behind at Pickfords or they were nicked prior to shipping, as everything that was on the manifest arrives safely. Just another irritation to sort out.

We have been looking at houses and gosh, what an incredible choice. Americans certainly know how to build stunning houses – as for the kitchens and bathrooms – sensational. Someone said that life in heaven should be as follows: You must marry a South African, drive a German car, eat French and Italian food and live in an American house – how true!

Lesson learned this week : A Credit score is THE most important thing to get going in the US! And the key contributors to a credit score are a mortgage and a credit card! Even car finance is not taken as seriously as a credit card record. The only problem is that you don't have a hope in hell of getting a credit card unless you have existing credit. So, if you don't have existing credit, you can't get a credit card! Solution? You have to apply for them. Problem! If you apply too much and too often, and get turned down too many times, this is a big black mark against you. So, what do you do? Well, nothing - you are stuck in a circle of doom. In desperation and after being turned down about six times by various credit card banks, we are advised to stop applying immediately as this is damaging our future chances. We decide to dump the problem fairly and squarely in our bank manager's lap and tell him to fix! Now we wait to see what happens in the next few days.

Watching the media and especially the news on TV is an interesting experience. Local news TV stations cover Charlotte and its immediate surrounds. The World News TV stations, however, include items on stuff almost exclusively in the US or to do with US people, but does not include Europe, South America, Asia and never Africa! CNN International is not broadcast in the US at all, and CNN here is also only national news. It seems to me that the US population is not interested in what is happening outside the US, although come to think of it, the country is so enormous, with so much going on, that they would most likely have to have a 2-hour news broadcast to incorporate the rest of the world's news.

Little do we know that within a very short space of time, the average American will be faced with the "discovery" of two new countries, Iraq and Afghanistan, until now virtually unknown to all but a few "fringe" and "alarmist" intelligence analysts.

Having witnessed the abolition of the death penalty in South Africa in 1995, we are surprised to see that 31 US States still adhere to this practice. North Carolina executed another man yesterday - This was the lead article on Sunday Aug 26 ....

"Stephanie Ewing grew up without a mother because Clifton Allen White beat her with a shovel, tied her up and slashed her throat at least 6 times. The 28-year old Charlotte woman bled to death, leaving her sister to clean up the blood. That was in 1989 and Stephanie was only 7. Early Friday, she held hands with her aunt and cousin as she watched White die a far more peaceful death than her mother's. White died a clinical death, strapped to a gurney like a patient with a blue sheet up to his neck. He said goodbye to his wife and sister, a goodbye Stephanie Ewing never had. I watched. White winked twice and nodded as if to say - I'm ready. At one point he appeared to smile - an odd gesture for someone about to meet the state's ultimate punishment. White's sister, sitting in the first two rows of chairs, blew him a kiss at 1.59am. White had already been strapped down for an hour. He turned away from his relatives, looked toward heaven and mouthed a prayer. I watched his chest expand and then collapse. It was 2.01am. The combination of thiopental sodium and pancuronium bromide appeared to make him drowsy. Then White closed his eyes and died. Warden Lee pronounced White dead at 2.23am. A corrections officer drew a beige curtain, blocking White from view and ending the show. Now there are 220 inmates on North Carolina's death row instead of 221. I felt for White's relatives. They too are suffering the loss of a loved one. But my heart returns to the 7-year-old girl who grew up without a mother. I feel for the woman who never saw her daughter's prom dress and who will never get to bounce grandchildren on her knee. She will never get to watch her daughter get married, because a man in a drunken rage cut her life short - literally. That man died in peace with his body intact. A mortician will not have to sew him back together. Death

penalty opponents stood in protest outside the prison. One said it's not a deterrent. Maybe it's not. But the death penalty is predictable. If you plot to kill someone in North Carolina and brutally follow through, then you risk being put to death. It's that simple. It's the law."

Heavy stuff for breakfast reading on a Sunday morning with your Post Toasties, before joining the majority of "Charlottans" heading off to church to rejoice in the Word of God! I think that perhaps the New Testament never arrived with Mr Columbus, and that these folks still adhere to the 'older' version! There is an irony that executions here take place at 2am on Saturdays and not on Sundays - wonder what the Jewish folk in this Judeo-Christian society think about that?

Dianne and I are busy getting the business moving and are astonished at how much we can get done with decent internet speeds. Back home with dial-up in South Africa, that little "wheel-of-death" gave us plenty of time to get a coffee, check the mail and read the paper. We are planning for our first ExecuRead campaign that starts on Tuesday 11 September.

America is a VERY strange society! And they don't speak English. They speak American! Or rather 'Mer'can. They drive on the pavement (the road), they walk on the sidewalk (the pavement), they pee in the bathroom (the WC or toilet), they don't know what a loo is and being pissed means being angry. You sit on your fanny! (your bottom). A guillotine (for cutting paper) is a paper-trimmer, cellotape is Scotch-tape, Tippex is Liquid-paper, a car's bonnet is a hood and your luggage goes in the trunk (the boot). A 4x4 is an SUV (a sports utility vehicle), which is pronounced vee-hi-cle! So while most folk think that it's all about immigration, the real challenge is acclimation aka acclimatization!

Speeding is a serious No-No. The speed limit ranges between 35 and 55 miles per hour. Exceeding the speed limit by more than 15mph means suspension of your driver's license for 12 months. Any and every speeding violation of more than 10mph over the speed limit is notified to your insurance company - you are a high-risk driver and your healthcare and vehicle insurance is loaded for a period of 3 years!

And yet, for a country of 300 million people, the system just seems to work. You can do very little without a social security number, and linked to your Social Security number is your credit score that is calculated by the three main Credit Bureaus in the country – Equifax, Experian and TransUnion. And your credit score, a measure of your fiscal health and responsibility, determines whether you get credit or not and at what interest rate, whether you can rent an apartment and often whether you can get a job. And for many immigrants, this is somewhat of a culture shock – we are not accustomed to the penalties imposed on a minimum payment that is just one day late.

We are surviving. Not having earned a cent in the last two months, with another couple of weeks to go before my first ExecuRead classes are scheduled to start, the stress is taking its toll. We are lonely and miss our families and close friends. We see a lot of our first friends in the USA, the Christies, South Africans who came out here 21 years ago, lost everything when their container got washed off the ship and then lost their son Michael in an auto accident a few years after their arrival in Charlotte. They still have their South African sense of humor and seem to enjoy us as much as we enjoy them. But friends of six weeks simply cannot replace friends of 10, 15 and 20 years or more.

The kids are enjoying life here but have become very dependent on family as they still have very few friends. This move is not easy. It's somewhat like being in solitary confinement. The important thing is for us not to lose sight of the big objective - a big business opportunity, a great education for the children and a new life for ourselves. Noble ideals, but still not easy.

Day 39. Wednesday August 15, 2001

To my Dad

I wrote this letter just before we left South Africa, planning to send it to you as soon as we arrived in the USA on July 8. As fate would have it, this computer (and this letter) went to Istanbul, Miami and Atlanta before arriving last week. I thought that most of it would be out of date, but after hearing from Fiona that your foot is playing up again, perhaps this letter still works. I have been trying to call you via the Net2Phone system, but have just been advised that the South African Government has blocked Net2Phone to South Africa as it deprives Telkom of some revenue, so will find another route as we still have not found an international call carrier.

A Letter to Mum & Dad

Now is not the time to be sad, nor to have regrets. It is a time to be brave and to accept that all birds must leave the nest sooner or later.

I have travelled a long road to reach this point in my life – I am risking everything on this venture and I need to know that I have your support and strength behind me. To a very large extent, you have contributed to this decision – you have given me the strength to be bold and to make decisions as great as this one. Similarly, you also instilled in me the family values and compassion which delayed this decision for so many years.

Why am I embarking on such a major upheaval so late in my life? A good question, and one which I cannot easily answer. Perhaps a multiplicity of reasons :

Mid-life crisis – I have been teaching speed reading for 25 years in South Africa and firmly believe that few other careers could have been as financially and intellectually rewarding. I doubt whether there is anyone in the world who has as much experience in this field as I now have. And I know that no other course in the world is achieving the level of results that my course is achieving. I am getting bored and I need a change.

My Children – In as much as you succeeded in producing a litter that were different, that were not suited to the routines of the corporate establishment, (and let's face it Dad, you have been swimming upstream your whole life!), so too have I produced a couple of mavericks, both of whom are going to require some very careful nurturing if they are to realize their ultimate potential. Sarah will need international schooling and training all too soon and hopefully I can endeavor to make the move before she does. Michael has no future in South Africa – he is too male, too pale and too much of a cyber-geek to survive in a country where the great majority are 2-dimensional philistines. Kalil Gibran said that we do not own our children – they are on loan to us. And when children leave, there is a degree of pain. You experienced that when you left me, a tearful 12-year-old, at Rondebosch Boys High School the first time (and probably every time you returned me to boarding school!). And there was pain when I moved to Johannesburg. Both of these moves were big in pain but small in distance. Unless I plan appropriately, I run the risk of losing both my children on inter-continental moves when they get to the same age as I was when I moved to RBHS.

South Africa – This country is no longer my country. It is fast becoming a waste-land, the deteriorating play-ground of gangsters with their hands in the cookie-jar. A land where life is cheap and values even cheaper. Where corruption, greed, exploitation and waste are the norm rather than the exception. Where race discrimination is worse than it ever was under apartheid. While I love the country, I am learning to hate the people of this country. And while I still believe that there is some hope for South Africa, I cannot afford to gamble with the lives, health, security, education and future of my children.

Business – There is a big and growing demand for my skills in the USA and in the UK. With companies in both countries, I believe that I have the ability to fast-track my wealth-accumulation. Should circumstances indicate a return to South Africa, those dollar and pound earnings will ensure that I am independently financially self-sufficient and not the victim of a currency that is in free-fall.

But there is a cost and a price to be paid. And you and I have been paying this price for many years now. From a parent/child father/son mother/son friend relationship, I effectively left home at the age of 12. From that moment onwards, my relationship with you changed and could never be re-captured. Boarding-School – a wise decision? Who knows? For every argument "For", there is an argument "Against". My childhood friends, Peter Burger and Mike Daneel, returned to Hermanus and both lost their fathers. I left Hermanus and yet also "lost" my father to geographical distance – none of us REALLY got what we wanted.

My solution has been to shun adversity and to reject all negatives. I only see positives in this move. We are making the American Dream a reality and you gave me the tools to do so. I am not leaving South Africa – I am adding the USA and the UK to my sphere of operations. I am not losing friends but gaining new ones. An email is still only a local call, regardless of whether it is to Johannesburg, Sydney or Charlotte and a telephone is still only a piece of plastic with a microphone and speaker, regardless of how much wire and fiber-optics are connected to the pole outside Hoy House. (The Stewart family home in Hermanus where we have lived since 1955 and where my mother and sister lived until very recently.)

What does change, is the illusion of reality. For centuries, people believed that the Sun rotated round the Earth. Copernicus proved otherwise. And yet reality defies the senses – we see the sun rise in the east and we witness the sun moving across our sky to set in the west. We have never witnessed the earth moving and yet we are expected to believe that it is not the sun that is moving from east to west, but the earth that is moving from west to east.

You have allowed yourselves to become affected by this illusion. For the past 12 years, the distance between Hermanus and Johannesburg has been as great, practically-speaking, as the distance between Hermanus and Charlotte. What does it matter how far apart we are geographically if neither is within your physical reach? Your inability to cross the geographic divide has been more than amply resolved with email, fax and telephone and other than the telephone dialing code, you would be none the wiser if I was calling you from Charlotte, Johannesburg, Cape Town or from a house across the street.

All I want from the two of you is for you to stick around for a lot more years. Just as you are afraid to say goodbye, so too am I. I am not ready to say goodbye to either of you. You are like a pair of favorite "vellies" (hand-made shoes from soft animal leather). I have gotten pretty used to you. You fit well. You may be getting a bit tattered and with a hole or two, but you are my Linus-blanket. And I wouldn't want it any other way.

Dad, I know you sometimes get a touch depressed about your health. Your comment about feeling bad because you could not help with packing up the Hermanus Penthouse is a load of twaddle – you deserve your day in the sun. For too many years you carried the load in this family. It's time you sat back and let someone else take the wheel. Feeling sorry for yourself does no-one any favors. Least of all yourself. If you are going to sit on your bum, enjoy the feeling. Relish in your laziness. And if you cannot enjoy it, then get up and do what you want to do, regardless of any pain and in the full glorious realization that your will to succeed is more powerful than any minor discomfort. So you have a hole in your foot? Okay, that's bad, a tough break, but it's a damn side better than having a hole in your head. And if the worst comes to the worst and they cut off your foot, that's a damn side better than losing your sight, your hearing or your speech. Hell, I think the last time I ever noticed your foot was as a kid when it communicated with my bum, and that was only figuratively in any case! Whatever happens, no negatives, no depression and no giving up. As Hemingway said, "man can be destroyed, but never defeated."

Mom, you keep the faith. Spiritually you are one of the toughest people I have ever had the honor and pleasure of knowing. And one of the gentlest.

I love you both. Bruce.

The world, as we know it, has changed. Irrevocably.

Day 68. Thursday September 13, 2001

It's two days since we were having breakfast and watched thousands of people die, and two 110-story buildings disappear in a cloud of dust. No-one knows the body count – the recovery crews have ordered 30,000 body bags, and seven more buildings are at risk of collapse from the earth tremor caused by the WTC collapse – the tremor measured 2.5 on the Richter scale.

The nation is in shock. Fortress America has been breached. It has touched everyone. The wackos are out in force. Last night, in response to a crank call, the Empire State Building was evacuated. This afternoon, another crank call resulted in the Capitol being evacuated. Within 15 minutes of the disaster, people on the internet were auctioning fragments of the plane that crashed into the North tower. In Charlotte, there are cops on virtually every street corner. On-street parking in Charlotte is prohibited – only in parking garages after vehicles are checked.

Strangely enough, we are in shock too. And we are confused. We are immigrants. We are not Americans. So why would something like this have such an impact on us? We realize that our decision to move to America was not just a business decision, but an emotional decision as well. We had turned away from South Africa and we had turned to America and for some inexplicable reason we are seeing America as our country. While South Africa is a place, America is more than that. It's an idea, a concept, an emotional destination.

Talking to Americans, the picture is equally confusing. This might be the biggest single day tragedy to hit America since the Battle of Gettysburg. Pearl Harbor: 2,390 lives lost, Okinawa: 6,800 lives lost, D-Day: 10,000 lives lost. These were WW2 battles. Sept 11: who knows? The average American doesn't really understand or appreciate what the real world is all about. Within Fortress America he has, perhaps understandably, become comfortable, secure and complacent. Terror outside Fortress America does not touch him and he cannot identify with external terror. He has the luxury of being able to intellectualize terror. Suddenly that terror has walked in through the front door and he no longer has the luxury of being able to say shame! It's in his face. And he cannot fully accept that Fortress America is no more. And now Bush talks of war. So far, the mood is one of stunned horror and shock. Slowly, as the full impact dawns and the piles of body bags become rows of husbands and wives, brothers and sisters and as the thousands of orphans seek new homes, the horror and shock will be replaced with anger. Someone has pulled the tail of this very big and very powerful sleeping tiger. But how do you declare war on a nation that comprises multiple countries largely comprising Bedouins, camels, tents, fleas and lots of sand and rocks? You cannot bomb his home – with a few sticks and a piece of rag, he is back in business. One suggestion is to invade the entire Middle East and turn it into a single-country free-zone, occupied and managed by the big 7 countries. Others caution about the draft and the humiliation of another Vietnam.

And then we have the real rocket scientists – pocket knives and box-cutters are now prohibited on aircraft and luggage security will become intolerable. And I cannot wait to see Mrs Posh in her $20,000 First Class seat having to eat her steak with a 'spork'! Or sipping her Dom P from a plastic cup because of a ban on wine-glasses! They don't appear to have thought about the fact that a twisted and broken aluminum soft drink can makes a lovely jagged edge, just perfect for cutting throats! Or that the average martial arts aficionado has far more deadly weapons at the end of his arms and legs than any lunatic with a box-cutter. Of course, we should not forget that no amount of passenger security will stop another disaster, especially if the terrorist is a pilot, in the cockpit, trained by the USA at a USA flight school. How many more Manchurian Candidates are there? It now appears that 10 Arabs, with forged pilot's documentation and weaponry have today been arrested at JFK and La Guardia airports, trying to board internal USA flights!

At the risk of sounding totally perverse, one must acknowledge the absolute brilliance of the deed. No need to smuggle weapons onto the aircraft. The aircraft is the weapon itself, courtesy of the airline. And no need to fill the aircraft with bombs, just a few tons of fuel, again, courtesy of the airline. And add this deadly concoction to the top floor of a very high building and gravity will do the rest. Multiply this by 2 with a careful interval of 18 minutes and you can add hundreds of rescuers to the 'bag'. And because of the proximity of other buildings, it looks like the 'bag' will reach 7 to 10 buildings in Manhattan alone. All for the price of a couple of airline tickets, paid for with a credit card that will most surely 'bounce'!

Something that we talk about privately, is how the wheel has turned. It was not too long ago that the USA condemned South Africa's policy of 'hot-pursuit'. When the South African Defense Force pursued terrorists into the neighboring Southern African countries, the world yelped about the sovereignty of those countries. When South Africa said we make no distinction between terrorists and the countries that succor or harbor them, the world made us a pariah. Regardless of the motivation or the semantics of terrorist or freedom fighter, atrocities committed on civilians are unconscionable. And we think that the average American has finally come to realize that while he may call this an act of terror or an act of war, and while the Muslims may call this an act of freedom, the bottom line is that innocent people died. Hopefully, America will wake up and start listening to other allegations of terrorism around the world. If the civilized nations of the world band together to bring an end to terrorism, then possibly some good will come out of this madness. Right now, we grieve with all of America. And selfishly, but perhaps understandably, hope that America comes out of the bunker before our stash of Rands and Dollars runs out.

On the home front, we are settling in to what we now view as our new home country. I am obviously worried about the huge societal change prevailing, but fortunately we have the resources to access vast amounts of data on virtually every aspect of business life, and so we spend every available minute sending out mailers to companies, colleges, schools and universities. We accept that we have to build a ground-swell of awareness about what we do and sooner or later, the repetition of publicity will bear fruit. It is so easy to forget that the successes we enjoyed in South Africa were the fruits of many hard years and lots of seed-planting.

We are grateful for the dozens of emails over the past two days wishing us well and sending best wishes for our safety. And to answer the question all have been asking, "No, we are not coming home. America is our new home. We are now asking the question – what can WE do to help America?"

We have North Carolina Driver's Licenses, a huge step in the immigration process! We booked our appointments shortly after arriving in the USA, downloaded the instruction manuals from the internet, did some study and waited for the big day – which was supposed to be Tuesday 18. Arrived at the DMV (Dept of Motor Vee-hi-cles) with hundreds of others, and thanked providence that we had booked our appointment. We eased through the mob to the front of the queue only to be told that the computers were off-line and that we would have to wait until the computers came online again. DMVs are planned and built by the same people all over the world and the queues are just as long as in Johannesburg so we feel quite at home. Anyhow, after two hours with no computers on line, we gave up and came home.

This morning we call to find out if the computers are operational. No, call later, they say. Many calls later, we are summoned – come now, the queue is not too bad. So we rush across town to join the queue that has grown considerably. Come hell or high-water, we are staying for the duration. We are given a number and told to sit and wait. We read books. We snooze. We talk to the Mexicans and the African Americans. And we wait. For hours.

And then the PA system calls us. First, we have our eyes tested, documents checked, vee-hi-cle license and insurance checked. Then we wait. We have passed Test 1. Then the PA tells us to go to computer terminal #4 to do the test. It is a touch-screen terminal and it asks you 25 questions about rules and regulations, road signs, and driving law. Multiple choice. Pass mark is 80%. We are warned. Less than 80% and you go home. Di and I are terrified. Some of the questions require a Ph D in wacko-thinking – If your car is running heavy on the right-hand side, what's wrong? Choice of answers: The Steering is faulty – wrong! The tires are faulty – wrong! The suspension is faulty – Yeah! Di goes first (ladies first of course!). She takes a long time! She is flushed! I am trying to see what answers she is giving but at my age, even with my new eyes (I had Lasik surgery just before we left South Africa), I can see squat! She passes. 80% on the dot. 20 correct and 5 incorrect. And off she goes for the driving test. 20 minutes later she is back, smiling. She passed!

I head for the computer. It tells me that if I am not sure of an answer, I can skip it and come back to it later. Sounds OK. So cautiously I start the test. Remember, I have not written a test since university days and that was when John Vorster was Prime Minister of South Africa in the 70's. I answer some, and I skip some and then the computer stops and starts flashing TEST COMPLETED! "WHAT?" I yell. What happened to the test? Why can't I try the ones I skipped? Because you answered 20 out of 25 and got the 20 correct. You don't need to attempt the ones you skipped. Now let's see if you can drive.

I am led outside by this two-tone blonde – the front half of her head is blonde and the rear half is brunette. I do not have the cojones to ask her why. She tells me we are going for a drive. That this is a test. That everything has to be done by the book. I start driving, one hand on the wheel.

"Mr Stewart," she barks "this is a test. You need both hands on the wheel!"

Sorry! And I am barely a mile down the road when "Mr Stewart, you are doing 45mph in a 35mph zone! Are you in a hurry to fail this test?"

I gulp. "No Ma'am. Sorry Ma'am. It's just that I have not been this nervous since my first date as a teenager!" God, the woman actually giggled!

"Stop here," she says. "Now 'back-up' (reverse) the vehicle."

So, I am really cool and zoom backwards using the rear-view and wing-mirrors.

"Mr Stewart, you are not driving a truck. Look over your shoulder to see where you are going!"

Jeez! Does the woman think I've the neck of a fucking owl?

We head back to the testing station, and if I have not already done it all, she barks again. "Mr. Stewart you are doing 47mph in a 35mph zone. 3mph more and I'll suspend your license before you even get it! What's with the heavy foot?"

"Well Ma'am, I drove a Corvette in South Africa."

And she mellowed. She also drives a 'Vette and her name is Stuart! "Here's your license Mr Stewart, but watch yourself!"

And there are hilarious sides to immigration as well. Sarah had to write an essay and we get an urgent call from the school about Sarah's inappropriate language. Sarah wrote about the geese sleeping on the warm pavement (road), forcing Mom to hoot her hooter to move them along. The teacher has deleted the words "hoot her hooter" and replaced them with "honk her horn"! You see, hooters are boobs and are not to be displayed or depressed by motorists on public roads!

Day 89. Thursday October 4, 2001

Business is very slow in this New America. Bush keeps talking about getting things back to normal, but there is nothing normal about knowing that America is going to strike the Bin Laden groups and that Bin Laden is going to hit America again. The media don't help as they thrive on tragedy and disaster. The newspapers and TV are full of discussion panels about Bin Laden's biological and nuclear capabilities. With stories about Smallpox, Anthrax, Sarin and DX nerve gas. About how many people in America would die if you took 50 suicide terrorists, infected them with smallpox and sent them around the USA on planes, trains and to shopping malls. Also veiled hints that Bin Laden has nuclear capabilities because of his relationship with other nuclear nations. South Africa has not been mentioned per se, but one cannot help thinking that the USA supported the ANC (African National Congress), declared an arms embargo against South Africa, and supported the ANC in taking over South Africa. Now remember that South Africa is nuclear capable, and South Africa helped Israel, and now the ANC is as thick as thieves with Gadhafi who is as thick as thieves with Bin Laden. Ergo, what Nationalist South Africa did for Israel, ANC South Africa is probably doing for Bin Laden. And whatever happened to the five tactical 'nukes that South Africa built with the enriched uranium from Pelindaba and the nuclear know-how from Israel?

So, it's not business as usual. It's called "Operation Save Ass" – how to survive in a country at war when you're a new immigrant, have an almost stagnant business and the clock is running before you need to renew your visa and prove to the USCIS that you are meeting your visa requirements.

Living in the South, sooner or later every immigrant has to learn about NASCAR. Stock car racing in the United States has its origins in bootlegging during Prohibition, when drivers ran bootleg whiskey, made primarily in the Appalachian region of the United States. Bootleggers needed to distribute their illicit products, and they typically used small, fast vehicles to better evade the police.

Frank and Kathy, parents of one of Michael's classmates, invited us to a Ducks Unlimited function at a place called DEI. Didn't know what we were in for, but what a wonderful surprise. Ducks Unlimited is a Duck Hunting and Conservation organization with over a million members. From their DU events and hunting licenses, they are buying thousands of acres of land which is returned to wetlands for bird conservation, thus ensuring an endless supply of birds to shoot during the hunting season when they spend a fortune on camo clothing, boats, motors, 4x4s, retriever dogs and floating duck decoys to attract real ducks and geese. They were having a fund-raising auction and the function was being hosted by Dale Earnhardt Inc. Dale Earnhardt is to NASCAR what Schumacher is to Formula One Racing. For the first time since we left South Africa, we quaffed lovely red wines and the best fillet mignon in months! This however was our first introduction to NASCAR. Dale Earnhardt was killed at Daytona earlier this year, but has left an empire that is now being run by his son, Dale Earnhardt Jr. We are taken on a tour through the plant – quite awesome – this is where they build the NASCARs for the Pennzoil, NAPA and Budweiser NASCAR teams. The plant was built at a cost of $50m and DEI's annual volume is $800m. Everything is controlled by computer, so they can maintain the exact specs of every car – exactly 6 pounds of paint on the chassis and interior of the car, exactly 3 pounds of paint on the exterior of the car. Cylinder heads are machined by NASA-grade computer-controlled high-precision machines so that every tolerance is controlled. In the engine shop we see rows and rows of engines – each one costing $60-grand – all ready to get dropped into one of the NASCARs, ready for final tuning. These little babies push out over 800bhp. The sheer size of things they do in this country is staggering.

Over dinner at DEI, Kathy asks me whether I have ever seen a NASCAR race. Never, I reply. Well, how about joining us at NASCAR on Sunday – we have a box! Now Kathy is no slouch – at the Ducks Unlimited auction, she bid $1000 to do 3 laps in a NASCAR with Richard Petty, a NASCAR driver (another NASCAR racing dynasty family), followed by 8 solo laps in a NASCAR at any racetrack of her choice – Charlotte, Daytona, Talladega, Darlington or Indianapolis. These little toys run around a 1.5-mile circuit at an average speed of 180 miles per hour (that's nearly 290kph!).

Sunday Morning – 7.30am – Michael and I are off to Lowes Motor Speedway with Kathy and some of her friends, all racing enthusiasts. It's only about 40 miles away, but there are 200,000 other fans heading the same way and it will take us 3 to 4 hours to get there!

The stadium is massive, the organization unbelievable. We park miles away and 5 minutes later a shuttle-bus picks us up and takes us the rest of the way. We collect the tickets and then collect the head-sets and scanners – these are head-phones which protect your ears and which are connected to scanner radios so you can intercept the radio broadcasts and the communications between the drivers, pits and spotters (spotters are team members who sit on the roof of the stadium and who give advice to the drivers – who is threatening you, who is creeping up on you, who is in the pits, when to overtake, where a gap is opening up.)

We get seated and watch the opening ceremonies. The race is 500 miles – 334 laps around a 1.5-mile circuit. Top speeds are 180mph plus. The sweeper trucks brush and vacuum the track – even a tiny piece of road-debris can be fatal at these speeds. Two F16's with missile pods fly overhead – they have been allocated to patrol the stadium just in case some jihadist decides to land another airliner in a stadium with almost 200,000 people, including me and my boy. When the F16s come overhead, the people start chanting U S A, U S A, U S A – quite stirring hearing all these voices booming out U …. S …. A ….. U …. S …. A …! Then, just as the race is about to begin, the big screens show President George Dubya Bush announcing that America has launched the strike against Bin Laden. Well, the crowd goes mad – cheering and shouting and whistling. Shit, the craziness of it all – one moment we are all crying because we got hit and then we are having a party because some other civilians are being nailed!

Soon we forget the war and it's NASCAR – 43 big V8s pushing out a combined 34,000 horsepower. The noise is unreal. And the whole place shakes and vibrates. They go tearing around the circuit at 180 miles per hour until there is a crash. Then the pace car pulls out and forces everyone to slow down to a respectable pace while they remove the wreckage and the sweepers sweep the track, wash off the oil and fluids and re-vacuum the whole place. Then the pace car slips into the pit-lane and it's balls to the wall again until the next crash. They do this for 500 miles. 8 crashes, 40 slow laps behind the pace car and the average speed for the whole 500 miles was 133mph including the 40 slow laps. Then all 200,000 people pack up and head for the biggest traffic jam you can imagine. We catch the shuttle back to where our cars are parked and we have a "tail-gate" – we pull all our SUVs (4x4's) and pick-ups (bakkies) into a laager, bums towards the center and we have a cook-out – a gas cooker on the back of a pick-up, and tons of food. Boerewors (South African sausage) (if you can call it that) is cooked to a cinder, steak starts looking like a briquette and hamburger patties turn out to be deadly weapons they are cooked so much. Then we stick marshmallows on sticks till they are runny, slap them between two bars of chocolate, then between two sweet crackers. They are called "Smores" (i.e. want s'more!). And we drink tons of Light Beer. No hard-tack and only Bud Light or Miller Lite because it takes longer to get smashed and there are less calories! Yea, the logic of eating 10,000-calorie 'smores followed by a Lite beer! We wait until the traffic calms down and then head home – almost a 14-hour day to enjoy a 4-hour race! As they say in the good ol' U S of A …. Yeeeeeh Haaaaa!

Blood-money

Day 106. Sunday October 21, 2001

We've just earned our first income in post-9/11-USA! $25 tax free. Just enough to fill the Durango. We've been getting a touch depressed about the slow pace of business, so decided that anything is better than nothing. Still no progress with my radio talk program, as they are still interviewing scientists who want to tell us about how bad the bioterrorism warfare is going to get, and how to recognize anthrax, and what to do if you open that envelope and white powder falls out of it. My media releases don't get into the papers because terror, drama and tragedy sell more papers than my penmanship.

How did I earn my first $25 you might ask? Well, this is a story that I'll be able to tell my grandchildren one day. You know, about how easy it is for the kids today and about how tough it was when I was a youngster during the Terror War of 2001.

Well, it was like this, grandchildren. America was at war. Our soldiers were fighting the Arabs in the desert and we were being poisoned here in America. We all wore gas-masks and we had to put our mail in the microwave or steam-iron it before opening it, just in case the envelope was full of anthrax. Lots of people were losing their jobs and we had no money. So I decided to search the newspapers for something to do to make some money. And there it was "Earn $$$ for Plasma". And so off I went. I filled in lots of forms, had my photograph taken, and got plugged into a machine that took my temperature, measured my pulse and blood-pressure, tested my blood, weighed me and measured me. Then a nurse made me strip to my underpants (thank God I was not wearing my holy ones!). She felt all my glands, made me cough, checked under my tongue, behind my ears, behind my knees and between my toes (just to check that you have not been shooting needles, son!). Then asked me if since 1977 I had slept with a man, been in prison or paid a woman for sex. The first two were easy. When I paused on answering the 3rd question, she raised her eyebrows and asked me why I was hesitant about that one. Well, I answered, 'Is my wife's allowance a gift, entitlement or payment?"

Then I got sent to a large room with 30 recliner-chairs and lots of large machines. The technician explained what was going to happen and did I still want to proceed. What the hell, at the end of the procedure they were going to give me a fruit-juice, a peanut butter cracker and some money! They put a pressure cuff around my arm and then stuck this large needle in the vein of my arm. The machine's lights show "DRAW", the cuff tightened and I had to keep clenching my fist. My blood flowed out of my arm, down the tube and into a reservoir. Then when the reservoir was full, the cuff loosened and the machine told me to relax my fist. The machine said "Hold". The reservoir of blood started spinning in a centrifuge and the plasma, a clear straw-colored liquid, rose to the top of the reservoir and flowed into the plasma bottle. The red hemoglobin settled to the center and bottom of the centrifuge and went into another container where it was mixed with an anticoagulant. Then the machine said "Return" and started pumping the hemoglobin back into my arm. When the reservoir was empty, the machine said "draw" and started sucking my blood out again. This cycle happened 5 times until they had separated 903ml of plasma from my blood and returned all of my hemoglobin. Then the machine said "Close-down" and fed a 500ml dose of saline into my arm just to make sure that my blood-pressure did not drop too much. The saline was quite chilly and I could feel this coldness spreading in my arm. The whole separation process took about 90 minutes which was too long because I had not had breakfast, had 2 cups of coffee and was quite dehydrated. Most of the others finished the plasma separation in 3 or 4 sessions. I plan to do better next time. And Voila! They paid me $25! I converted 1 liter of my plasma into 20 gallons of Premium Unleaded Dodge Durango Go-Go Juice. And I now do this twice a week. The Sunday money feeds the car and the Wednesday money feeds the family. And who says you cannot make a living in this country out of a little blood-money!

Visiting the Mountain People

Day 120. Sunday November 4, 2001

We have just returned from a fabulous weekend away. Woke up on Saturday morning to find perfect weather and nothing to do – business is dead as the proverbial Dodo and we are not sick with anthrax, so life is great! Decide to take a drive out along the Blue Ridge Parkway, which stretches all along the foothills of the 2,200-mile Appalachian Mountains from Virginia, through North Carolina and into Georgia. (The book, A Walk in the Woods, by Bill Bryson will be made into a delightfully funny movie starring Robert Redford and Nick Nolte.) We planned to head down to Asheville, about 120 miles SW of Charlotte. What a great trip. Went via Boone which is really in the sticks (hence the saying 'out in the boonies' which means the same as 'out in the boondocks'.) Got side-tracked with so many little places to see, only arrived in Asheville late Saturday afternoon and after a whole day in the car, were not too keen to drive home again. So booked into a Motel! You know those weird little places you see in American gangster movies where the fellow in the front office has greasy hair and stubble and walks around in his off-white wife-basher vest? Well, we found it – greasy hair, stubble, vest and the local resident old-timer sitting on a rocking chair wearing dungarees, a hat and a piece of straw between his few remaining teeth! $59 and we get a room with 2 double beds, 4 concrete pillows, windows that won't open and a too-hot air-conditioner that is controlled from the office by the Hollywood extra with his stubble, vest, greasy-hair and poor inglis!!!

I break the news to the kids – we are sleeping over in Asheville .... YAAAAAA! And you have a double bed! .... YAAAAA! And you have to share with your brother/sister...... WHAAAAAT? NO WAYYYYYY! Ok then sleep on the floor if you like.

We park the car and go for a walk-about and some window shopping. Stunning little town with one of the biggest hospital complexes we have ever seen – something like Johannesburg General and Groote Schuur hospitals combined and then some! Remember, this little town is way out in the mountains. We find little artsy-shops and glass shops that make your eyes water. Prices of glass articles from about $500 up to about $15,000. And about every type of architecture under the sun. When young George Vanderbilt visited the place in 1880, he decided that it was quite nice, purchased 125,000 acres and built the largest private residence in America -- Biltmore Estate -- and then started bringing his pals out for a DW (dirty weekend). A lot of them liked the place and it soon became the hidey-hole for the rich and famous – hence the diversity of culture and architecture.

As we are going to have an early start, it's to bed by 10pm. Well, this is called fun. The kids have not had much experience sleeping with anyone (thank God!) and find that 2 squiggly worms in one bed doesn't work. Sarah is a real possum and burrows under as many blankets as she can find. Michael likes to be cool and doesn't like to be smothered, so between him kicking the blankets off and Sarah pulling them back on again, they are in for a great night. In the meantime, Di and I are trying to acclimate (acclimatize for you non-Americans!) to a double bed that is somewhat less than our king-size bed in Charlotte. Di is too cold and I am too hot. The windows won't open, so I ask grease-ball to turn down the heat, leave the door open to get rid of the fug and go for a coke. 1am and I eventually get to sleep. 2am and I hear Michael squiggling around in his bed. He has turned 180 degrees looking to get warm now because Sarah has all the blankets. He is curled up like a fetus with his head to the bottom of the bed. I turn him round and dump some blankets on him. He wakes up, says AAAAAAH! and goes straight back to sleep. I try to sleep but the hard pillow under my head against my ear is giving me a cauliflower ear and the bugs are biting me and it is getting too hot again. I'm exhausted and too hot and so I start breathing deeply. I DO NOT SNORE! 6am and the kids are shaking me and saying Dad, please turn down the volume – we cannot sleep! Bugger off, it's Mom who is snoring – go wake her up! Oh, what the hell, might as well all wake up and go see what the world looks like. Di and I have back-aches out of hell from the beds. Crawl into a shower to get old bones working again. And of course, we only get 2 towels. "Vot do you hexpect for 59 bucks???" Because this overnight was a last-minute decision, we have Di's hairbrush but no razor or tooth-brushes or deodorant or clean underwear, which doesn't faze "I'm Hungry" because he's a grubby little bugger who has to get force-washed when he smells too much like a hamster's cage. My 18-hour beard and fury teeth make me look and feel like a wino. The girls are OK because they carry a panel-beating kit in their hand-bags and can do a surface paint-job and perfume deodorizer, but there is no way that this old wino is going to walk around reeking of Chanel!

It's a quick breakfast of bacon and egg rolls and hash browns at McDonalds and these intrepid explorers are off again. The colors are simply unbelievable. The kids think our predilection for fall-colored trees is crazy but they enter into the spirit of things by appointing themselves as fancy-tree-spotters!

It's difficult to imagine that in just a few weeks all this color will be gone and that this whole area will be blanketed under snow with a thriving skiing industry for thousands of visitors. Most of the Blue Ridge Parkway has gates every so many miles which can be closed to seal off sections of the Parkway when the snow, ice and fog gets too thick.

Anyway, a great weekend and our first real break since we arrived here. We feel revitalized and willing to take up the fight for survival once again. And our immigration attorney in Florida has just reminded us that we already need to start working on our visa renewal which expires on February 15 – all he needs is financial statements showing that we are in business, how many workers we are employing and what their salaries are, and of course $2500 for the visa renewal application please.

After 9/11, America started taking its security very seriously. The Patriot Act basically suspended all human rights – the government has unlimited powers to eavesdrop whenever and wherever it chooses to, and suspected enemies of the state can be arrested, detained indefinitely and without charges, trial or legal representation. And because of the glaring gaps in technology and security communication between organizations such as the Department of Defense, the CIA, the FBI, etc, a new federal department, the Department of Homeland Security is formed. The idea is that until 9/11 we had dozens of streams of security data, all disconnected and with little interconnectivity. All of the data relevant to the 9/11 attacks was known by various agencies. The problem was that no-one was able to connect the dots. With the formation of the Department of Homeland Security, all these independent streams of data will be channeled into one large stream. And into this massive intelligence security agency, the previously independent Immigration and Naturalization Service (INS) was morphed into the United States Citizenship and Immigration Service (USCIS). More importantly, whereas the legacy INS was about regulating people coming into the USA, the new USCIS, with its anti-terrorist security mantle, is more concerned with keeping people OUT of the USA. This will have a massive impact on our future in America. Indeed, because we are already in the system, albeit the old INS system, our records will have to migrate into the new USCIS system. Equally ominous, the USCIS will now have multiple Service Centers, located in California, Nebraska, Texas and Vermont and each of these Service Centers will handle different types of immigration matters.

Now there's a saying that "if it aint broke, don't fix it". Equally true is "if it's broke, don't fuck it up anymore!"

Wanna BJ?

Wednesday November 7, 2001

I have a training opportunity in Atlanta, GA and rather than fly or drive, I decide to take the iconic Greyhound bus – only $72 for the 500-mile round trip. You cannot make reservations, so it's first come first served. Bus leaves at 12noon so you better be here by 11am. Interesting joint! Definitely for the budget-conscious traveler! Everybody speaks either Southern or Spanish, neither of which are music to my genteel and somewhat hard-of-hearing ears.

The bus-driver, a pleasant fatherly-looking chap, late fifties (old!) but with the build and aviator-shades so popular amongst drill-instructors of the US Marine Corps, comes onto the PA system with a few words of welcome … "Welcome to Greyhound …. Have a pleasant trip …. If using a radio, walkman or cd player, headphones only, no loud voices, no drinking of alcoholic beverages, no smoking of cigarettes, cigars, pipes or marijuana. If you need to speak to me APPROACH ME SLOWLY – DO NOT CREEP UP ON ME OR RUSH TOWARDS ME, ANNOUNCE YOURSELF BEFORE YOU GET CLOSER THAN 10 FEET FROM ME, MAKE NO SUDDEN MOVES AND ENSURE THAT YOUR HANDS ARE OPEN, IN FRONT OF YOU AND IN FULL VIEW AT ALL TIMES!" Shit! What have I let myself in for? What sort of passengers does this guy think he has on board? And then I remember the incident recently where a passenger slashed the driver's throat and crashed the bus up the road in Tennessee. So, for the next 5 hours, including a wee-stop, it's a very quiet, subdued and immaculately behaved bunch of passengers. Amazing what a little up-front "Don't fuck with me" advice can do!

In Atlanta, later that night, I check in to a Days Inn hotel/motel type place. Nice and cheap. About $45 incl taxes. I'm tired and hungry – just been teaching for 4 hours. I ask the receptionist whether there's a pub or restaurant nearby where I can get a drink and a snack. Nope, closest is MacDonald's, about 10 blocks away – or try the vending machines! Ergo, supper is a Coke and a Kit-Kat. I get into my room, been there no more than 10 minutes when there's a knock on the door.

"Who's there?" I ask through the closed door.

"Room service," a voice announces.

Maybe some advice on where I can get a decent meal? I open the door. She's tall, looks a bit like the model, Iman, but a lot more tatty. "Yes?" I ask.

"Looking for a girl?"

"No thank you," I respond, quite emphatically.

"Wanna BJ?"

"No thank you!" Shit, is this what this place has come to? Where the hookers knock on your door to sell their services? Aren't they supposed to stand on street corners, under street-lights, wearing black leather mini-skirts, fish-net stockings, see-thru tank-tops and looking like what's-her-name from Pretty Woman and wait for you to cruise them? I was even too scared to ask how much, just in case she saw this as the opening gambit in negotiations! For a moment my ego might have smiled that even at 50 I am worth a roll in the hay, until you accept that in this line of business, if there's not a wallet attached to the willy, even Mel Gibson is going to luck out!

It's this that makes this move so interesting and exciting – sure, the economic uncertainty is not too pleasant, but life is so different – every day we experience something new, something different, something happy, something sad. Life has become interesting again, now that the country is getting over 9/11 and is starting to become bored with Anthrax. In South Africa, I think I was becoming bored with life, and short of joining Arthur Murray, we had to do something different. We all ran successful businesses or had successful jobs, we all had the security of our homes, we spent time with other secure people and we all bitched about crime and corruption and swapped stories about which of us had had close shaves with bandits. Now it's changed – nothing is secure for us, nothing certain. Everything is changing. It's a new beginning in pretty much every way.

I get back to Charlotte and the Christies have invited us to "drinks" - aka a surprise birthday dinner for me - a slap-up dinner, a bottle of Chateauneuf-du-Pape 1982 and a bottle of 12-yr-old Chivas as a birthday present, plus a birthday card that says "the nice thing about being 50…is that you can start all stories with….in my day!!" A fitting end to my first half-century on this planet.

Don't you just love kids?

Life is becoming normal for the children – they're demanding pocket-money again! However, the pickings for the kids have been lean. When I earn, you can start getting pocket-money is the rule. Yes dad, but you are earning $50 a week from the plasma-clinic – why can't we have some of that for pocket-money? And who said the little darlings are not all blood-suckers at heart?

Michael, forever the total schlenter, has realized that the tooth in the slipper and some dollars from the tooth-fairy is a sure bet, notwithstanding the lack of funds here. He knows that I am the tooth-fairy. I know that he knows. The fact that I have all his missing teeth is a dead give-away, notwithstanding the fact that I tell him that the tooth-fairy buys the tooth from him and then sentimental old me buys the tooth from the tooth-fairy so that I have a memento of my little babies. But as this is the only way that he is going to wheedle a few dollars out of the tooth-fairy and me, necessity is the mother of invention – the moment he feels a tooth being remotely loose, he starts wiggling it around until he can pull it out or convince Mom to pull it out for him. This morning he marches into my office, gap and all, holding a freshly-plucked tooth in his hands and smiling bloodily at me – "c'mon dad, let's cut to the chase – save the tooth-fairy some effort, get a good night's sleep tonight and just give me the bucks right now!" What can you say?? At age 7 he has now lost or managed to self-extract 7 teeth. Poor Sarah however – at 12 she's only lost 4 of her milk-teeth and is destined to be the only octogenarian still with most of her milk-teeth. Hers are all as solid as rocks – all 4 had to be pulled by the dentist and most of them had roots that are longer than the average permanent molar.

Friday November 23, 2001

We've just experienced our first American Thanksgiving – a celebration declared by Abraham Lincoln in 1863 – the last Thursday in November to give thanks to God for the salvation and abundance granted to the American people. Although I'm not sure the American Indians share this sentiment. Thanksgiving is as big as Christmas and what a bash.

The Christies invited us to their street-party last Saturday. Started in 1945 by a couple of WW2 veterans who were neighbors in this particular street in Charlotte and who survived the war, this street party, restricted to only residents of the street, has now grown to over 120 guests. We're invited because we're 'staying' with the Christies for the weekend.

It all starts at 5am with the building of a huge BBQ fire, like a massive pizza oven. While waiting for the coals to get ready, we quaff gallons of very fiery Bloody Mary and attack a large sack of enormous oysters from the Gulf of Mexico. Then, because the properties in this area are huge and very wooded, the old-timers start unpacking their stash of moonshine. A number of them have illegal stills and spend the year preparing bottles of moonshine and jars of moonshine fruit – plums, peaches, cherries, strawberries, etc. Some of the stuff has been aging for 8 years and more – the liqueur is lethal and the fruit enough to floor a jumbo. While everyone gets quietly smashed, stories are told of WW2 and Vietnam as most of them served in both wars. Once the coals are ready, some 20 – 30 large whole pork loins are placed on the fire and then the top is closed with sheets of corrugated iron to convert the whole thing into a braai-smoker. We drink a lot more, tell more stories, while regularly opening the cooker and turning the roasts. The marinade is made of all sorts of things and tastes divine. Everyone has his role, function and title. The "Master-Baster" (referred to as the "masturbator" after a few Bloody Mary's) is responsible for ensuring the correct flavor. At lunch-time the meat is done and so is the cooking-committee, so we all stagger home to sleep for the afternoon while the "cutting-committee" comes in and totally shreds the meat into something with the texture of saw-dust, and the "salad-committee" comes in and starts laying out loads of salads and tons of dessert (that's pudding for you Brits reading this). Then the families all start arriving from about 4pm, play games and have a magician-show for the kids and dads and then a serious feast until about 9pm. They have electric golf-carts to ferry you home if you are too old and too doddery to find your way home in the dark, or if you are young and too pickled to find your way anywhere, or both. This party is always on the Saturday before Thanksgiving and allows you to recover on Sunday, which, after a mixture of Bloody Mary, oysters and moon-shine, you really do need.

It was in this part of the world that NASCAR originated – the good ol' boys, during prohibition, developed their driving skills for the race from their hidden stills to the speak-easy's with loads of illegal booze. The first to get to the customer, gets the sale and sets the price, hence the fast driving! These stills are often highly sophisticated and are still illegal in North Carolina where the booze outlets, called ABC's, are all owned by the State. I am told that if you are a "shiner" and want to go legit, the state will set you up with a regulated and registered still, monitor and buy your production, all for an up-front investment of $100-grand.

Then on Thanksgiving Day, we head off to SouthPark mall for the lighting of a 60-foot Christmas tree and the most incredible fireworks display – I suppose it is only in the USA that you celebrate Thanksgiving by lighting a Christmas Tree, having a Santa Claus and paying homage to Guy Fawkes simultaneously.

Di sends me off to the dumpster to get rid of the bags of garbage. Now I'm the ultimate scrounger, so I spend a few minutes poking around in the dumpster to see who has been throwing away whatever. Some months ago, I salvaged 2 mahogany-veneer side-tables and 2 table-lamps, which, with a little work, have turned out beautifully. Well, this time, the dumpster looks even more interesting – a quick check around to see that no-one is watching and I'm into the dumpster. 10 minutes later I start unpacking the haul – 1 foam overlay for a mattress, 2 goose-down pillows, 1 large goose-down duvet and cotton duvet-cover, 1 quilted comforter with matching pillow-case, 12 cotton dinner-table place-mats and 6 cotton-embroidered serviettes and I large inflatable bed – all new and most of the items still with price-tags and price-stickers. About $500 worth! We're at a loss to figure out why someone would want to throw this away – it was not covered in white powder, so don't think this is an anthrax booby-trap, so either someone had a domestic squabble, got thrown out of home with his/her stuff or it was shop-lifted and possession became too dangerous so dumpster was the logical solution. The price-tags don't tell me where the stuff was acquired from and I don't see much benefit in placing an advert in the newspaper "One set of fine linen and goose-down bedding found in dumpster on Thanksgiving. No sign of occupant. Will owners please queue at 3 Beacon Hill Lane?" Just to be totally safe, we're getting everything washed and dry-cleaned. So, at last we have finished the guest-room – we are storing a bed and "chester-draws" aka chest-of-drawers, for a friend, have a dumpster bed-side table and dumpster bed-side lamp, and dumpster-duvet and dumpster-pillows! Between this haul and my $50 a week for my plasma, who needs to work? Arms getting a bit sore now – two bloody great needles every week and then one of the technicians stuck me badly, needle right through the vein so the old arm swelled up and now all bruised. Had to stick me a second time – this is the worst part – they clean the arm with iodine and of course when the needle goes in, so does a bit of iodine and it stings like hell. They paid me an extra $5 on top of the $25 plasma fee ($5 for the pain of the unsuccessful needle stick!)

An American Christmas

Christmas Eve : 2001. This is without doubt the most difficult part of our new life. A year ago, at this time, we were in Hermanus, enjoying friends, family, kreef (lobster) and fine wine, warm weather and the Cape ocean. Here we have no friends, no family, no kreef, cheap wine and it's freezing outside. Not even a snow-flake.

The kids know the status of the finances, so we're all in this together. We decided not to lavish on a Christmas Tree and all the decorations this year – waste of money and will draw attention to the fact that the base of the tree is also somewhat bare. Told the kids that we were going to have a lean Christmas THIS YEAR ONLY!

Michael comes home from school and announces that he can prove that there is no Santa! Oh Yeah? I challenge. Yup, he says. If I get a tiny, small, cheap present, then I know it's from Dad 'cause we know he's poor. If I get a serious present, then I know it's from Santa 'cause he isn't poor. There's the proof! Well, I begin to explain, Santa has to visit a number of poor communities in the USA and around the world and is going to be especially busy in New York and Washington this year, so maybe Santa won't even come to Charlotte this year…. A kick in the shin from Di reminds me that having Michael announce to the kids at Country Day School that Santa was pulling out of Charlotte, would cause chaos!!

And we do the immigrant/tourist thing over weekends. Go to visit Brattonsville, the village in South Carolina where a lot of the movie Patriot was filmed. See Mel Gibson's house, the tomahawk that he bloodied the Brits with, and the cellar / kitchen beneath Aunt Charlotte's house where the family hid from the baddies. Out in the woods we're able to load and fire a long musket and learn how to throw a tomahawk. Get some great pics of the kids with bloodthirsty grins and brandishing an evil-looking tomahawk. I explain to them that the poor Brits that Mel chopped to pieces were probably kith and kin of Granny Jennifer in Hermanus! (Bit of poetic license but it gets their attention!). Sit on Mel Gibson's veranda and rock in his rocking chair – very relaxing – must get one of those – there's nothing quite like sitting in a rocking-chair on your stoep (aka veranda) keeping an eye on the slaves!!!! OOOPS!! Not very PC that! C'MON GUYS, RELAX. I'VE GOT MY TONGUE IN MY CHEEK! And I'm on a movie-set for goodness sake.

Then a drive to McAdenville, (aka Christmas Town USA, pop 651) just south of Charlotte. A town founded in 1771 where, in the 1860's, a wealthy local left his entire estate to the town on the understanding that the town set up Christmas lights every year. And that's what they do. From the beginning of December until after Christmas, they light the town – every house, tree, pole, shrub, signpost – everything that can possibly be strung with Christmas lights is strung with Christmas lights – a whole town. And from sunset to 10pm every night, cars stream through the town. It's bumper-to-bumper with your lights off for a 60-minute drive through fairyland. Absolutely stunning. Apparently, the residents have got used to the nightly invasion and have accepted that popping down to the "store", for a six-pack does not entitle your missus to ask where the hell you've been when you get home 2 hours later!!

Di and I are hanging in here. I think Di misses her stuff more than I do. She desperately wants to start entertaining again and having her things around her – her pictures, family albums, personal stuff, furniture etc. She's the budgie, the finch, the love-bird. She's been without a nest for 6 months now, and it's beginning to take its toll. Also, the concern about her Dad who is not well. We try to rationalize that the road we have decided to take will have its price to be paid, but as we all know, you cannot rationalize emotional feelings.

We also have the uncertainty about our status hanging over us – our visas expire on February 15 and we have to get them renewed or leave. We are confident that we will get the renewal, but the uncertainty is a burden, especially as our business activities were badly impacted by 9/11.

What's all this white stuff?

On New Year's Day the news announces that there is a storm warning for Charlotte, due to hit us. We envisage tornados, thunder and lightning. Nothing of the sort. From a beautiful sunny, blue sky, but chilly morning, the temperature suddenly plummets, the blue sky turns grey-pink and the next moment it's snowing. Within a few hours we have a couple of inches. By Thursday morning it's up to about 7 inches and the world is white with snow. Early morning radio and TV broadcasts announce that all schools and most of the shops are closed. Snow is so uncommon in Charlotte that they don't know what to do when it snows, so they just close everything and stay at home. However, every wombat with wheels comes out from under his rock and goes for a drive to check out the scenery. They end up in ditches and piling into other cars. Total chaos with over 100 accidents recorded on Thursday morning (and this is with most places closed!).

We decide to close up shop as well, get dressed in our cold-weather gear and go have some fun in the snow. Within 5 minutes, we realize we're a touch under-dressed for this type of weather. Our woolen clothing just absorbs the snow, melts and freezes us to death. Then when tobogganing, the snow falls down your neck and up the back of your shirt, melts and freezes you. The cold also tends to shrink your bladder. Now the girls are used to sitting down for this operation. However, Michael and I soon realize that the equipment we are familiar with has sort of disappeared in the cold. After a few futile attempts to encourage the poor little blue-fellow to vacate his jockeys, only to have him violently retract at the first hint of the below-freezing outdoors, and usually at that critical moment when he is just starting to do what we want him to do, again resulting in most of his efforts ending up inside your trouser-leg, rather than outside, we decide that while it may be more time-consuming to go indoors, undress and sit, it is certainly a lot safer and drier.

Within a few hours, all our clothes are soaked with melted snow. Our neighbor kindly offers her snow-gear and suggests that we look at buying something more conducive to survival. It is −5 C at this time. We head off to Sports Authority to see what the prices are like. First, we have to dig the Dodge out of the snow and brush off a whole bunch of the stuff that's accumulated on the roof and hood, aka bonnet. Then with much caution we try our hand at driving in fresh snow and ice. What a breeze. With 4x4 and diff-lock it's a Sunday afternoon stroll. A little bit hairy when you try to stop and you hear the noise of the ABS system unlocking the wheels as they begin to skid.

Now shopping here is different. As you get closer to Christmas, the prices get higher and higher and only suckers shop just before Christmas. Immediately after Christmas the sales start. And these are serious sales with discounts of up to 40%. Then after these few days of sales, they get rid of the rest of their stuff by offering discounts of up to 40% off the sale price. And we walk into one of these sales. The poor guys did lousy Ski-wear sales for Christmas because of the poor economy, so started their first big sale straight after Christmas. Then they launched their second big sale precisely at the time that the first big snow hit Charlotte in 10 years. Snow-jackets discounted by 60%, farmer-john snow-pants discounted by 60%. We decide that good cold-weather gear at these prices is cheaper than a single visit to the doctor, so we do the works – snow-jackets, snow-pants, snow-gloves, snow-boots, and head-bands to keep the "weeks" ('ears' in Stewart-speak) warm – at less than $400 for the 4 of us. Then we are ready to play. Spend hours tobogganing on the slopes outside the apartment – warm and dry as toast.

Friday morning, Michael's face looks like a red balloon. Angry red rash, swollen and very itchy. Tried everything to alleviate the swelling and irritation. Eventually cortisone ointment. It appears as if he is allergic to the cold! Fortunately, other than the itch, he feels fine and is not going to miss the snow and spends the whole day on the slopes with a gaggle of girls wanting to toboggan with him. A very strange kid this one. He's generally not into girls, shuts his eyes when he sees people kissing (when he sees the 'look' that people give one another on TV and hears the 'music', he shuts his eyes and shudders 'DAD, THEY'RE GONNA DO IT! YUCK!'') and yet he is so friendly and charming when they want to lend him their toboggans and pull him through the snow and spoil him rotten. There's got to be a lesson in here somewhere! I think I shall have to watch his 'action' more carefully! 9pm comes on Friday night and he is still not home – we go looking for him and he is still on the slopes, warm as toast, happy as a bird and still with the birds.

Sarah on the other hand is all high-fashion. In her powder-blue snow-jacket with matching headband and cream cashmere scarf round her neck and covering her lower-face, one would think her blue-eyes came from the same store. Sarah and Di are pretty much the same clothing and shoe-size now, so watching them shop together is a treat. They also have extended wardrobes making mixing-and-matching that much more fun. They even ended up buying identical fashion snow-boots!

Michael's allergies seem to come and go – for days he will keep them under control and have no asthma attacks and then suddenly all hell breaks loose. Last night, Michael gets an attack and we needed to borrow a nebulizer from some friends. It's 10pm and minus 3. Daddy, go fetch. The roads are still full of ice, the windscreen keeps freezing in the ice-rain and my better judgement tells me that this is simply not a good idea.

So today, we decide that we have to buy a nebulizer. Now in South Africa, we'd simply drive down to the pharmacy and buy one. In America it's not that easy. You need a prescription from a doctor. Why? Well to make certain that you don't buy one in order to nebulize glue, petrol, spirits and whatever else you can get your hands on. Fine! So we track down Michael's Dr Fraser at the Carolina Asthma and Allergy Center and get him to agree to prescribe one of these machines. Then we start calling around to see who has one for us. Ouch! Wal-Mart has one for $96. Eckert Drugs wants $339 for theirs (apparently has a rechargeable battery unit to make it portable! Hell, at that price I would expect it to at least make me a cuppa Joe at the same time!). We settle on $120 from Apria Healthcare which they deliver to us and demonstrate within an hour from time of order. Not bad. Then we have to fill in the forms. Tons of paperwork, declaring that we know what the device is and what it is used for and how to use it, that we indemnify the world from any liability arising from our free choice to operate said device by ourselves and without the supervision of the manufacturer, distributor, agent, government or George Dubya, that we indemnify etc, etc from any liability, injury or consequential damage arising out of our choice etc etc to self-medicate, etc etc. Then forms to indemnify the salesman from any liability arising out of his visit to our home, indemnifying him, his company, the world etc etc from any duty to advise us as to the security, safety of our home or the appropriateness of this dwelling as being suitable for the safety and well-being of the person being treated etc etc. 6 forms later, duly signed in triplicate, dated and witnessed with a copy for us and a copy for you and a copy for the Department of Health and it's good luck with your purchase and we hope it will give you many hours of reliable service. Please call us in 6 months at which time we will be pleased to offer you a service call to replace the filters and answer any questions you may have! I suppose all this shit is so that little jonny-swamp-dweller doesn't get his hands on one of these things, over-inflate his pet alligator beyond the point of no-return, gets covered in gore from popped-alli and then sue the manufacturer for damages. Like the kid who sued the microwave company for millions when he tried to dry darling doggy in the microwave.

Before leaving SA, I had the Lasik laser treatment on my right eye. I now have my good right eye for long-distance vision and my good left eye for short-distance vision. Because I never had time to get the right lens of my spectacles replaced with clear glass, I just removed the right lens. It makes me look a bit like a down-and-out, but at my age it goes well with salt-and-pepper 3-day old stubble. I use my specs for driving at night – it helps my night-vision, and I use my specs when lecturing – it goes with the bow-tie and helps my image. However, it still looks ridiculous having a missing lens. So I tootle off to the local specs-shop and ask them to please supply a plain glass lens for these specs and / or a plain plastic lens for these other specs.

"Sorry, you need a prescription!"

"What? For a piece of plain glass or plastic? "

"Yes."

"How do I get that?"

"Go for an eye test and get a prescription."

"Well, I don't need an eye-test - There is nothing wrong with my eyes. I don't need to pay someone $150 to tell me my eyes are fine and then pay you an additional $25 for one plain glass or plastic lens!"

"Then why do you need a lens if your eyes are fine?"

"I don't need a lens for my eyes – I need a lens for my vanity."

"Sorry, but you still need a script for a lens."

"Why?"

"Because you are not qualified to know what type of lens you need, and we are not qualified to diagnose what lens you need, and if we supply you with a lens without a script, then we are liable for any damage you may suffer, as well as any damage you may cause, arising out of your eye with its non-prescription lens!"

So I continue with one lens in my specs. It's a good ice-breaker when I rub my eye without removing my specs!!!

Tonight, we begin the first of our 5 ExecuRead marketing mini-lessons in Charlotte, aimed at giving people a taste of what I do and hopefully encouraging them to sign up for the full training course. If these mini-lessons don't deliver, it's home-schooling for the kids and full-time dumpster-foraging for me. Hold thumbs for us as we can no longer afford to come back to SA.

Not that South Africa is such a pleasant prospect – what with the Rand at 12 to the dollar and the government congratulating itself on their sterling efforts at maintaining the strength of the Rand and with the dancing former-president deciding that Bin Laden is not such a bad guy after all. Those with long memories will remember the international repercussions for PW's Rubicon speech and that little minister of police's comment about Biko's death leaving him cold. Well, those were nothing compared to the general feeling here about Mandela and his support for Bin Laden. We are generally surprised at how little South Africa is mentioned in the media here. However, in the past few days, there has been loads of comment, shock and criticism that Mandela of all people and a Nobel Peace Prize winner to boot, should side with the world's #1 public enemy.

Don't come back to New Jersey!

Day 207. January 30, 2002

Just returned from my business walk-about to do some teaching in DC, New Jersey and New York. The planes are cramped little bug-smashers (propellers) because so few people are willing to risk flying in the post-911 era, so they park the big jets and fly the bug-smashers. This is my first bit of serious business travel since arriving in the USA. Oh Boy! I get to Baltimore-Washington airport, 30 miles north of DC, hire a car and drive to DC and promptly get lost, even with loads of maps, and end up going the wrong way up a one-way street. Cause a traffic-jam and then while doing a U-Turn, get stopped by the police who are very officious but very understanding and guide me to Massachusetts Ave with the instruction to proceed for about 20 blocks and then turn right into 6 St SE. Of course, Massachusetts Ave reaches a huge round-about with about 12 streets going off it, very few of which have signs, and of course I pick the wrong exit and get lost all over again. 3 hours later I quite accidentally find Hereford House, my B&B, run by Ann Edwards from Kent, who welcomes me with a lovely pot of English tea, an old Labrador and a King Charles spaniel – both of which immediately adopt me!

That evening I set off for Georgetown University, 6 miles away, across town and the quadrants. 90 minutes later I arrive there, having done the scenic route! Absolutely no parking to be had. I have to park in the staff parking area, but because the shuttle does not run after hours, I have a 20-minute walk to Healy Hall where I am doing my seminar. The temperature is below freezing. When the first people arrive, I am told not to expect too many attendees as it is Martin Luther King Day. Now in the South, we don't celebrate this to any great degree, but in the "Chocolate City" (a rather un-PC description of Washington DC given to me by my African-American friend who works for GovCo), everything comes to a stop. Secondly, there is no on-campus parking for students or the public so people go home and call or email me to say they came, couldn't find parking and so went home. Had about 8 people there, all keen, but not enough for a course. Set off for Hereford House at 9pm, get lost, ask bus-drivers, taxi-drivers and filling station people to show me where I am on the map (which they can't as none of them read maps) and again quite accidentally find home just after mid-night! I'm getting a touch tired of having a car in this city!

Then off to Dayton, New Jersey – a 4-hour drive through stunning countryside. Lots of snow, blue sky and the Chesapeake River is beautiful. Huge bridges, lots of cities and my navigation working well, I think. Now a short drive to Newark Airport to dump the car – it's a liability and I cannot take it into NYC. And here the problem starts. Newark Airport is huge and is under construction. I can see Alamo Car Hire but it's on the other side the interstate freeway and it's rush-hour traffic. I follow the signs, get into a serious traffic-jam, and then the signs suddenly stop and I end up on a long bridge, going in a direction not exactly appropriate for getting to Alamo. Illegal U-turn on the bridge and back-track to the airport. Start all over again and end up on the same bridge going the wrong way. I have now been trying for 2 hours to get rid of this beastly car. Another U-turn but less successful this time! The U-turn needed a 3-point turn, the car stalled and within the next 60 seconds I have caused a monumental traffic jam. I am spotted by the bear-in-the-air and it's sirens and a whole bear-pack. They pull me over, and tell me to get out of the car. It's hands-on-holsters time. And I lose it, totally. Tell them that I am trying to find the (expletive) Alamo Car Hire so that I can return this (expletive) car because I have been driving around this (expletive) neighborhood and airport for 2 hours and would someone PLEASE arrest me and remove this (expletive) vehicle from my possession and take me to the (expletive) airport which I have been trying to get to, without the (expletive) car for the past 2 (expletive) hours. All of this while standing in my bow-tie, with my trench-coat and Indiana Jones hat and best British accent. I am sure they think I'm a little bit odd, take pity on me, and escort me to Alamo. Give the girlie at Alamo a real turn when she sees me pull in with 3 cop-cars with flashing lights top-and-tailing me and a chopper over-head. Everyone is very nice, but they suggest, of course very politely, that I refrain from driving in New Jersey until I am more familiar with directions!

Getting rid of the car is a blessing. I catch the train into NYC and oh-so-easy, a cab to the Seton Hotel, on E 32nd Street. Just a hole in the wall with a grease-ball behind the grilled reception desk and most of the rooms rented out by the hour. Only $60 per night for central NYC. A rickety elevator to the 3rd floor and behind a mauve door is my room – tiny and not totally spotless but with a comfortable bed and a brand new lovely shared bathroom down the hall. I think that the stunning bathroom is the clue to the nature of clientele – cleanliness before comfort.

I do not have time to go and see Ground Zero – you need a ticket, although it's free, but required, for some reason or another, and this will mean more cabs to the Seaport Terminal. Spend a couple of hours at Times Square and 42nd St. Amazed at how the city has been cleaned up. No more porn on the streets, the hookers are under-cover and the sleaze-shops are almost invisible. Just loads of people, stunning girls in long-fur-coats and a parade of stretch-limos that never stops.

Immigrant Lesson learned – No matter how successful my business might have been back home, America was not waiting for me to come here.

Day 210. Saturday February 2, 2002.

Go to America my girl, do good and do it well!

After a very harrowing and sad past week, with Dianne's Dad being so ill back in South Africa, we have just received the call from South Africa.

Nick, Dianne's father, had been ill with a mysterious blood-loss for over a year and eventually decided to have an operation to determine where the blood-loss was occurring and repair it. The doctors advised against the operation – said Nick's heart and lungs would not handle the strain of major surgery. Nick insisted, had the operation and survived. However, post-op complications set in, he fought bravely for over a week, but finally decided that the fishing would be a lot better on the other side. Those who know him know of his dislike for hospitals and sickness. In his last months, he became increasingly frustrated at his declining health and I think his decision to have the op was a final throw of the dice – all or nothing. It is sad that he won the battle only to be laid low by a curved ball that had nothing to do with his illness or the surgery. Personally, I think he always knew that he would win, whatever the outcome.

Nonetheless, it's terrible being so far away from him and the family at this time, and we feel so helpless. Sadly, Dianne never saw him at the end and was unable to say goodbye at his funeral. His last words to her when she left South Africa for a new life in America were "Go to America my girl, do good and do it well!"

These are the very real costs one pays for leaving your loved ones and family so far away when making a move like this.

Like all Americans, we watch George Dubya do his State of the Union Address. He says a few words and then pauses, while the whole Congress gives him a standing ovation. Then another few words and another standing ovation. I think they measure the success and acceptability of the speech by the number of standing ovations received. Very insightful speech – We are at War. We will continue to fight this war, notwithstanding the fact that it costs America $30 million per day to fight this war, a billion dollars a month. We know that Bin Laden is only one of tens of thousands of terrorists, and when we have finished destroying terrorism in Afghanistan, we will look for other countries that harbor terrorists, and we will continue the war for as long as it takes. To meet this challenge, we are going to build the US Economy and we are going to reduce taxes. Now this is a nice one – a double-speak oxymoron. Reduce taxes to build an economy to spend $12 billion tax-dollars a year on looking for terrorists. So far, more Americans have died in Afghanistan through accidents than through Afghan bullets and bombs. The reality is that accidents will happen, and when surrounded by a lot of very deadly stuff, accidents tend to be pretty final. One can only speculate as to whether the scourge of terrorism against the USA could not have been prevented if America had spent all this money on building up the economies of these countries? Or if Uncle Bill had sorted them out when he should have.

For us here in the USA, it is a very bad time. The awful realization that when we left South Africa and said goodbye to family and friends, in some cases, this would mean farewell forever. Our dreams of being able to return soon to South Africa for a holiday, disappeared in the flames of the World Trade Center. Dianne and I agonized over whether she should return to SA before her father's operation, after the operation, or for the funeral. It was not an easy time. I have to keep traveling to make the business work, kids have to be delivered to, and collected from, 2 different school-campuses, Sarah has choir, theatre and opera, often until mid-night. Many friends offered to keep the children while Di and I would be away from home, but we felt that this was too much of an imposition – Sarah's late-evening concerts and rehearsals, and especially Michael's health situation. It now appears that he suffers from bouts of anaphylaxis. During the snow in January, he spent many hours tobogganing in the snow. Later that evening he developed a severe rash on his lower face, which swelled up like a balloon. At the same time, he became totally listless, couldn't keep his eyes open and could barely walk. We assumed tiredness and an allergic reaction to the hot chocolate that he had been drinking. It now appears that he had gone into anaphylactic-shock caused by the physical exertion and extreme temperature. We have done some research into this, and it appears that his situation was a lot more serious than we thought. We now need to keep epinephrine, an "epi-pen", on hand in case this happens again. Another reason why we cannot really leave him with friends for any extended time. In this litigious country, it is too much to expect friends to give Michael an adrenaline-shot if he needs one. Stopping him from exercise is not desirable – he needs to strengthen his lungs and improve his fitness. He is already the fastest 1-miler in his grade and has just received his high-yellow belt in Tae Kwon Do. It appears that he is allergic to just about everything, and that virtually anything can push him over the edge and result in either asthma or the more extreme anaphylactic-shock. So now we have him on a very extreme diet of just about every suspect food-stuff, lots of PediaSure to keep his vitamins up, and we monitor his weight, pulse, respiration and blood-pressure on a daily basis. Once we have him stabilized, we will start introducing one foodstuff at a time to evaluate his reaction, or lack of reaction, before trying a new foodstuff.

Notwithstanding this, it was very painful for Di to decide that her place is here in the USA. From the reports and emails, Nick had a great send-off. After the service, a wake at Dianne's sister, Libby, and Paddy's home, which, by all accounts, was exactly what Nick would have wanted. Somewhere he is back on a trout-stream, where, I am led to believe, the fish are in abundance.

To all who sent the dozens of emails and who made the numerous phone-calls, thank you. We were feeling awfully lonely, lost, sad, abandoned, scared and very aware of what a huge place you filled in our lives in South Africa and how much we lost when we left SA.

Buying a car with a weak credit score … and a good friend!

At last, my training courses seem to be picking up and I need to use the Dodge, which leaves Di without a car. The only solution – buy a small, cheap-and-nasty back-up car. But how to do this with no money and no credit rating, but good prospects?

And this is where we get our first dividend from having the children at Charlotte Country Day School. One of Michael's class-girl-friends is the daughter of the owner of Scott Jaguar in Charlotte. So, a quick call to Scottie – can you find me a cheap but reliable 2nd car from your stock of trade-ins. Why? he asks. I tell him the numbers. No problem, come around and let's see what we can do for you. Bye the way, what's your Social Security number, he asks.

We get to Scott Jaguar, drool a bit over the XK's and S-types and say "one day!" Meet with Scottie and his sales rep, Brian Hill. Here's the deal, says Scottie. I have run your Social Security number through the credit bureaus and through Jaguar Finance. Not great. However, I am willing to go to bat for you on this one. Jaguar has just released a new model – the 2002 X-type.

And there she is. Pacific Blue, Sand/Ivory leather interior, 3-liter V6 230HP, 5-speed automatic, ABS, traction control, all-wheel drive, premium optional extras package and CD sound system. $40k. I'll knock off my dealer mark-up of 10%, subtract a residual of 52%, give you a 3.25% interest package, throw in a 40,000-mile unlimited warranty with full-service package and you take the car on a 39-month lease at $500 a month. All you pay for is fuel and tires. Interested?

And so we have our "2nd-hand, cheap-and-nasty", Jaguar-style! Now all we have to do is figure out how to keep the payments going.

My Visa comes up for renewal on February 15. Hold thumbs that the US Immigration people are in a good mood. Our South African attorney in Florida says no problem. But then have you ever met any attorney who says you have a lousy case – these guys make their money out of selling straws to drowning people, and at $2500 for my renewal only, (Di's comes up for renewal in a month's time), would YOU tell me I have a lousy case and lose out on $2500?

A quick note on credit scores.

In the USA, a credit score determines your life. Unlike most other countries, you must have debt – well-managed debt. But here's the paradox. To get debt, you need credit, and to get credit you need to have debt. The process for establishing a credit score is the 1-2-3 rule : ONE mortgage, TWO installment loans i.e. fixed period fix repayment loans such as a car-lease, and THREE revolving credit loans i.e. credit cards and store-cards.

The best credit score builder is a mortgage, but impossible to get once you arrive in the USA – lenders want to see at least two years of US tax returns. So you have no choice but to pay cash or rent – neither is a good idea for a number of reasons.

However, once you have a mortgage with regular on-time repayments, your credit score rises quickly and this opens the door to installment and revolving-credit loans and these accelerate the rise in your credit score.

Really smart people, which we are obviously not, purchase a US property while still domiciled overseas – with a Dollar down-payment and a sound foreign credit history, they are able to finance the investment home with a US mortgage secured with their foreign credit history. Add a tenant to rent the property and pay the monthly mortgage costs, and you start building a sound mortgage account history. Once you get to the USA and get a Social Security number, which is then linked to the mortgage account, the history becomes yours … retroactively …. and your credit score rises dramatically. And this immediately attracts lenders with offers of credit cards, store-cards and finance offers.

If only we had known this before we came here.

Day 252. Sunday March 16, 2002.

Reality sets in.

The thrill and excitement of a new country has waned and we are facing the harshness of reality. We have still not had a decision on my visa renewal, and the lawyers now want another $2500 for Di's visa renewal that expires next month. You will all have heard the news that the legacy-INS (Immigration & Naturalization Service) recently granted work-visas to the 2 dead pilots who destroyed the WTC, these visas being granted 6 months after the applicants died. Bush says he is "real hot" about this and will take the INS to task. Now this may or may not have implications for Di and I – we seem to fail on a number of requirements for a visa – we are not jihadists, we cannot fly jets and we are alive!

And not for the first time do we question our wisdom and reasons for leaving South Africa and moving to the USA. It's something that can become corrosive and we re-commit to making this work. Years later, talking to students of mine in the US Navy Special Warfare Development Group, aka SEAL-team Six, they tell me that even thinking of failure is failure itself.

The War is now costing the US Economy $2.5 billion per month! Added to this is the realization that we are totally out of our depth in this country. America is an incredibly complex society that generally welcomes immigrants, but rarely waits for immigrants.

While in New York, I make the pilgrimage to Ground Zero. Train from Grand Central (42nd St) down to 14th St and then subways to Fulton St and then a short walk to Ground Zero. Navigation is easy with the twin towers of light – 2 banks of 44 x 7000-watt spotlights shining vertically into the sky – pretty impressive.

Ground Zero is both impressive and disturbing. After 6 months of round-the-clock work, they are still at it. The whole area is ablaze with countless floodlights and a hive of activity as hundreds of people and tons of equipment continue to remove the mountains of rubble. The area is extremely cold and damp and they continue to spray a fine mist over the work area to keep the dust down. New Yorkers have developed the New York Cough – a result of the tons of dust that covered the city on September 11. Every truck leaving the site travels through a huge white plastic tunnel – a car-wash – where high-powered sprayers wash the truck, especially the wheels and underside, primarily to stop muck from being carted into the streets, but also for a more macabre reason.

Every load of rubble is taken to a sorting area where it is dumped onto conveyor belts – sorters pick through the millions of tons of debris, looking for body-parts. And this is the other reason why the trucks are washed as they leave the site – to ensure that a large truck leaving the site does not start dropping clumps of mud on the streets that may or may not contain human remains.

The barricades around Ground Zero have become a shrine, very much like the flowers for Princess Diana. This is however a shrine with a difference. Very few flowers now, but tons of items. Banners with hundreds of messages and signatures, flags from all over the world with messages, thousands of photographs of missing people, mini-shrines with a photograph of a father, his dressing-gown and slippers, his reading glasses and the last book he was reading, his cigarettes and lighter, pipe and tobacco, a glass with a can of beer. And even at 11pm, hundreds and hundreds of people, many of whom return night after night, maintaining vigil while the clearing of Ground Zero continues. I see families standing together weeping. Some shrines are manned around the clock – with some 3000 people still missing, speculation exists that some may have survived the collapse of the towers, and resulting from the horror and trauma, are suffering from amnesia and are existing in the shadow-world of New York's homeless, unknown, un-remembering and uncared-for – the hope is that one day, these poor souls will start remembering what happened and will possibly head back to the last place they were at – the WTC – and that families might recognize them.

At the risk of generalizing, the American society we have interfaced with is a very strange one. A society that jointly has managed to dominate the world and virtually every facet of modern society. While every other country is a place, America is so much more. America is an idea. A unique mindset. America is a society that initially appears to be made up in part by false, shallow and colorless individuals. Perhaps people who choose to reveal nothing of themselves to outsiders. People play the game here – they are so polite you could scream. The most common phrase is "y're welcome!" And "I want to share something with you". Feed them slop and they will say "Thank you, a wonderful meal." Why? Because it's easier to be kind than to be honest. To be kind and to walk away, than to be honest and have to explain why. It's a superficial thing. The paintwork is pristine but it's hard to see what's underneath. If there is a problem, throw money, manpower and machinery at it. It's like soldier ants – individually, of not much significance, but enough of them will destroy a building. And I think this is what makes this country work. Lots of ants, each with its own tiny task to do and a national pride that gets it done so incredibly well. And each ant has been so well-trained not to deviate from its task nor to encroach on the 'space' of another, to travel no faster or slower than the other ants.

And yet amidst all these peculiarities, we have witnessed extreme levels of generosity. At the national level, the support for the 9/11 victims, families and first-responders is nothing short of mind-boggling. And simple basic thoughtfulness – an unidentified neighbor left a VCR at our front-door – saw them on a special at Wal-Mart, thought of us with a video cassette of Dianne's Dad's memorial service but without a VCR to view the video, and bought one as a gift for Dianne and left it, anonymously, on our door-step. I think that the bottom line is that as faceless generic foreigners we are not always welcome in America. Yet once individuals get to know us, we are accepted into this peculiar society. It's a slow process. All very uncertain for us. But on balance, while we most likely left this move for too late in our lives, we made the right decision to come here.

Day 295. Sunday April 28, 2002

For the past couple of years, I've been doing some on-and-off studying for my Master's degree in Education. I never really figured on getting the degree itself, as all I really wanted was the knowledge. But after 9/11, like so many Americans, I wanted to contribute to the re-building of America and the safety of America. 9/11 was clearly a failure in American intelligence and I figured that perhaps by enhancing the reading efficiency levels of intelligence analysts, I could do something to contribute. I certainly had the time to devote to study, and to do some research into the application of my ExecuRead Methodology and Techniques to the reading requirements of military intelligence analysts. This was very theoretical, as I had absolutely no access to intelligence documents and could only focus on what was in the media. But this did give me direction and renewed motivation. And earlier this month I completed my last exam and added a Master's degree to my resume. Now with more than 25 years teaching experience and loads of statistical information on hand, I may just take a stab at getting my Doctorate.

Day 300. May 3, 2002.

Still legal.

Good news. We have just been advised by the USCIS, aka legacy INS, that my visa has been extended for another year until February 15, 2003. Notwithstanding our first year being somewhat disastrous, largely because of 9/11 – virtually no income, no taxes and no employees – they seem to think we have the potential to make a difference and have allowed us to stay. We are now eligible to start the process of filing for a "green card" and permanent residence. This is somewhat of a mixed blessing – the past year has been pretty brutal. What with the trauma of 9/11 and Dianne's father dying, coupled with little to no business and the extreme loneliness of the new immigrant, we were almost looking forward to being kicked out and having to retire to Hermanus and the misery of eating freshly grilled lobster with a chilled Cape wine, while watching the sun set over Walker Bay, with no more than the sounds of the surf and the blowing of the Southern Right Wales to disturb the peacefulness. Instead, the fight for survival continues in this very strange society.

Special note here. The USCIS has again ruled that it is satisfied that I meet the requirements for the L-1 visa. Specifically, that:

1. I WAS employed in an executive / managerial position with the South African company, and

2. I AM employed in an executive / managerial position in the US company and

3. there exists a qualifying relationship between the two companies.

A couple of months later, Dianne will also receive an extension to her L-1 visa, but for 3 years, until May 2005. Why she got a 3-year extension while I only got a 1-year extension is puzzling. What is however important is that the USCIS has again ruled that it is satisfied that Dianne also meets the requirements for the L-1 visa. Specifically, that

1. she WAS employed in an executive / managerial position with the South African company, and

2. she IS employed in an executive / managerial position in the US company and

3. there exists a qualifying relationship between the two companies.

Day 388. July 30, 2002.

When 3 comes before 1.

Time has flown and we have already passed our first anniversary in the USA.

Here's another hurdle that faces potential immigrants like us. Assuming you have filed a successful petition for a Visa, such as an L-1A (executive/managerial transfer) or H-1B (skilled worker) or B1/B2 (business / tourist) visa, the USCIS issues a Visa Approval Notice. This allows you to BE PRESENT in the USA legally and to do whatever the visa permits (like work for remuneration in the case of the L and H visas) or attend business meetings without remuneration in the case of the B1/B2 visa. But this Visa Approval Notice is not a visa – it does not permit you to TRAVEL TO or ENTER the USA. If you are already in the USA, fine – you have legal status to be in the USA. But if you need to travel internationally, you have to include in your travels a visit to the US Embassy in your country of domicile to submit an application to have the Visa Approval entered into your passport as a Visa to travel to the USA. And there is no guarantee that this application will be granted. So even though you have permission to BE in the USA, you may be denied permission to TRAVEL TO the USA. Equally bizarre, even with a valid visa in your passport, when you arrive in the USA, Customs and Border Protection have the authority to deny you entry INTO the USA.

So, it's a 3-step process. 1. Get permission from a US Embassy or Consulate to travel TO the USA ; 2. get permission from Customs & Border Protection to ENTER the USA and 3. get permission from the USCIS to BE IN the USA. But just to complicate matters, you have to start with step 3, the most expensive part, even though there's no guarantee that you'll get through steps 1 and 2. And little do we know it, but in the not-too-distant future we'll have a very personal encounter with this legal conundrum.

With a renewal of my visa, and with a Visa Approval Notice in hand but not yet in my passport, I am offered a teaching assignment for the military in Canada. But while it will be fine to exit the USA and enter Canada, I will have to return to the USA via South Africa and the US Embassy in Johannesburg or Cape Town. Look at a map and you'll see what I mean.

Business is still slow, so we decide to cut our cloth accordingly. Sarah is not enjoying Charlotte Country Day School and offers to move to something less exotic. However, the school board allocates her to McClintock School where you need a flack-jacket, a large supply of condoms and a midshipman's vocabulary. Definitely not the place for my darling daughter! But short of moving to a new address that is zoned for a better school, Sarah is about to experience another side of life. And I am motivated to find time to work on my Doctorate.

Michael gets taller and skinnier by the day. He loves Charlotte Country Day School and has made many friends. In addition, we seem to have his asthma under control at last (possibly only for the Summer). He eats his vitamins every day, watches what he eats (which means he eats loads of mozzarella cheese and tomato pizza for breakfast, lunch and supper and for all the snacks in between.) He continues to smell a bit like a hamster as we don't make him wash all that often – we have some research that keeping kids too clean may contribute to allergies – the theory is that if your immune system is fully occupied fighting your own dirt, then it does not have time to get affected by environmental and foodstuff allergens. Sounds like a crock of shit to me, but Michael is a boy and loves the idea of not having to wash all that often and for whatever reason, his asthma is minimal. He is such a beautiful boy with his blonde hair, tanned skin, big brown eyes and shiny white teeth – but you need to love him (or hamsters) lots to cuddle him.

The weather here is murderous – temperatures of over 100 degrees F with energy-sapping humidity. As I write this, it is 1am and the temperature outside is 90 degrees F! It has cooled down as it was 99 degrees at 7pm this evening. We keep the air-conditioners on all the time and try to ignore the electricity bill every month until the weather cools down in the fall.

We decide to dig into our savings and get away from the heat for a week and to head to New York for an 'educational'. Manage to get 4 cheap air-tickets to New York and a reasonable hotel on the west side of Manhattan. A 3am wake-up for the 3-hour 150-mile drive to Raleigh airport to catch our flight to LaGuardia – tickets from Raleigh are half the price of tickets from Charlotte. Of course, I am singled out for a full airport security check, much to the consternation of the children. Then a 90-minute flight to NY in a small 45-seater jet (we don't use big jets in the USA anymore – they tend to land in inappropriate places!)

By mid-morning we are in Manhattan. First stop – a big pizza for Michael who needs about 5 - 6 meals a day – this kid either has a metabolic system the size of a NASA rocket-booster or a serious worm! Then a major walkabout and parade of excursions – a visit to the Museum of Natural History, a trip up the Empire State Building, a boat-cruise round Manhattan Island, a visit to the Sony Electronics Wonder Museum, then to Toys R Us's latest store on Times Square (which has a full sized Ferris wheel and Jurassic Park dinosaur in the entrance) and to FAO Swartz (two seriously huge toy shops – look-see only mind you), then a walk through Chinatown (so Sarah can buy a copy-Gucci), Little Italy, Greenwich Village and Soho, Ground Zero, Ellis Island and the Statue of Liberty (now closed to the public in case some crazy decides to blow up this icon of American freedom and liberty.) Then to Cheap Tickets at Times Square to stand in line for last-minute tickets to see Phantom of the Opera – the kids are mesmerized, although after 15 years since I last saw the show in London, I am a bit disappointed. In London we saw the 3rd night after opening with Michael Crawford and Sarah Brightman. Americans are able to throw huge amounts of money into a show, and the set and costumes are brilliant. But the voices do not quite make it.

We also spend 3 hours queuing for tickets to see the new Thoroughly Modern Millie show which has won all the Tony

Awards. Again, a brilliant show but the voices are lacking. Then off to the Intrepid Sea and Space Museum on the Hudson River, 2 blocks from our hotel. Stunning and not to be missed. Home of the USS Intrepid – a WW2 aircraft carrier that has been turned into a museum, including everything from the first submarine ever built, to the latest in aero-space technology – from lunar capsules to Tomcats to AWACS to the still-classified SR-71 Blackbird. Intrepid was the victim of 3 kamikaze hits during WW2 and was recommissioned temporarily after September 11 to house the 750-man FBI team of investigators into 9/11. Next to Intrepid is USS Growler, the only nuclear submarine open to the public, including cruise-missiles. Tours through the sub are strictly controlled and well-observed. And next to Growler, the QE2 – not part of the museum, but on a quick stopover on its way around the world with its complement of 'poor' people who had to fork out a minimum of $100,000 for a berth in the bilges! Don't have my bow-tie with me so cannot nip in to see if my god-mother Gillian is in the neighborhood – last I heard, she was buying Spain or something equally exotic.

Day 456. October 6, 2002

My parents have their 52nd wedding anniversary tomorrow – congratulations Dad and Mom – not many people can claim so many years together. And thank you for sharing 51 of those years with me.

And my baby daughter Sarah becomes a teenager on October 18 – currently rehearsing for her two performances in Mahler's 3rd Symphony, conducted by world-renowned conductor Cristof Perrick. With 103 instruments and 120 voices it should be quite spectacular. It has never before been performed in Charlotte, so it will be somewhat out of the comfort zone of the normal classical audience here. Next on her calendar is a performance of Benjamin Britten's War Requiem, which may or may not be opportune, depending on Bush and Saddam. She is changing every day – the move away from Charlotte Country Day was the best thing for her. We had to settle for McClintock Middle School (which she finally loves!), where she is in Grade 6 but has been put into the Scholar-Program where she does Grade 8 math and communication and is getting straight A's. She travels to school on the yellow "cheezer" (school-bus), plays the French-horn (in addition to the flute), speaks 'Southern' when at school, speaks South African when at home, sings Italian with her singing tutor and reads half a dozen books a week.

Michael is still at Country Day – loving it and has become quite outspoken. Ended up with a pesky little girl sitting next to him who never stops talking and who keeps copying his work. Now young Michael (turned 8 in July) is very holy about getting 100% for everything he does and hates people who crowd his space. In class, they are teaching the kids how to tell the time – give them a sheet of paper with lots of clock images and ask them to write down the time displayed in the picture. Jessica gets everything wrong, so copies from Michael (who has been able to tell the time since age 5 and whose comment is that it's only in America that 8-year-olds have to be taught how to tell the time). In defense, he starts writing down the time in 24-hour format and this really confuses Jessica (and unfortunately also the teacher!!). Then he switches tactics and next to the image writes down 4 different times – Eastern, Central, Mountain and Pacific. Now this really confuses Jessica, so she asks Michael what the 4 times mean, Michael tells her to keep quiet and they both get into trouble for talking in class. In order to "nuzzle" her, he eventually demands that Jessica be relocated to another seat. Becoming quite anal-retentive this son of mine. Very much into his soccer and just loves his math. Becoming a total computer geek. Such a beautiful child and still smells like hamsters.

I am still plugging away at the business and trying to concentrate on my Doctoral studies. We became very demoralized a month ago and started the corrosive debate that perhaps America was not for us. Then out of the blue, when we were at our lowest, I received calls from a Medical Center in New York, from Kenan-Flagler Business School and from Unifi Corporate University, all wanting courses. This could be the turn-about – we have spent so much time and money in planting seeds, maybe we will soon be rewarded with harvesting a crop.

In the lead-up to the first anniversary of 9/11, the local newspaper, Charlotte Observer, calls us to do a story on immigrants and how we've been affected by 9/11.

We have a love-hate relationship with this country. We tend to lose sight of the fact that immigration is never easy, even less so when you have left an established life-style. And even less so when you are getting fairly long in the tooth. In the long run, this move will be great for the kids. I doubt that I will ever really get used to the changes – I should have accepted the US job from Coca-Cola back in 1983 when I had youth and a secure job-offer on my side.

In what country is South Africa?

November 2002. And the roller-coaster ride just keeps on going.

The D.C. Sniper, John Muhammad, has been offing strangers up north, much to the chagrin of the law-enforcement agencies, and mothers have been forcing their kids to wear the latest Washington fashion statement – a flack-jacket and bullet-proof helmet. Looks a damn side better than the anti-anthrax gas-masks that make people look like armadillos. And now in Charlotte, you can go and collect free issue special iodine tablets – the idea is that because we all live so close to 2 nuclear reactors, in case of one or both being blown up by terrorists, your thyroid is at risk and will start absorbing the radioactive iodine, so if you quickly take these tablets, you can saturate your thyroid with good iodine and it won't absorb the radioactive iodine. Someone needs to point out that if we lose 2 Charlotte nuclear reactors to terrorists, my thyroid is the least of my concerns.

Other than having to downplay all of this to our two young children, another thing that has emanated from the sniper-saga is another fat legal bill for me – with 9/11 and the USCIS giving visas to the dead terrorist pilots, they got all antsy and only gave me a 1-year renewal.

Three months later, they were back to their sloppiness again and gave Di a 3-year visa renewal. Now it appears that the USCIS had 17-year-old Lee Malvo (the Jamaican juvenile accomplice of John Muhammad) in custody some months ago, found that he was an illegal with no job and no address and instead of holding onto him, they let him go free, pending a deportation hearing 10 months later! More mud for the USCIS and another tightening of the immigration laws.

After an enjoyable and successful course for 23 MBA students last week, Di and I are off to New York to exhibit at the NY Expo. We are meeting some of Di's friends in Connecticut when we are there, as we are starved for some mental stimulation – very tired of explaining that Robert Mugabe is not the president of South Africa, that South Africa and Zimbabwe are two separate countries, that Egypt is quite a drive away from South Africa and that while Australia may have been recently 'colonized' by South Africans, the 'river' dividing the two countries is more than a quick swim, and that gold is not mined in Fort Knox.

While in New York we catch a train to Riverside, Connecticut (near Hartford) to see some old friends. Di has not seen them since a skiing trip to Austria in 1982 and Nick and Tracy have been living in the New York area for about 16 years. Nick's claim to fame is that he produced the highly successful international ad campaign for …"Some things may be priceless, but for everything else there's MasterCard". He is also Michael and Vanessa Prior's nephew – small world!! (When Di and I were working for Consol, a large glass, plastic and paper packaging company in South Africa, we were tasked with building South Africa's first museum of glass. We met Michael and Vanessa Prior, serious antique dealers and the four of us travelled the USA, UK and Italy buying glass artifacts for the museum. When Sarah arrived, Michael Prior graciously agreed to be her god-father.) Nick meets us at the station and we head back to their beautiful home, filled with paintings and furniture from South Africa, for drinks and it promptly begins to snow. After a wonderful long lunch at their yacht club on the Long Island Sound, we catch the train back to NYC exhausted! Nick and I have been meeting in

NYC occasionally as he has some great ideas about getting my business moving.

For the last three days we have been besieged in the latest battle of the Civil War between the North and the South – a freezing cold front has moved South from Canada while a tropical front moved North from Florida. These two armies met in the Carolinas on Wednesday. Warm air rose above the cold and resulted in a storm of ice-rain – no wind or fireworks, just a deluge of rain that freezes as it hits the ground. Everything coated with a thick layer of solid ice. Trees cannot carry the weight and come crashing down, smashing power-lines, cars and houses. The interstate highways are closed, as are all the schools. A state of emergency has been declared with over a million people without electricity. Estimates are that it will be 3 weeks before full power is restored. School gyms, conference centers and fire-stations have been converted into refugee-shelters for those who have no heating. The Red Cross has come to the fore with stretchers (known as cots, here), blankets, toiletries (for those who forget theirs at home!) and warm food. Shops are empty as deliveries have been suspended. Many of our friends have left home and moved in with others who have power and heating. During the day and night, you can hear the sound of trees crashing to the ground under the weight of the ice.

The roads are coated with black-ice, and with this being such a rare occurrence in the Carolinas, every yobbo with a car is out sight-seeing, resulting in wrecked cars all over the place. Few people know how to handle 4-way uncontrolled intersections (without traffic lights) so they either all go or all stop at the same time – the stopping is fine – it's when they all go at the same time that there is a spot of bother for all concerned.

We have been fine – no power-outages and our TV and fridges are full, so, with the kids at home and the cars frozen solid, we have been snug as bugs. I had a course to teach in Greensboro on Thursday. Took me half an hour to thaw enough ice off my car just to get the doors open. Then heard on the TV that the interstate was closed. Called my client in Greensboro and begged off for a week.

The kids have been having a ball playing on the ice. Michael finds out the hard way that bicycles and black-ice are a bad mix. Sarah is now champing at the bit to get up to the mountains where it has been snowing heavily. So it's up to Appalachian Ski Resort on Sunday.

War-talk

February 2003. War Diary – I am in DC this week. Drove up from Charlotte on Monday morning. Loads of this crappy white stuff all over the place. Thank God for 4X4. Keep getting into snow-drifts and having to take "d'tours" (Yank for detours) so Mrs Garmin works overtime in keeping me pointed in the right direction. The Texan Cowboy has oiled his six-shooter and is really keen to get hisself some scalps. But the country is spending so much time talking instead of doing, that Saddam has more than sufficient time to prepare himself for war. There is ongoing news-coverage about what the FBI says is likely to be a major attack against the USA and the prediction is something "very dirty".

While in DC, the news tells the nation to prepare for war – you need 3 days of food and water in the most secure room in your home. Also, all your medical supplies, warm clothing, cell-phones, torches and portable radios with lots of spare batteries. And a large supply of plastic-sheeting and rolls of duct-tape. In the event of a chemical or biological attack, seal yourself in your secure room by closing up all windows and vents and doors with the plastic and the duct-tape and listen up for emergency announcements, especially news of where to go for government issues of antibiotics and Potassium Iodide in case of a "nucular" aka Nuclear attack.

In DC, you can see those really cool Hummers with Stinger rocket pods for shooting down the baddies – they are moving about the streets and getting into position near strategic buildings. Nothing like seeing it this close to get the indigestion into top gear. And on all flights into Washington DC, you better not need to take a leak in the last 30 minutes of your inbound flight. 30 minutes prior to arrival in DC, any attempt to leave your seat will result in the plane making an emergency diversion away from the city and you being arrested by the on-board air-marshal. So, plan to take your dump in international airspace or after you have landed.

I had been in New York and Philadelphia the previous 2 weeks and the preparations for war were not as obvious – Colin "Goebbels" Powell had not yet made his Security Council "d'bute" (yank for debut) where he spelled out all the "d'tails" (yank for details) charging Saddam with his dirty deeds. I just love the logic. "This picture shows a de-contamination vehicle and some trucks outside a building. Ergo, there are chemicals in the building. Now this picture shows that the trucks and de-con vehicle have gone and the inspectors could find no chemicals in the building. Ergo, the chemicals have been moved and hidden." Simple, isn't it? Like seeing a fire-engine parked outside a house. The next day the fire-engine is no longer there. Stupid me, I assumed there was a false alarm about a fire. I didn't realize that someone had moved the fire and hidden it!

Some people are getting down to some frenzied emergency shopping. Many of us are taking a more pragmatic approach. Personally, I don't think my old body is flexible enough for me to bend down and kiss my ass goodbye (and quite frankly, that is not the view that I want fixed in my mind for all eternity), so the idea is to simply take a deep breath. All very dramatic and alarmist.

Driving back to Charlotte from DC, I get my first speeding fine. Finished teaching a class at Georgetown University's McDonough Business School in DC at 9pm, still feel wired and decide to do the 7-hour drive back to Charlotte. Give Mrs Garmin the directions, set the cruise-control and off we go. Speed limit is 65mph so the cruise–control is set for 68mph. Imagine the scene. It's after midnight, the temperature is just below freezing, the roads are deserted, there is a full moon – a lovely night for a relaxing drive. Two hours into the trip I see I have company some distance behind me. No problem, my speed is fine and all is well. And if I have a breakdown, help is close by and I won't freeze to death waiting for a tow-truck. Next moment, the lights and sirens come on. I pull over with a Virginia

Bear behind me. Knowing how trigger-happy these guys are, and wondering what the problem is, I turn on the interior lights, open my window and place both hands on the steering wheel. In my wing-mirror I see the cop heading towards me from behind, one hand pointing a very big flashlight (torch) at me and the other hand on a very big pistol on his hip. (These guys use a .40 caliber with hollow-points). He asks for my drivers-license and registration papers. They're in the glove-compartment I tell him. May I remove my hands from the steering-wheel to get them? Permission granted. I do so, noting that the glare of his flashlight does not leave my hands and neither does his grip on the .40 caliber. Off he goes back to his car to make sure that I am not Osama Bin Laden or Saddam Hussein. Comes back satisfied that I am Mr Stewart from dopey Charlotte, NC. Shit! Nothing exciting here! Do you know at what speed you were traveling, Mr Stewart? Why yes officer, as a matter of fact I do. A little over 65mph – set into my cruise-control and I am sure that Mrs Garmin also recorded my speed quite accurately. Yes, I agree with that Mr Stewart. You went through a static radar trap a few miles back and were recorded at 68mph. I then paced you and also recorded your speed at 68mph. So what's the problem, I ask him? You were in a 55mph zone he answers, with no hint of a smile. Here is your summons to appear in court in Stanardsville Virginia or you may pay an admission of guilt of $5 per mph over 55mph i.e. $65 plus a processing fee of $47. Now since I admitted my speed and even have a GPS unit to prove my "guilt", I hardly think it's worth the effort of a 700-mile round trip to Stanardsville Virginia to plead my case, even if I could find this piddly little town again, but I think it's really rich having one of America's finest skulking around in freezing temperatures waiting to catch me, while the rest of the nation is hiding behind Stinger-carrying Hummers and embalming their homes in plastic sheeting and duct-tape, not to speak of the more aromatic enjoyments of having a family insulated in a sealed room with no washing facilities and an open bucket for less savory ablutions. And the FBI says there are over 3000 suspected Al Qaeda terrorists in this country, just waiting to trigger a nuke or toss some anthrax into the wind! What does this guy think? That he'll catch Al Qaeda terrorists in a speed-trap? In Virginia? Oh well, I suppose the poor bugger deserves to screw someone. I am tempted to suggest that he might try spending cold nights in more comfortable activities, but decide silence to be the better part of valor. You never know with these people – they take their jobs very seriously and his sense of humor may have been as icy as the rest of him.

News from the home front. The children seem to have compartmentalized the threat of a nuclear and/or biological terrorist attack. Sarah is comfortably top of her class at school, even though she is in Grade 6 and doing the Grade 8 advanced curriculum. She is now the lead French-horn player in the school orchestra. Michael is still the ultimate geeky nerd. A whiz at math and science, loves his computer and has developed a serious sense of humor. Gets very peeved if he makes a silly mistake in math, but is totally laid-back when it comes to spelling. Either gets 100 percent correct or 100 percent incorrect, depending on how he feels that day. When his teacher blasts him for poor spelling, he quips that spelling is for people who don't know how to use spell-check on their computer! He is now the second fastest 1-miler in his grade, and figures to be the fastest just as soon as he can breathe as much air as the other guys – still gets asthma when he smells his own sweat and runs like the wind until he starts sweating and then runs out of air. He has good days and bad days. He is so lean – built like a greyhound. All brain and spirit, but eats continuously and zero body-fat.

Clearly the move to the USA is more than justified by the education our kids are getting. Yes, it's tough on the parents, especially as we get older and have to face starting at the bottom rung again, but it's a worthy sacrifice. And Di is into the restoration business. Digs up furniture that people turf out. Strips it down, sands, seals, glues, stains and varnishes. Rocking chairs, coat-stands, table-lamps, wall-units – stuff looks better than new.

I have again had to apply for a renewal of my Visa. Last year they gave Di a 3-yr renewal but only gave me a 1-yr renewal, so I have again had to fill in loads of paperwork and give the lawyers another $2500. Not that I have had any experience with hookers, but I would imagine that the only difference between getting screwed by lawyers and by hookers, is that with hookers there is some expectation of an enjoyable ending to the whole procedure.

Day 618. March 17, 2003, 03h00. US At War.

Pangaea 2003 – Outside, the mist lies still in the calm night. In many churches all over the country, prayer meetings are held for peace. On countless street-corners, candle-light prayer vigils are being held to pray for peace. In other corners, speculation reigns – how soon before we go to war? In a chilling broadcast, Saddam Hussein cautions that any invasion of Iraq will be met by retaliation anywhere in the world that is accessible by land, sea or air. And on the local news, Charlotte's mayor, Pat McCrory announces that all of North Carolina's hospitals have been placed on emergency alert. One can only wonder how we reached this point so soon. And we've only been in this country for 20 months.

In his State of the Union address, President George W Bush manages to secure 77 standing ovations during his 60-minute speech. (I had a Jewish woman in my NY class – says her mom got most upset – she remembered a similar incident in the Reichstag in 1939). He's come a long way since his early presidential days. Now it's 'sound-bites' to a nation that changed on September 11, 2001. What has happened in the short period since the Florida Supreme Court resolved a dead-locked presidential election? How did a president who had the support of less than half of the nation, become the idol of Americans in the post 9/11 year and then as quickly find his popularity decline to less than 50% by early 2003? What is an increasingly desperate and frustrated president likely to do to capture a second term in office?

In some quarters it is being argued that America is colonizing the world. Ridiculous? America's annual defense budget now exceeds the rest of the world combined. America controls Space, with very little of planet Earth not subject to American satellite scrutiny. And now America comes face to face with the UN Security Council. Some news commentators have stated quite unambiguously that

America IS the United Nations. President Bush has asked the Security Council for support in a War against Iraq, but has made it very clear that UN support, while desirable, will not affect his final decision. America sees itself as the world's policeman, as the custodian of world affairs, as the paterfamilias of the modern Pangaea.

Thomas Friedman, the foreign affairs columnist of the New York Times, wrote that the first salvo of WW3 was fired on July 17, 1996 with the downing of TWA FL800 off the Long Island coast. At the time attributed to an exploding fuel tank, subsequent investigations revealed credible evidence of FL800 having been downed by a terrorist missile, and covered up by the Clinton administration to protect the airline industry and the Atlanta Olympics. Within the past few months, accusations are being leveled that the missile that downed FL800 was in fact a US Stinger, fired by the US military to down FL800 which had been hijacked by terrorists and filled with Semtex. It is being hotly debated whether President Clinton was correct in concealing this from the public.

Whatever the debate about TWA FL800, the nation was ill-prepared for 9/11 and in a single day, the world changed. A bumbling President Bush received the support of 100 percent of Americans. Dividing lines between Republicans and Democrats were abolished. If you were not behind George Bush, you were un-American. And George Bush declared War. The people loved the 'sound-bite'. Few stopped to think …. War Against Whom? … What Nation? …. What Country? How do you fight an ideology that has no nationality, wears no uniform and has no country? So, the enemy had to be personified – the enemy was given a name – Osama Bin Laden – and Bush promised his head to the American people. But Bin Laden proved no easy target. Few Americans realized that Bin Laden was no idiotic untrained desert Arab, but a multi-millionaire Saudi businessman who was trained by the USA to lead the Afghan rebellion against the Russian occupation. After spending years as an Afghan 'Freedom Fighter', Bin Laden has proved to be a somewhat elusive 'Terrorist' and rather difficult to secure as a trophy for President Bush's 2nd term election campaign. Americans started asking why Bush was taking so long to tame the 9/11 terrorist. Bush's ratings started to decline. Action was needed. The side-step from Bin Laden to Saddam Hussein must rate as one of the slickest sleight-of-hand moves in modern history. Suddenly, Saddam Hussein became public enemy #1. Interestingly enough, another creation of America's foreign policy. Now this man was a far more interesting target – he controls a country with lots of oil – a fat prize for a president with a mission to prove himself. Remember – the US runs on oil. Lots of oil. Our biggest supplier, Venezuela, is having some difficult times and the supply from South America has slowed to a trickle. Should Bush be able to secure a Middle Eastern oil-field for America, this would further enhance America's international power-base. America tends to have a firm belief that if it's not owned by America, it should not be worth owning – South Africa's gold industry learned a bitter lesson here.

However, Bush has a problem. By no stretch of the imagination can he sell an oil-motivated US invasion of Iraq to the US people and the rest of the world. So it's back to bait-and-switch – terrify Americans and the world with stories of Saddam Hussein's brutality, human rights contraventions and weapons of mass destruction. Then hide behind the UN – give an invasion of Iraq some international respectability. Let there be little doubt that even with UN support, who will control a post-invasion Iraq …. and the oil-fields. As to brutality and human rights contraventions, who is Bush trying to kid? America does nothing if there is not a return on investment. America doesn't give a hoot about human rights. In South Africa, human rights were traded for Black American votes. In the rest of Africa, human rights were traded for domination over the Soviets. Once the Soviets were out of Africa and Mandela was in the Union Buildings, human rights violations had served their purpose. And as for the so-called weapons of mass destruction, what's so unique about Iraq? America, Russia, China, France, Germany, India, Pakistan, South Africa, North Korea, Israel and others all have weapons of mass destruction.

There is little doubt that Saddam is a nasty piece of work. But what do you expect – he was trained by professionals in Langley,

Virginia? And perhaps he does need to have his claws trimmed. But this pending fight reminds me too much of those kid-fights we had at school. We strutted and postured and threatened and all too soon we attracted a huge crowd – and it was the crowd that forced the first blow to fall – after all, who has the guts to be the one to back off first. And I fear this is what we have got ourselves into. Almost 300,000 troops on the borders of Iraq. Most of the carrier battle-fleet in position for a first strike. And last week we watched news footage of the B-52 Stealth bombers leaving US soil. And footage of the new 21,000lb bombs - called MOAB's (Mother of all Bombs!). As one military observer noted, these are so big that they not only remove the building, but the foundations as well. We have spent months threatening Saddam, and months talking about the invasion, and months bragging about how quickly this will all be over – it's Blitzkrieg all over again, or so we think. The general consensus is that we have had too many testosterone- and adrenalin-hyped-up troops sitting around for too long and that we cannot expect them to sit around much longer. They are getting bored and the weather is warming up. It's going to hit 85 F (36 C) there today. They might do most of their training in the heat and humidity of the Carolinas, but this weather is small potatoes when compared to the heat of the Arabian Desert that goes up to 130 °F (55 °C) (we've been there, in Oman and the UAE, when the authorities closed tourist-access to the desert because it was dangerously hot!). So it's a case of either take a dump or get off the pot!

Now I'm no military strategist, but I figure that with so much fire-power aimed at Iraq, the wisest thing for a sane man to do would be to step off the plate. However, a crazy, but clever, insane man, who has literally hundreds of suicidal fanatics available to his cause of Muslim Fundamentalism, might just figure on doing something really nasty right here in our back-yard, where we least expect it. All those fancy Humvees with all those pretty Stinger missiles parked all over DC and NY awaiting air-attacks, but quite vulnerable to a ground attack by a couple of fanatics wanting to grab those assets in order to plant Stingers into some pretty big downtown buildings. Or all these juicy nuclear power plants parked all over the USA. Or a few bags of some chemical or biological nastiness in downtown Manhattan, DC, Seattle, LA or San Francisco. Lord Kitchener demonstrated that few soldiers fight well when concerned about the safety of their homes, women and children.

One should not forget that with the exception of Powell and a couple of others, few of the politicians here are former military people. If an invasion of Iraq is justified on military grounds, it should have been done months ago. The world might have squawked a bit, but if the troops had revealed all of those piles of weapons of mass-destruction that Bush says he has proof of, the world would applaud and say 'wow, we never knew it was so bad – just as well you invaded.' However, now it is in the hands of the politicians who are looking to cover their asses before an invasion, just in case things don't quite pan out as expected. One of my neighbors, a retired US Marine says this is Vietnam all over again – a war that will be started by politicians and a war that will be ended by politicians once the body-bags start coming home.

Personally, I figure that Bush should withdraw from Iraq, come home and issue a warning to the world – commit an act of terror and America will immediately, and without notice, attack and invade any country which hosted and supplied the terrorists. If necessary, train and maintain a special global-anti-terrorist strike force for the task. We have the money – since 9/11, the so-called War on Terror has cost the USA over $1 billion per DAY - $365 billion dollars in the first year after 9/11. You can buy a lot of strike-drones and train a lot of SEALs with that many potatoes.

As for the Stewarts in Fortress America, we are well. At dinner parties, talk about South African crime has been replaced by talk about War. The declining SA economy has been replaced by a declining US economy.

Sarah has another singing gig – she is one of 2 sopranos in the children's chorus of the opera Carmen at the Belk Theatre. She is doing really well at school – still top of her class and recently represented McClintock Middle School at the regional event of the national US Science Olympiad in Charlotte and walked away with a Gold Medal. Brains and a voice, although we are not certain where her voice is going. Her tutor says she has the full range of a mezzo and soprano, so she should become quite versatile.

Michael is still pretty much a 4.0 GPA student in math and science. Still lives on rice, mashed potatoes, pasta, pizza and vitamins. Found him some waffles that he can eat without a reaction to the eggs, so he scoffs waffles for the protein and carbs, and tins of sliced peaches. So tall and thin. But very much a hamster – eats minute quantities at a time, but eats 10 times a day. Always has a snack close at hand – with him, everything is immediate. When he gets hungry, there's no waiting at all. Similarly, when out in the car, and Michael says "Stop the Car", you ignore him at your peril. He comes home from school, and eats. Homework is done in the car and within a few minutes of getting home. It's a matter of pride that he gets his homework done quickly and correctly, and he gets very pissed if you ask him whether he has done his homework – gives you a flat cowboy stare and asks "is that a serious question?" Knows exactly how each of his classmates is doing too. Says one of his friends writes really well …. And then totally deadpan "which is just as well – if he couldn't write well, he would have to take a job at Burger King!"

The kids are handling the talk of war quite well. We haven't quite done the full emergency thing with gas-masks, duct-tape and rolls of plastic and setting up an emergency room, although I have noticed that Mommy Di has been quite busy – plastic containers with medical supplies nicely labeled, a special container with Michael's medicine and face-masks, all nicely labeled, and yes, I did see a couple of rolls of duct-tape and a couple of bottles of chemical-toilette stuff. But little things, like the school asking us to pack a special medical kit for Michael, which the school will keep with their emergency evacuation kit, makes one realize that we live in interesting times. We also tend to have more batteries than usual, and the cars get filled up when only half-empty and cell-phones are always kept fully charged. We try to build a small stock of emergency snacks, but find that we all suddenly started experiencing these small emergencies that necessitate nocturnal visits to the War-cupboard. Which reminds me, I had better prepare a large quantity of biltong and koeksusters in case we have to go into Laager. (If you've not tasted South African biltong (aka jerky), you're under-privileged. And if you've not tasted South African 'koeksusters', you've never lived!)

Day 629. March 28, 2003. Not quite a "quickie".

First of all, we are just 'fahn'. We've eaten all the biltong and koeksusters while watching the war on TV. "Shrub" (that's code for the little Bush) is really pissed because his re-election campaign is not going according to plan. His little excursion to go collect the scalp from the bully in the sand-pit has gotten a bit bogged down.

When we decided to go and nail that irritating man in Iraq, we were assured that this would be a quickie. You see, when mah daddy went over to "eye-rack" 12 years ago, he sorted Saddam out in only 100 hours. Now, today, we have much better weapons, and in any case, Saddam's army is going to 'hands-up' at the first sight of our over-whelming forces.

Well, now as they say in the classics, assumption is the mother of all fuckups. You see, Saddam didn't go to the same gentleman's school as the boys from Queensbury and doesn't know the rules. After all, he was trained by the US Military Bad-Asses!

Now, when I was a kid and got into scraps with the other kids from the neighborhood, my daddy told me that in a fight, it's not how you fight, but who wins.... And the best idea is to kick the other guy in the balls first. Even better, kick him when he least expects it. And he who fights dirtiest, fights best. Then the fight is over before it has even started.

And here is our little problem. We sent 300,000 troops to Iraq with lots of B-52s, F-117 Stealths, B-2 Stealths, lots of Apaches and lots of Black Hawks and thousands of cruise-missiles and Tomahawks and even a whole fleet of those really fancy M1 Supertanks. We sat on Saddam's border and tried to make him chicken out and run away. Mistake #1. Then we invaded without a formal declaration of war. Other than imposing ridiculous Rules of Engagement on our fighting soldiers, the absence of a declaration of war by Congress denied our troops many of the much deserved and much needed benefits accorded to soldiers in times of war. Mistake #2. We also announced that our fight is with Saddam and his cronies and not with his people. Mistake #3. Suddenly we find that this fellow uses human shields and won't come out into the open where we can nail his ass, reckons that a white flag is a great way of getting us to drop our guard, so they can get real close to shoot us, and even seems to have an endless supply of US army uniforms and civilian clothing. So our boys see a bunch of civilians, go up to them assuming them to be buddies and then get their asses shot at. Or see a bunch of other yanks, go up to have a Budweiser and get nailed because we couldn't see the big mustaches under the gas-masks. And we take prisoners, and give them water, food and medicine, while they take prisoners and give them a bullet in the head. IT'S JUST NOT FAIR. DIDN'T ANYONE TELL HIM ABOUT QUEENSBURY RULES AND THE GENEVA CONVENTION? WHY WON'T THEY FIGHT FAIR SO THAT WE CAN KILL THEM IN A FAIR FIGHT!? And then there is all this fucking sand that keeps getting in the electrics. It's all the fault of the French. They made us start this war in March and everyone knows that March and April are full of sand-storms. And the Iraqi troops won't come out and fight in the desert where the M1 Supertanks can work to best effect. Instead, they are skulking in Baghdad with their women and children as human shields. And in Baghdad, the US is outnumbered 5 to 1, and while they hide behind human shields and shoot us, we are not allowed to shoot them through their human shields. After all, we've got 500 flipping EMBEDDED journalists with us – who came to record our blitzkrieg victory but who are instead a big inconvenience – witnesses with TV and camera and all.

"Shrub" now says this was never expected to be a short war and it will last as long as it takes to win. Another war of attrition. 'Nam 2. Russia and Syria are now actively supplying Iraq with military supplies – especially night-vision goggles and radar-jamming systems. So now the enemy can also see in the dark, and the cruise-missiles are getting totally confused and dropping all over the place – result – Mr US Grunt won't shoot a human shield, but it's OK for missiles to wander all over the skies, getting jammed until eventually taking out a chunk of desert at $600,000 a pop or flattening a school or hospital and giving the protesters even more to rant and rave about. Donald Rumsfeld warns the Syrians that if they continue to supply Iraq, we will go after them as well. Ergo, Shrub is building a list of people NOT to invite to his next party at Camp David (nice Jewish name this! I understand it used to be called Shangri-La) – Top of the list is of course Osama BL, then of course Iraq, then France and Germany for not supporting him, then Russia and Syria for helping Iraq, then Turkey for stuffing around with over-flight rights. Laura is getting peeved – not much of a dinner party with only the Brits and Aussies and with Spain and Portugal and then the rent-a-guest crowd.

The TV is solid War – even Nickelodeon has news updates for the latest pictures and news about how many of their people we're killing, and how many of our own kids they have killed and we have killed. Websites are up where you can go and place bets on how long the war will last. Over $1.5m in bets has already been placed.

If the world was one big family, the Brits would be the parents – leaders in their time but now a bit elderly and would rather wear their robe and slippers while having a cuppa-tea; also, a touch laid back and not too keen on shaking things up. The continentals are really the cousins of the Brits/parents, tend to be over-shadowed by the Brits/parents and are more of an irritation than of any real benefit. America of course is the adolescent teenager – requires instant gratification, terribly materialistic, thinks he knows everything, believes that the world revolves about him, not interested in other views and opinions, somewhat prone to temper-tantrums even if everything gets broken in the process, and tends to be a bit of a bully, regardless of the consequences.

I'm spending a few days teaching in Atlanta – very relaxing, as the class is small and the hotel is empty – people staying at home with their Jerky, Krispy-Kreme doughnuts and Duct-tape. Even the hookers are absent. Looking forward to my next trips to DC and NY as they now have Humvees with Stingers on the streets and Black Hawks patrolling the skies – Remember the movie "Black Hawk Down"?

Sarah is busy rehearsing for Carmen, and also for her first solo recital. Very disappointed at not being able to go on the June tour to Washington State and Canada. She doesn't have a visa to get back into the USA. We are also awaiting our visa-renewals which should get here in late May or early June, but then we have the problem of getting the Visas into our passports – this can only be done by a US Embassy and you only find these things OUTSIDE the USA – so we have to leave the USA in order to get a visa to come back into the USA!! Asinine if you ask me! We cannot risk sending her to Canada and then hoping that she will be able to get to an embassy to get a visa to come home to her daddy. We are trying to find out whether we can courier the passports to the embassy in Toronto for the visas without actually having to go there ourselves, but have a feeling that the USCIS and Department of State will freak if there's not a body attached to the passport.

Latest news is that the War has been put on hold in Iraq as the US troops have run out of food! Apparently, the supply lines are too long and some of the troops have been without supplies for a few days now.

Latest internet betting : 90% of the bets are that Shrub will remain in power at least until Monday, and that the US will still be fighting the war in Iraq as of June 30.

Day 700. June 7, 2003. Kalli-fornia to Florida.

Just back from DC, and we are packing for a 2-week holiday in Florida. Things have been rather hectic over the past 2 months. I have been teaching in New York, Florida, Los Angeles, San Francisco, Houston, Dallas and DC. It's time to re-introduce myself to a wife and two children who have seen very little of me this year.

A friend in Florida has given us his timeshare apartment for a week in June – on the beach in Ft Lauderdale, so we will definitely get some time together as a family.

On a really positive note, the USCIS has again renewed my L-1 visa, this time for 3 years until February 2006. (Forgive me for repeating this again – you'll see why later on.)

This is now the third decision from the USCIS that it is satisfied that I meet the requirements for the L-1 visa. Specifically that :

1. I WAS employed in an executive / managerial position with the South African company, and

2. That I AM employed in an executive / managerial position in the US company and

3. That there IS a qualifying relationship between the two companies.

Listening to C-Span and the House Judiciary Sub-Committee debate on the new Patriot Act, makes one smile. Remember South Africa's 30-day, 60-day and 90-day detention laws that caused such an international uproar? How detention without trial was against civil rights and all that shit? Well, in terms of the Patriot Act, 'Shrub' has the power to declare any person or group of persons as being 'combatants' in a war, and as such, they may be arrested and detained without trial, or court appearance, or access to legal representation, or habeas corpus, INDEFINITELY! So Mr Attorney General John Ashcroft, when could these unfortunates expect to be released? When the circumstances precipitating their classification as combatants ends! Wow! So, in the war against terrorism, if I have a darkish complexion and a big moustache and happen to look a little bit like an Arab wanted by the FBI, and am arrested, possibly as a result of mistaken identity, do I have access to an attorney and witnesses and a court-room, to try to prove my innocence? Yes. When? When the circumstances precipitating your classification as a combatant ends! You mean, when the war against terrorism ends? Yes! And all this time we thought the good ol' US of A was against South Africa's detention laws because they suspended civil liberties…

Day 721. June 28, 2003

Bush declares Victory!

Since Shrub strapped a jet on his back and headed off to one of the aircraft carriers to announce our "Victory", the 100-thousand soldiers still in Iraq are getting very pissed off that they have not been able to come home to a ticker-tape parade, more have died since victory was declared, than during the War itself, the WMD's have not been found, OBL and Saddam have not been found, the French and Germans are saying "we told you so" and cousin Tony is wondering how to explain his adventurism to the British public. Meanwhile, we are all rubbing our hands in the satisfaction of another job well done and don't screw with the US of A! My heart goes out to the troops who have become pawns in games played by politicians who invariably have little to no skin in the game.

While on holiday in Ft Lauderdale, we decide to give the kids a taste of open water snorkeling. After getting them fitted out with mask, snorkel and fins, we charter a boat to take us for a cruise along the inland waterways and out to sea to a reef some miles off-shore. Climbing down the ladder is too lady-like for Michael, so he decides to do a 'giant-stride' off the boat and ends up with his fins halfway up his calves! Getting them off is less easy. Sarah is a duck-to-water and ends up doing some great dives down to the reef. Michael is a touch more hesitant about the open sea, as he has recently seen the film "Finding Nemo" and is convinced that he will come face to face with Bruce, the delightful Australian Great White Shark, and is concerned about his diet, notwithstanding his new resolution that "fish are friends, not food".

Talking about Finding Nemo, a TV personality here decided to have her kid's birthday party at an oceanarium. All was going well and the children were loving the antics of the seals, dolphins and penguins, until the daddy penguins started getting amorous with the mommy penguins, and the children started asking questions. In total embarrassment, the parents asked whether this exhibitionism could be curtailed until the children were a bit older. "No problem," said the keeper, "we'll just start feeding time a bit earlier and dish out some fish." Well, as the first fish was greedily grabbed and swallowed by the first penguin, the party dissolved into screams of horror, anguish and protest as the children watched Nemo being swallowed by the penguins! Needless to say, the party was not a success and tearful children returned home somewhat earlier than anticipated.

Back on the dive-boat, things start getting a bit out of hand as well. After sitting in the car for a 14-hour drive from Charlotte to Ft Lauderdale, one starts to experience the usual problems of bowel-immobility. Not having anticipated going out to sea for so long, Di and Sarah had taken a pill the night before, to loosen things up a bit. While the four of us were snorkeling on the reef, Sarah was the first to return to the boat with indications that things were seriously on the move. Directed to the 'heads' by the skipper of the boat, she soon finds that it is a no-contest between the capability of the 'heads', and the challenge she is imposing on the system. So she drops back into the ocean to come call Dad to do some repair-work. Meanwhile, Mommy Di suddenly realizes that she is also 'in need' so to speak. Returning to the boat, she enters the 'heads' and staggers out a few seconds later with a look of absolute horror, shock and consternation on her face at what she found there. "Bruce!" she calls, "you have to get here, right now!"

Now there are some things that Dads should never have to do, and this is one of them! There is no way that we can ask the skipper of the boat to enter that tiny room to repair the damage, so trying not to gag and with undying love for Sarah in my heart, I enter this chamber of horrors, realizing that Sarah must have reduced her body-weight by no small amount. This is going to be no easy task. Nor a quick one, in spite of having Mommy Di lurking just outside, dancing around and extolling me to greater and hastier efforts. All in vain. Her need becomes more urgent than my abilities, and faced with the only alternative to the open deck of the boat, she desperately plunges back into the sea to go and explore a distant portion of the reef, fortunately down-stream of the boat. She might have gotten away with it too – the smile of total relief on her face is not all that obvious. She should, however, have remembered that she is on a reef very rich in fish-life, and she should have remembered how we always used to take hard-boiled eggs with us on our scuba-diving photo/video excursions to attract the fish and drive them into a feeding frenzy. If she had only looked behind her, she would have seen the ocean boiling with fish-life in a feeding frenzy the likes of which I, and the skipper of the boat, have never seen before. As you can imagine, we decided to put our penchant for fresh fish, and especially sushi, on hold until we have extended our vacation somewhat further down the coast-line! (After this, I shall possibly never be forgiven once Di and Sarah find out that their personal embarrassments have been penned into immortality!)

After a week in Pompano Beach and sated with sun and sea, we head south to the Florida Keys, 150 miles of islands and bridges extending into the Gulf, and ending at the most southern tip of the USA, Key West, only 90 miles from Cuba. One of the most beautiful places on earth – warm, clear tropical seas as far as the eye can see. The town of Key West is very Hermanus-y, small streets, tiny shops, lovely old homes, full of charm and character. See Ernest Hemingway's home and stop off to visit Sloppy Joe's Bar where he and others of his time, were regular drinkers.

All in all, we're getting used to this country and are feeling a lot happier now that we have a fairly steady flow of business. No great shakes, but people are starting to ask for me at last. We think that things can only get better. On July 8 we will have been here for 2 years, and feel we have paid our dues in sacrifice, uncertainty and hardship, and are better able to handle the sadness of absent family and friends. We know we will never rebuild friendships to any similar extent, but still feel that Sarah and Michael will be the true beneficiaries in the end.

We are saddened to hear that our great friend and doyenne of international dive-travel, Lyn de Lacy Smith, is seriously ill with cancer. We have known Lyn for many years and have traveled all over the world with her, to some of the most exotic dive-locations in the world – the Maldives, Singapore, the UAE, Oman, Egypt, the Red Sea, Malaysia, Borneo, Great Barrier Reef and the South China Sea. Lyn and underwater video specialist, Gordon Hiles, also part of our team of dive-travelers, are now the owners of our former home in Fourways, South Africa.

Day 997. March 30, 2004

Putting down roots.

Lyn de Lacy Smith has headed off to the Big Blue. We spoke with her a couple of times during her final days and she was chirpy to the very end. I'll never forget her final comment to me … "cancer is a guaranteed way to lose weight!" Bon voyage to you, Lyn-girl. We miss you every time we don a t-shirt from our many travels around the world.

We've finally decided that we need to put down some roots in this country. Another serious oversight by so many immigrants like us. Owning property and having a mortgage is the biggest single contributor to a good credit score. So not only has our credit score suffered over the past two years, but we've also missed the 4% to 6% growth in the property market, and we've been paying rental with after-tax income and missing out on the mortgage interest deduction. We call our realtor-friend Ann Christie and ask her to find us a house.

When she brings us into an area called Providence Plantation with hills and swamps and loads of trees and streams and shows us quiet streets called Houston Branch, Cotton Planter and Rhett Butler Lane, we are hooked. And thus starts the process of buying a home in the USA. This is a serious business. Firstly, you fill in the contract – more like a book than a piece of paper, with a million and one checks and balances to make sure that both buyer and seller are fully protected.

Then we call in the Home Inspection Service – they check the property from top to toe and make a list of everything that is not 100% - they even find a cracked roof-truss left by the builders 8 years previously. Every fault and flaw is documented - dripping taps, dead light-bulbs, dirty carpets, cracks, bad wiring, rubble in the crawl-space under the house. None of this 'voetstoots' stuff here – we get a list of over 100 major and minor defects. Then in comes the land-surveyor to check the boundary markers, house-plans and improvements, just to make sure that all is well. Then in comes the Heating & Cooling guy to check the furnace-heat, air-con and gas feeds, just to make sure that the furnace is not leaking CO into the house and that the equipment is still 100%. We get all these reports and they have found a bundle of faults – big and small. We give the reports to the seller who now needs to fix everything at his expense or to refuse to fix and allow us to walk away from the deal. Everything gets fixed and we have another inspection. This time they find a small crack in the furnace-manifold – something that must be fixed as it will soon start leaking CO into the house which will kill us all – just another $3k to lighten the seller's bank account.

Then it's mortgage time! The real test of our credit in this country. We are referred to a hot mortgage guy at Chase Manhattan Bank. Allan seems to know his stuff (but in hindsight he would have been better suited to selling 2nd-hand cars). He checks out our credit and verbally assures us that we can get an 80-15-5 deal at 6.125%. This means an 80% first mortgage, a 15% second mortgage and a 5% deposit, all fixed at 6.125% for 30 years. A sweet deal, better than we could have hoped for. We sign all the papers and closing is set for mid-October 2003. Closing is THE BIG EVENT! Buyers and sellers and their transferring attorneys all get together, check and sign all the documents and hand over all the payments, keys, warranties, reports and instruction booklets – all in one fell swoop.

The morning of the closing, we all head round to our new home, just to make sure that it is still there, and are about to go to the closing, when we get a call from our real-estate attorney to advise that the closing documents have not arrived from Chase Bank. Urgent call to Allan, to be advised that the documents are on the way from Atlanta and we will have to close the following week. Rescheduled for the following Monday, we get to the closing only to find that the loan has not been approved because Allan had not completed all of the loan documents. After numerous calls and much choice language, the seller is about to pull out of the deal and we are about to get faced with the arrival of our 40-foot container from South Africa with nowhere to live, as we have already terminated our lease at Providence Square Apartments and arranged for the container to be delivered to our new home the 2nd week of November.

Time to reach out to old friends – Nick in Connecticut. Formerly the marketing director for MasterCard (you know, the "Priceless" MasterCard ad campaign), Nick just happens to be the Chief Marketing Officer for Chase Bank in New York. An urgent call to him is our last hope. Don't know what Nick said to these Suthern Folk, but things started happening all of a sudden, albeit now very cool and unfriendly. A new closing date is scheduled and we breathe a sigh of relief. The afternoon before closing, Ann calls me to advise that she has received the closing documents from Chase, but advises that the numbers do not seem the same as discussed. It's now a 90-10 loan at 6.375% and Personal Mortgage Insurance of a couple of points. Other than the higher interest rate and the PMI which will cost a couple of hundred bucks a month, the 10% deposit is a disaster – instead of going to the closing the next day with a down-payment check for $15k, I now need $30k which I don't have. Total disaster. I go sit outside with a beer and start figuring how to move everything back into Providence Square apartments and how to install the contents of Fourways and Hermanus into a small apartment. Then the phone rings.

Now this good fellow and I love biltong, but cannot palate the dehydrated road-kill they call jerky in this country. So we built a biltong cupboard with a huge fan on top and 2 to 3 times a month we go buy 40 to 50 pounds of meat, turn the kitchen into a blood-bath as we trim and slice, salt and spice the meat into respectable steaks for biltong meat, whilst consuming disrespectable quantities of red-wine and beer. This gets hung in the biltong cupboard and a week later we have about 15 pounds of dry 'billies', reputed to be best in town – even our Suthern Friends have come to the conclusion that when it comes to jerky, "those Yankees from Africa do it best!" (My next-door neighbor replaced his moonshine still with a beer brewing fermenter and we now trade biltong for great malty home-brew beer!)

Anyhow, back at the apartment, I'm chewing on some billies, staring moodily into a beer and the phone rings. It's my good friend, mentor and biltong-partner (who needs to remain nameless for certain legal and ethical reasons.) What's up, he asks. I tell him. How much are you short? About $15k, I tell him. Come around for a beer, he says – I'll have a check ready. Simple as that. Just a word, just a hand-shake.

So, we get to the closing and buy our house. Rent a truck, buy some beer, grab all the friends we can find, and move everything out of the apartment and into Providence Glen Road. 10 days later, the 40-foot container arrives and they unpack 300 boxes into the garage and onto the drive-way and move all the big stuff into the house. It's chaos – never thought we had brought so much crap with us – remember, for more than 2 years we have lived without the stuff from South Africa and had gotten used to a more Spartan life-style. A lot of fun opening 300 Christmas Presents! And for the next 3 weeks it's finding places for everything, re-boxing and storing that which simply won't fit, and connecting everything. Plus, a stream of friends and neighbors coming in to help unpack and explore – especially the locals who come to ogle at stuff you simply don't get in this country of plastic, chip-board and veneer.

The change to our lives has been tremendous. We're in our own home in the USA, just 28 months after leaving our lives and homes behind in South Africa. We're living the Great American Dream at last! We're in a great neighborhood and feel really settled. The kids catch the school bus outside our front door at 7.30am and are back mid-afternoon. They travel with all the other kids from the neighborhood, and so are able to get together for play-time after school and after homework. Quiet streets, minimal traffic and totally safe.

We recall that two years ago, when we arrived in Charlotte, someone told us that life would be tough until we purchased a home. That people still remember what the post-Civil-War carpet-baggers did. Came to the South, took what they wanted and then moved on. That locals will see us as carpet-baggers, until we put down roots by buying a home. And that until such time, there is little merit in investing time and friendship with us if we might just move on. How true that proved to be, and how even more true that will prove to be in later years, when the crisis hits us.

My friend Neville Christie has retired. Since arriving in the USA from Durban, South Africa, 27 years ago, he has been fascinated by, and an avid collector of American malapropisms, like the recent one on TV – talking about a very versatile football player who could play left-field or right-field, they described him as being the most 'amphibious' player of recent years. Since Neville has been taking the piss out of his colleagues for many years, they found his list of malapropisms and used it to write his farewell speech. Enjoy. See how many you can find…

*"It's a **Doggy Dog** World … or **Caulk** it up to Experience.*

***Undoubtfully**, 1938 was a very good year. Shortly after **Valentimes** Day, Neville Christie, a **gentile** giant, was born. The doctor cut the **biblical** cord and he came into this world screaming **bloody Mary**. Little did we know that this young baby would grow to be an astounding individual with a **photogenic** mind to **inspirate** us all. Would this child be the next person to build the Empire **Mistake** Building?*

*Neville spent his early years playing with a **frisky** and trimming the **scrubbery** and **indigent** trees around the house. His mother was concerned the way that little Nevey **woofed** down his food and that he may some day get sent to a **formitory** or be **incinerated** in jail. But everything was always **Crisco** (kind of cooking oil) clear to him. He wanted to go off to school to study something in **dept**.*

*As a boy he excelled in schooling and athletics. It was said he was terrific at **shalom** skiing, just as graceful as **poultry** in motion until he got either a torn **cartridge** in his knee or a **conclusion** of the brain. After the doctor gave him a **scam** however, he realized it was a **mute** point. Although class work could get **pedious**, Neville kept his **ears to the grindstone**.*

*One day, out of the **coroner** of his eye, he spied a nice gal named Ann who was leaning against a **black-flow** preventer and they **conversated** over a **craft** of wine while **Ozark** stuff played in the background **(Placebo** Domingo). At the **spare** of the moment they went skinny **dripping**. She was a good **suspect** and no **creamadonna**. The wedding was announced in the news **mania** and she became his bride after a suitable **dual diligence** period.*

*Don't **misconscrew** me, Neville was a good student. He went on to a career with Mobil Oil, that he hoped would one day find him in Saudi **Uranium**. But Ann said "what's the **incentitive** with that" and she wasn't moving to that den of **inequality** and gave him an **ultima** to move to America. On the **spare** of the moment, Nevey came home with a **vanilla** envelope with tickets on a **computer airplane accrosst** to New York (not to be used in **conduction** with any other travel.)*

*Unfortunately, there was a **flaw** in the ointment. El Nina had made the weather **erotic**, and while the coast bore the **blunt** of the storm, the weather was very **bazaar**. Their container, **slat** full with their furniture, was washed over-board. It was a total **fiesta**. Although very **flustrated**, Neville said there was no use getting **uptense** about things – "I strive under these circumstances". As usual, he would bear the **grunt** of it. Upon arrival in NC, they inquired at the Smithfield Harold (newspaper) "Do you have any furniture **to sale?**" After days of **flea** bargaining with a fine **tooth pick**, they picked up a **condenza**, a **cadenza** and a claw foot **chester** drawers. It was not an exercise in **fertility**. They paid the man in full because he would not accept a **parcel** payment.*

***Phrase** two of Neville's career started in **Sweet** 101 at Morningstar in 1980. He took to the construction business like a **horse on fire**. He was **kidding** butt from day one. On every **sight** he supervised the **compassion** testing, the **facial** boards, **riff** raff, railroad **tides**, **constantina** wire, fens, roof **trussles**, the **masonite** construction (whether it needs painted or not)* *ekksettera – anything that might **avoid** the warranty. He was careful to see that the fluorescent lights had **a good balance** so they wouldn't cause an **electronical** shortage. His long-term partner in the joint venture, Steve, said per **batim**, "everything Neville did worked like a **chime**."*

*With his job in place, Neville hired a **prostituting** attorney known for his excellent **Jewish** prudence, to pursue citizenship. He showed up for his interview with the Federal Bureau of **Instigation** and although they checked him for weaponry, he was only wearing a beautiful pressed shirt with a **mammogram** on the pocket. His efforts came to **fruitation**. Now the American dream was open to Neville.*

*He had always longed to live in a **condom** with **shudders** and a **Muriel** on the wall on a nice **cuddlesac** with a **labradog** (not one of those mean **rockwelders** that might cause a bad **experiment** with the neighbors), and a vacation home on Top **Soil** Beach.*

*Well, let's cut to the **chafe**. Neville is retiring and **eating** high on the cob, while building a third home on three **contagious** properties. Although we miss your collegic **aurora** around the office, we can picture what you are up to – **serenading** the steaks with horse **relish**, treating your taste **bugs** to your favorite foods – preparing **asparagrass** with **holiday** sauce or vegetable **melody**. No worry here about **very close veins, contract** lenses or hip **displeasure**. Your daily **threadmill** workout will keep **cadillac** surgery at bay.*

*Neville, we will always keep you on a **pedal stool**. Please consider this our standing **ovulation** for you. Not sure if we got the **punctuality** right, but we wanted to give you a taste of your own **medication**. We wanted to add our two **senses** worth. Great minds **stink** alike and we hope you appreciate the **jester**!"*

Day 1360. March 8, 2005

Almost four years in the States "en ahv nah learn ta spake Suthern which is much different than reglar Inglish." For example, we have learned about certain words which are really phrases. Such as :

Mayonnaise : "Ahv seen da Lawd with mayonnaise." (.... my own eyes).

Urinal : "Urinal ot of trouble." (You're in a lot ...)

Wijadija : "Bring ya truck wijadija?" (with you did you)

Innuendo : "A bird flew innuendo." (... in your window)

Axed : "I axed y'all to give it ta me." (Asked). Now this smacks of Chaucer, but I guess those that use the word don't know its origin.

Michael got rapped at school for arguing with his math teacher. The question was 'how big is the area of a square, 4-feet by 4-feet'. Mike said 16 square feet. The teacher said 4 feet. Mike said No. The teacher said the answer was given as 4 feet in the math curriculum book. Mike said the book is wrong. Teacher said she is bound by the book as laid down by the educational department. Mike said they are all wrong. So, naughty child!

He has officially tested at 143 IQ and is now on the Gifted Kids Register which means that he starts fast-tracking through the school-system and the universities start pestering him. It also means that the little shit now thinks he is smarter than his 'old man' (which he probably is!) and the arguments and debates start in earnest. And Sarah has been accepted into the International Baccalaureate program as from Grade 9.

Day 1420. May 27, 2005

The children and I are travelling to South Africa for a visit. Di unfortunately cannot accompany us as she is still a 'hostage' in the

USA. Her visa expired in May and her renewal has not arrived yet - if she leaves the USA without her new visa, she won't be able to get back in. Hoping it will arrive in time for her to join us, as I am pretty useless without her to look after me - becoming a bit absent-minded and will probably lose the kids somewhere.

We fly on Sunday 31 July and Michael goes into hospital on Tuesday 2 August to have his tonsils removed - they have been troubling him for years, are always infected and we think are the cause of him remaining so thin. It's time they came out and South Africa is the best alternative, as medical care in the USA can be prohibitively expensive.

Day 1566. October 20, 2005

Sad news. My dad, Bertie Stewart, passed away at 11h40 this morning in the hospital in Hermanus, a few months short of his 80th birthday. As she has been for their 55 years of marriage, Jennifer was at his side until the end. "Bon voyage and rest in peace Dad. Although missed, you will live forever in our memories."

The kids and I had a super trip to South Africa in August. Michael had his tonsils removed and I sorted out visa issues and a host of other pressing business matters. Then I headed off to Hermanus to spend a week of quality time at Hoy House with my folks. Dad was still very strong mentally, but physically very frail – for some years after breaking his ankle very badly, he had difficulty walking and this resulted in declining blood-circulation in his legs, compounded by having had two varicose vein surgeries, and a general physical degeneration. However, it was a miracle that I had the opportunity to while away a number of peaceful days just chatting about all those things that Fathers and Sons chat about. Sarah and Michael joined us for the last 3 days of our Hermanus stay, and valued the time with Grandpa Bertie and Granny Jennifer. A valued and treasured bonding experience, made all the more poignant when we said our goodbye's, as we all knew that we would probably not meet again in this life. During the past month, with Dad's declining health, our living so far away has posed its own burdens and we are grateful that modern technology enabled us to talk with him and with Mom on an almost daily basis.

We had a near-disaster at the USA Consulate in Cape Town. When we applied for our visas to return to the USA, they granted my visa, but refused visas for the kids to return to the USA. They needed Di's permission, as co-guardian, for the kids to travel internationally. I explained that Di was in the USA, effectively a hostage, because of delays in getting her visa re-issued, but this held no water with the US Consulate that applies the law without question or interpretation. So, an urgent call to Di to prepare a letter of consent, get it notarized and then couriered to South Africa, giving me permission to get a visa to take her children home to her! Dumb-ass legislators forgot to distinguish between one parent wanting to take minor kids AWAY from the other parent, and wanting to take minor kids TO the other parent. And what the law says, the elves implement, without question or interpretation.

Then the next crisis – the renewal of Dianne's L-1 visa to live and work in the USA is declined by the US Government. Apparently because she is no longer employed by Speed Reading International (SRI), which apparently no longer exists. After burning up some phone-lines, it transpires that my immigration lawyer is also the public officer of SRI. When I fired him for exorbitant charges, he resigned as public officer, changed his address and stopped filing annual corporate returns, all without notification to me. So, when the Florida Secretary of State sent urgent advisories about the pending dissolution of my company, everything was going to a non-existent mailing address. So, in October 2004, SRI was administratively dissolved by the Florida Secretary of State without any notification to me.

Meanwhile, as far as we are concerned it is business as usual. When the mess is revealed, it's grovel-grovel time, submit buckets of forms, copies of every bank-statement, invoice, class-roster and loads of affidavits proving the de facto existence of SRI and explaining why the mess occurred and why re-incorporation should be granted. Needless to say, plus a few checks for capital, interest and penalties. So now Di's application for L-1-visa renewal is back on track.

We are still sort of on track for our green-cards. Because our Florida immigration attorney seemed to be big on asking for checks payable to himself personally and small on providing formal invoices and proper payment receipts, we found a new Charlotte immigration attorney to handle our immigration and financial matters. Well-qualified with loads of testimonials from satisfied clients, a sterling success rate with visa and green-card petitions and a triple-A rating from the Better Business Bureau. More about THIS later!

We had the FBI take our finger-prints and sent these to South Africa for our SA Police Clearance Certificate which takes 8 weeks. (This is to make sure that we are not criminals running away from the fuzz in SA!) Really rich, coming from this country!! But then, in the American psyche, if it's the best, it must be American – almost a degree of pride in Al Capone, Bonnie and Clyde, Jeffrey Skilling (Enron) and Martha Stewart. God forbid we allow non-US criminals into this country to compete with our home-grown variety! Never quite sure whether it is the Arrogance of Power or the Ignorance of Power, or whether the one gives rise to the other!

Unfortunately, the envelope containing our finger-prints never made it to South Africa. Gone to that big mailbox in the sky. So I hand-carried another set to South Africa in August and Dianne's sister Libby has just collected our police clearance certificates. She has not called with any bad news, so we assume that we are not on the most-wanted list in South Africa.

All going well, Di can now schedule her green-card interview and once she gets her green-card, we all become permanent residents of the bad ol' US of A. Wishful thinking it would soon appear.

Then a small SNAFU-call from our Charlotte immigration attorney, Shante. Because I am the head of the family according to the USCIS – rather sexist I think - the green-card petition must (apparently) be in my name and not in Dianne's name. Just a minor administrative issue, she advises. We'll just file an amended petition and all will be okay.

On the family front, Michael, now 11, is as bright and cocky as ever. Now playing "major" league baseball for his Boston Red Sox Little league team, getting 100% at school, and bamboozling both teachers and students with his mastery of Trachtenberg Speed Mathematics. Sarah turns 16 on October 18, has a learner-driver permit (but no car!!), cell-phone, laptop and iPod, loves the International Baccalaureate program at high school, but we never get to see her – she leaves for school before the rest of us wake up and spends every minute of her time studying. Di is cooking on gas with a great array of PR clients and I play with them all as much as possible between teaching assignments that are becoming more regular and more frequent – 42 assignments so far this year. Our American Dream is blossoming.

While somewhere out there, Father Fate chuckles sardonically!

PART 2 : THE STORM

God grant me the serenity
To accept the things I cannot change;
The courage to change the things I can;
And the wisdom to know the difference.

Day 1874. August 24, 2006

The roller-coaster ride in this country never seems to stop. Last month, while on holiday with my Mom, who came to visit us after my Dad's death, we received the fantastic news from our immigration lawyer, Shante, that our permanent residence green-cards had been approved. Then the Wall Street Journal contacted me about doing an article on speed reading. Life was looking great. The WSJ article appeared end of July and business started booming. We now have solid bookings through to December.

But a month after my permanent residence had been 'approved' in July 2006, I still had nothing in hand. So I started making enquiries to see what the delay was. I booked an appointment to go and see the USCIS in Charlotte, and showed them my permanent residence approval notice, sent to me by immigration lawyer Shante. They entered the approval notice number into the system and it confirmed that permanent residence had indeed been approved.

Your green-cards should reach you soon, they tell me. A couple of weeks later, with no green-cards in hand, I am back at the USCIS offices in Charlotte. And again, the official enters my approval notice number into the system, and again confirms that permanent residence has been approved.

We start investigating our immigration attorney, Shante, and Oh Boy, what a voyage of exploration this was.

In September 2004, we had approached an immigration 'attorney', Shante, in Charlotte and briefed her to renew Dianne's L-1 visa which was due to expire in April 2005. This 'specialist' advised us to apply for permanent residence for Dianne, instead of renewing her L-1 visa. This we did, for a fee plus an additional $1500 for 'premium processing' – the US double-speak for palm-greasing. Instead of going to the bottom of the stack and waiting 450 days for a green-card, you legitimately pay for premium processing and get the whole job done in about 15 days. They don't call this "Scamerica" for nothing. Then Dianne's permanent residence application gets denied – I am the primary family member and I should be the permanent residence applicant. So we immediately file an application for Di's L-1 visa extension and also a permanent residence application for me. Some months go by and our 'lawyer' is full of self-praise about how well she has handled our case and how well it is going.

Then Di's L-1 extension application was denied because our company, Speed Reading International, had been de-registered due to inactivity. (And this is while I am chalking up air-miles traveling to and fro across this huge country with 5 time-zones, teaching class after class.) As mentioned earlier, our Florida corporate attorney failed to file annual returns. And in the absence of annual returns, the company was deemed to be inactive and was thus de-registered. Forget about sending out a reminder or making a phone-call. So we pay another wad of money to fix the problem and get the company reactivated, and then some more cash to file an appeal against the denial of Di's visa extension. And Voila…our immigration lawyer,

Shante, says she has received Di's visa extension and has Fed-Ex'd it to us.

In the interim, Shante also tells me that she has filed a petition to have permanent residence granted to me on the basis of Extraordinary Ability – I do a bit of a double-take on this one, as we are still getting "acclimated" to the double-speak here. "Exceptional children" at school are exactly that – they're exceptional because they are different. The un-PC word is handicapped. So I start wondering about what they mean by my 'extraordinary abilities'. But no double-speak here – I'm a specialist, have qualifications and am published, so they figure I'm a good candidate for enhancing the gene-pool. We complete many documents for our lawyer to file and write as many checks to compensate her for the excellent work she says she is doing on our behalf. Remember, in this country, it's all about the sizzle ... and to hell with the steak!

But the Fed-Ex envelope with Dianne's L-1 visa-renewal seems to have gone astray, and because of an oversight in her office, Shante had allegedly Fed-Ex'd us the original and had not kept a copy. But not to worry, she will get a duplicate from the USCIS and in any case, not to worry, as, WONDERFUL NEWS, my permanent residence has been granted and our green-cards will be issued on July 5, 2006, almost 5 years to the date of arriving in the USA on July 8, 2001. In addition, I get a couple of new clients, one in the Bahamas and one in Trinidad Tobago and the idea of spending 10 days vacationing in each country while teaching for 2 days, makes sense and sounds attractive.

Then 2 weeks ago, Di is lying in bed listening to the late late news and there is a news item about an attorney who is scamming his clients with bogus immigration applications. The news item mentions that the suspect has disappeared, but that he is believed to be in cahoots with another so-called immigration lawyer at a particular address. This address happens to be in the same complex as Shante, our attorney. First thing in the morning we try calling our lawyer, but there's no reply. We hot-foot it around to her offices, only to find that her offices are closed from Sunday through Wednesday. Something new and decidedly fishy!

We keep calling every number we have for her. Then we start sending faxes. No reply. I get my computer to start sending 101-page faxes with a single line repeated 500 times : "Shante…Call me. Bruce". I send this out every hour on the hour and get the message across. She calls me with apologies for not returning my calls, but she has been meeting with another attorney to have him assist her with her immigration case-load – her business has grown so fast that she needs to sub-contract. That she has passed my case to attorney Chris to handle the finishing touches as everything has been approved and we are just awaiting the final documentation from the USCIS and that attorney Chris will be able to accelerate this.

I call Chris, who knows nothing about my case. Another 100-page fax and Shante calls me to advise that she is meeting Chris, with my files and that I should be there at 3pm. I get there, only to find that Shante was there an hour earlier to meet with him. Exiting his office, she tells me that all is well and that Chris is totally happy with my case and that he will do everything to accelerate the issuance of our green-cards.

Shante scurries off and I get to meet the great white knight who promptly tells me that I am in serious trouble – that Shante is not an immigration attorney, her degrees, testimonials and Better Business Bureau rating were all fraudulently self-generated, that she knows only enough about immigration and tax matters to get herself into trouble, that her advice that we apply for permanent residence instead of extending our L-1-visa's was totally incorrect, that no petitions for L-1 extensions were filed or approved, that no petitions for my permanent residence were filed or approved, that we have lost a boatload of money, that Di became "illegal" in April 2005, that I became "illegal" in February 2006, that if Di leaves the USA she will be barred from returning for a minimum of 10 years, that if I leave the USA I will be barred from returning for a minimum of 3 years, that we have become the victims of a monumental fuck-up and that our case is FUBAR – if you saw the movie Saving Private Ryan, you will know what FUBAR means.

"But I have a permanent residence approval notice," I protest in shock and horror. "And on two separate visits to the USCIS in Charlotte, they confirmed that I have permanent residence."

Chris calls in an investigator from ICE, Immigration and Customs Enforcement, who confirms that the approval notice that I have, may have my name on it, but it belongs to someone else.

Here's the problem. The USCIS permanent residence approval notice contains a notice number and the name of the beneficiary. However, the USCIS case status system only works on notice numbers and with no reference to the name of the beneficiary. So, the number on my approval notice was a valid number on an approval notice for someone else. When I visited the USCIS they were simply confirming the case status of that particular approval notice number. That I was listed as the beneficiary meant nothing – the USCIS case status system does not reflect beneficiary names linked to approval notice numbers. All that Shante needed to do was to get hold of a successful permanent residence approval notice and replace the original beneficiary's name with my name. Then collect $5k from me for a permanent residence application and present me with a successful approval notice. I would become one of many clients scammed through this gaping hole in the US immigration system.

I call my Aussie friend, another one of Shante's clients, and fill him in on the situation. He's not concerned as "his permanent residence has been granted" he says. Check it out, I advise. An hour later he finds that he also got scammed for $6k and is about to become an illegal. Another South African, a teacher, is also down the tubes for $3k. And we wonder why we didn't decide, right up front in 2001, to say "to hell with becoming legal, let's just fly to Mexico and walk across the border like 11 million Mexicans have done." So, don't ever think the Mexicans are dumb! They know a whole lot more about how the system works, or doesn't work, than we give them credit for.

I swallow the bile in my throat, suppress the urge to go rip Shante's heart out, smoke a packet of Camel and start work from scratch with Chris, after, of course, coming up with another $5k just to get his attention, and fully realizing that being a lawyer is the only profession where your earning potential increases exponentially with the number of cock-ups you manage to fabricate and then have to fix. And by the way, advises Chris, "should our application for condonation of your illegality (in the absence of fault) fail, our firm also provides assistance for fighting deportation orders". Whether this fellow is going to be any different from the other "scamologists" in this country, only time will tell.

And another sardonic chuckle from Father Fate.

We are faced with this interesting little conundrum. Legally, because we now have no legal status in this country, we are not allowed to be in this country. Neither are we allowed to work. But we cannot fight an injustice without money and we cannot earn money unless we work and we cannot work without being in the country. And we cannot be in the country without fixing the screw-up. So we stay, we work and we pay. At least we will get free tickets out of the country if they decide to kick our asses out of here.

And then the realization hits me. If Shante was a crook with the immigration case, what has she been doing with my company and personal tax filings? I grab my latest two years of personal and company tax returns and hot-foot it down to the local IRS office and ask to meet with someone from the criminal investigation department. There's a little bit of scurrying around as it is apparently most unusual for people to ASK to see the IRS criminal investigators. I go through all sorts of security before getting shown into a very stark interview room where I meet with an IRS crime investigator. I tell her my immigration story and my concerns about my tax returns.

"Who prepared your returns?" she asks.

"Shante ....," I answer.

"How did you file your returns?" she asks.

"Shante did an e-filing," I reply. I hand over my latest returns and she immediately turns to the deductions page on my personal return.

"What are these two deductions?" she asks.

"No idea," I answer. "They are entered with item codes."

"Did you enter these codes," she asks.

"No, I don't even know what the codes stand for," I reply.

"They are for training expenses and other business expenses that you incurred on behalf of the company that were not reimbursed to you," she explains.

"That's ridiculous – I own the company and ALL my expenses are reimbursed."

She checks the other personal return. Same result.

"How did you know what to look for?" I ask.

"Sorry, I can't answer that question," she replies.

"Look, I'm a former South African Assistant District Attorney and I want to nail Shante. We're on the same side here. Now, is your answer 'can't' or 'won't'? "

"It's both," she replies. "This is now an active investigation. Can you give me Shante's office address?"

"Sure," and I do so.

As I am about to leave, she frowns. "Look, this is just a heads-up. I suggest you get a real tax accountant to go through every tax return that Shante prepared. Get him or her to check everything and to file revised returns if necessary. And do it without delay."

"Thanks for the advice. I guess I'll be hearing from your people in due course?"

She smiles. "C'mon, you know I can neither confirm nor deny that you will be audited. But whatever, it might be a good idea to take the initiative."

The following morning, the IRS raids Shante's offices and remove all her files. She will ultimately negotiate a plea-bargain, pay a substantial fine for tax fraud and spend a year in federal prison. And for practicing as an attorney without a license, I never hear whether the North Carolina Bar Association actually ever imposed the $25 "slap-on-the-wrist" fine on Shante for practicing as an unlicensed attorney.

Some months later I receive a notice from the IRS advising that my company and personal federal and state tax returns will be audited for the past 5 years and that I should report to the IRS with all documents and records blah, blah, blah. But I had spent my grace period fruitfully. Found a great Certified Public Accountant, Robert J Wilson, discovered Shante's shenanigans, filed revised returns and paid some back taxes, penalties and interest. The audit was a breeze.

Why did she do this? It was all about marketing. "If I cannot get you a refund from the IRS, then you don't pay for my tax services. I'm the Tax Lady!"

Between August and November 2006, I spend every available minute studying the US Immigration laws and preparing our new strategy with immigration attorney Chris. And on November 6 we file a comprehensive submission to the USCIS in Vermont, with affidavits from myself, my nephew Sean, attorney Chris and attorney Noel, testifying to a meeting with Shante where she admitted culpability, admitted to practicing as an immigration attorney without a license, admitted to lying to us and accepting sole responsibility for our lapse of legal status. And we include a statement from Shante, which she subsequently refuses to sign on the grounds of self-incrimination. We include the $1500 fee for 15-day premium processing, and on November 21 the USCIS gives us their response :

"The beneficiary's status expired on 02/02/06. This petition was filed on 11/09/06, almost 9 months later. It is the burden of the beneficiary to be aware of the laws & regulations governing his stay and abide by them. Please submit a statement explaining the delay in filing this application. Please note, it is the opinion of this service that incompetent counsel is not beyond the control of the beneficiary."

On the 27th we respond to the USCIS : The delay was caused by our understanding that our permanent residence had been approved on June 23, 2006. Between February and July 2006 our permanent residence case was pending, and according to Shante we were still "in status". Not being immigration lawyers ourselves, we relied on an advertised lawyer who is, we believed, an authorized USCIS representative. This is not a case of us relying on incompetent counsel. It is a case of criminal deceit, misrepresentation, forgery of federal documents and theft by false pretenses, perpetrated by an authorized USCIS representative. We include a copy of the bogus permanent residence approval notice and the two dates on which our permanent residence approval was confirmed by the Charlotte USCIS office.

On December 7th the USCIS approves my L-1 visa petition for the period December 2006 to December 2008, and sends us a set of L-1 and L-2 visa approvals for the family, but refuses to condone our 'out of status' period and refuses to grant us an I-94 extension of stay. By implication, we are illegally here and must return to South Africa to apply for a visa to return to the USA. But because of the non-condonation of our 'out of status' period, the kids and I will be prohibited from returning to the USA for 3 years and Dianne is subject to a 10-year bar from re-entering the USA. Additionally, because we have been here illegally, we can never apply for permanent residence. This decision from the USCIS is not subject to appeal, but we can file a notice for a new hearing if we have new evidence to present. The deadline for this is January 7, 2007.

This is not a good time for us. While I am getting my teeth into the immigration laws and have work to do with Chris, the uncertainty and total frustration of being helpless is murder on Dianne and the children. With just one month to find evidence for a new hearing, we cancel Christmas 2006.

Day 1989. On December 18th 2006, the "Keep The Stewarts In Charlotte" website goes live to get the word out, collect testimonials and seek audiences with influential people. We collect evidence of Shante's illegal, unethical and unprofessional conduct, her numerous identities and Social Security numbers. We prepare a civil law-suit against Shante and are working with the authorities to bring this person to justice. When we file our next response to the USCIS, due before January 7, 2007, we have to obtain the following :

1. A reversal of the USCIS decision of Dec 7, 2006
2. A condonation of our 'out of status' period from the last date that each of us was 'in status',
3. An extension of legal stay in the USA to give us time to file for and obtain permanent residence. This has become urgent as Sarah graduates from High School in 2 years' time, but until her legality of status is confirmed, she cannot start applying for college admission.

On December 22 we file suit against Shante and American Professional Services for damages and misrepresentation.

After a very un-Christmassy Christmas we are ready. On January 5, attorney Chris submits new evidence to the USCIS asking for a new hearing and requesting them to reconsider their decision. US Representative Sue Myrick provides a letter of support to go with the submission and we have the support of Senator Elizabeth Dole and Senator Richard Burr. We trust that we will be given a "Fair Trial."

On January 23 the USCIS sends us a new set of L-visa approvals for the family, together with an I-94 extension-of-stay allowing us to "travel" and which would normally mean we could return to the US if we ever decided to risk travelling outside the USA. However, the dates on this visa-approval are now changed from the previous validity dates of December 2006 through December 2008, to September 2006 through September 2008 - leaving a more than six-month gap in our L-1 visa history, which is required to have consecutive and valid dates from its inception to its conclusion after 7 years. If it has any gaps in it, the US Consulate in South Africa is obliged to refuse a re-entry visa to anyone who has had this lapse in status, and because the lapse is for more than 180 days, we would be subject to a 3-year bar from re-entry. These visas are useless to us. We believe this has been done on purpose to prevent us from returning to the US if we choose or are compelled to leave for any reason. We also find it peculiar that they have arbitrarily selected September as an alternative month to December. What should in fact happen is that the visa approvals should be valid from February 16, 2006 (when our last valid visas expired) to February 16, 2008 making the dates consecutive within our existing visa dates.

And then, to our total surprise, on January 30, we receive yet MORE visa approval notices - now with NEW dates that have reverted back to the first set of visa approvals we received in December 2006 - valid from December 6, 2006 through December 6, 2008. Clearly someone doesn't know what the hell they are doing! Wasting time, money, manpower and creating even more confusion for all concerned.

On February 9, 2007, Chris sends a request to Senator Richard Burr's office requesting assistance.

"Thank you for taking the time to speak with me this morning. As discussed, I am a bit puzzled by the recent notifications received from

USCIS on behalf of Dr. Bruce Stewart and his dependent family members. As background, I filed an L-1 petition on behalf of Dr. Stewart. The application was filed while he was out of status. In the context of the petition we acknowledged that he was out of status but argued that his failure to maintain his status was due to an extraordinary circumstance that was through no fault of his own. I'm sure you are familiar with the facts on that issue. In any event, I specifically requested that the USCIS approve his petition and accompanying extension of stay while restoring his L-1A status retroactive to the date that he fell out of status, in February 2006. My argument was premised on section 214 of the Immigration & Nationality Act, as amended. In addition, I filed extensions of stay in L-2 status for his spouse and children.

"We were overjoyed when we were informed that the petition and his extension of stay was approved. However, our excitement was mixed with confusion at seeing that the I-94's were dated from September 2006 through September 2008. Now, we have additional I-94's for each family member bearing approvals from December 2006 through December 2008. We have two issues at this point.

"First, why was the L-1A and L-2 status of the family not restored "nunc pro tunc" to the February 2006 date? The dates chosen by the Service bear no relation to the request that was filed. In fact, they appear arbitrary in nature. We would like clarification as to these dates. Furthermore, we would like the I-94's to reflect the correct beginning approval period : February 2006.

"Secondly, we are concerned with the permanent residence applications of the Stewart family. Specifically, any I-485 application filed pursuant to an employment-based preference category must be filed with proof that the applicant (and any dependent family members) had maintained their previously accorded non-immigrant status. These rules can be found in section 245 of the INA. Section 245(k) allows any applicant who has not continuously maintained their non-immigrant status to have their status adjusted to lawful permanent resident as long as the alien has not, for an aggregate period exceeding 180 days, failed to maintain a lawful status. Presently, with the dates provided by the Service, the Stewart family has been out of status for a period exceeding 180 days.

"While we could argue that this failure to maintain status was through no fault of their own when we file the I-485, our position is that we have already advanced sufficient argument on this issue. It is noteworthy that the Service accepted the argument and approved the L-1's and extensions of stay. However, their approval does not properly reflect the validity dates that were requested. To avoid having to make a superfluous argument during the adjudication of the I-485 (which will be filed in the very near future) we simply request that the Service error be corrected and new I-94's be issued reflecting approval dates beginning on February 14, 2006.

"At this point, since you have a direct line of communication with the Vermont Service Center, we respectfully request that you contact them and articulate our concerns. We are pleased that they have accepted our argument and have seen the hardship that the Stewart family has gone through as a result of the actions of Shante .... We just want the issue to be fully resolved. Should you have questions please feel free to contact me. Respectfully,.."

Day 2046. February 12, 2007

WONDERFUL NEWS. Our attorney calls this morning to say that the Vermont USCIS has FINALLY got with the program! They have back-dated our visa approvals to reflect no gaps in our status, valid until February 15, 2008. We await the new visa documentation to confirm this and once received, we are now able to proceed with the Permanent Residence applications AGAIN. They say things are better the second time around...

February 16. At last, we have the new L-visas with the correct dates on them in our hot little hands! Dated February 16, 2006 through February 15, 2008! Excellent job done by our attorney Chris and his staff, as well as the office of Senator Richard Burr. We go for our physical examinations, yet again - TB / HIV / Syphilis, etc - and poor Sarah's veins are not cooperative, and so, after much puncturing in her arms and hands, she has to go back next week to try again for her blood work. As soon as the results come back, we can submit the next stage, the I-140 petition for Change of Status from Non-Immigrant to Immigrant status. Once this is approved, we can then proceed with the Permanent Residence I-485 petition.

The L-visa is a non-immigrant visa that only allows temporary stay in the USA. It does not allow you to apply for permanent residence. If you want to stay permanently, you have to file an I-140 petition to change your status from non-immigrant to immigrant status. And if this is approved, then you can file your I-485 permanent residence petition.

By March 3 we have completed our medical exams, and our I-140 petition, for change of status from Non-Immigrant to Immigrant Status, is ready for submission by our attorney. On the advice of Chris, we have decided that to save time, we will file the I-140 petition simultaneously with an I-485 petition for Permanent Residence. This is filed on March 28. It's now a waiting game. We have no idea how long it will take the USCIS to adjudicate our I-140 petition. Now I can get back to earning some money to feed this voracious immigration beast. Fortunately, a number of my bigger corporate clients are regulars and book group courses with me multiple times each year.

In addition to my teaching assignments for AARP in Washington DC, Credit Suisse in New York and San Francisco, and Babcock & Wilcox in Akron OH, we see a further step in our permanent residence petition – we are instructed to have our Biometrics taken on May 24 at the USCIS Processing Office in Charlotte - fingerprints and photo's - the next step in the Permanent Residence application process. Processing time for green-card applications is currently running at 8 months.

On June 25, my family receives what's called "Advance Parole" - documents to enable us to travel in and out of the US. Strange terminology – gives the impression that we are felons about to be paroled! Essentially it means that because we have applied to change our status from non-immigrant to immigrant status, as a prelude to petitioning for permanent residence, our L-visa status is suspended. Accordingly, if I were to travel internationally on this "suspended"

L-visa, the USCIS would deem me to be abandoning my petition for permanent residence. So, with an Advance Parole document, I am permitted to exit and re-enter the USA on that document and without relying on my L-visa. That's the good news. But our attorney advises otherwise! He says wait until the green-cards arrive before you travel – remember, once you are out of the country there is no guarantee that you will get back in. And I guess that pulling in the help of the politicians to sort out the Shante debacle may have ruffled a few feathers at the USCIS. So we are back to square one on that one - going to miss a family wedding on June 30 in South Africa.

Day 2248. September 4, 2007

Such a beautiful day here in the Carolinas. We have just exited the month of August, one of the hottest months on record with 30 days of 3-digit heat – over 100 degrees F. The hottest we recorded on our deck was 110 degrees F (43 Celsius). Even our hot-tub reached 91, without the heater, so no relief there.

We had a lovely 2-week beach holiday in Lauderdale-by-the-Sea in Florida. Sarah has been pestering us for a SCUBA course and persuaded Michael to join her. They received a pile of material to study before the course, devoured this in one evening and got certified as PADI Open-Water divers in 2 days. Then Di and I hired some gear, chartered a boat and headed out to sea for some lobster-diving.

Interrupting our Florida vacation, I had the honor and pleasure of being a 4-hour guest-speaker at the Pennsylvania Conference of State Trial Judges – my subject was on speed reading and how to apply these skills to the judicial system. Quite an experience having 250 judges in the audience, even more so the socializing each evening.

Sarah spends a couple of weeks with a driving-instructor to get her competent enough to take her driver's license test. We bite the bullet and buy her the little Toyota Scion XA, primarily because she needs a car to drive to school and also because I am trying to avoid driving the Dodge 4x4 around town – too big to park and lousy fuel-economy. It's a boon to Sarah – her school bus arrives at 5am which means waking up at 4.15 and now, instead of spending 3 hours a day on the bus, she can drive to school and back in less than an hour, giving her more time for homework.

Getting her drivers-license is a nightmare – when she arrives at the testing station, they want either her social security number or a valid visa in her passport. Problem – being a non-resident alien, she has no social security number, and because we have not been back to South Africa in years, the visa in her passport has expired. But we do have valid I-94's – authorizations to live in the USA. "Not acceptable," says the Department of Transportation (DOT). Sarah needs to go back to South Africa to have the I-94 converted into a visa! We try to explain that the I-94 allows her to BE here, while the visa allows her to COME TO the USA. And since she is already here, she does not need a visa in her passport. "Tough," says the DOT. The law says she must have a Social Security number or a visa and makes no mention of an I-94. Sarah is in tears. We figure there must be someone in the DOT who knows about visas and I-94's, so we start visiting one testing-station after another. Finally, we spot a Mexican girl behind the counter, and if anyone knows about I-94s it will be another immigrant. When she asks for Sarah's Social Security number or visa, we just smile and tender the I-94 document which she accepts without blinking an eye, books Sarah in for the driving test and half an hour later returns Sarah and her new car to my anxious care. Enough to make one scream. Cannot really blame the DOT elves – they have to apply the law. The problem is with the politicians who make the laws and don't know enough about their own system to make laws that actually cover all the bases. But then if you look at the palookas who run this country – if they are not taking long vacations and overseas trips, they are out campaigning to raise funds for re-election to another term on the gravy-train.

While we are loving our vacation in Florida, two hurricanes are brewing. One for the USA and the world, and one for us personally.

By the time the 2007/2008 US Housing Market Crash comes to an end, 5 trillion dollars in pension money, real estate value, 401k, savings and bonds will disappear from the US Economy, 8 million people will lose their jobs, 6 million people will lose their homes and 5 thousand victims of the crash will commit suicide. Just in the USA.

And although we are totally unaware of the first seeds of impending disaster, since we have placed our trust and faith in attorney Chris, we receive a confusing notice from the USCIS on August 23, 2007 – a request for further evidence, an RFE, with regard to our application for permanent residence. We are confused, as the evidence they require is essentially asking for everything that we originally submitted in support of our L-1 visa petitions back in 2000 -- proof that we HAD a business in South Africa, that we WERE employed by the business in South Africa in executive / managerial positions, that we ARE employed in executive / managerial positions in the US company, full company organograms and job descriptions of all concerned, and that the US company enjoys a qualifying relationship with the South Africa company. All of which was submitted to, and accepted by, the USCIS and the legacy INS in September 2000 in support of our application for our L-1 visas, and which has been re-submitted on numerous occasions with the ongoing renewals of our L-1 visas for the last 6 years. The return date for this evidence is on or before October 4, 2007.

I ask attorney Chris to explain the insanity of asking for reams of documentation that they already have.

"This is clearly a boiler-plate standard RFE," says Chris. "Possibly some overworked USCIS examiner who wanted to go home and rather than spend time itemizing exactly what he wants, simply found it quicker to ask for everything. Not a problem – we'll respond to the RFE and point out that we have already submitted everything."

And that is what we do. This appears to be an ongoing bureaucratic saga with our files located in the Mesquite Texas, Vermont, Lincoln

Nebraska and Kentucky processing centers, and that the volume of documentation that we've submitted over the past 6 years has become so enormous, that these people find it easier to simply issue a standard blanket letter of request each time a decision is called for, rather than reading the documentation and making an informed decision on the documents they've already received. As we are property-owning, company-owning, tax-payers in this country, perhaps we should be forgiven for thinking that the USCIS finds it easier to make our lives a misery, than to do some serious work in fixing what is clearly a very dysfunctional system.

I will, in due course, find out that the I-140 / I-485 petitions are treated as totally new petitions, and that no attention whatsoever is paid to evidence submitted in support of a non-immigrant visa. The net result is that the case is treated *de novo*, and that a request for everything means exactly that. Everything. Why Chris down-played the importance of the RFE and advised that it was not necessary to submit everything asked for, I will never know. Was it ignorance of the law? Negligence on the part of an attorney trying to juggle too many cases? Or an honest mistake? Or was it my fault for not being a hard-assed client and not over-ruling my attorney and giving him firm instructions to comply exactly with the terms of the RFE? Whatever. The hurricane had been spawned and we continued our lives in blissful oblivion, little knowing that the storm will hit on January 9, 2008.

Unexpectedly, I receive a call from a British management consultancy in the United Arab Emirates, looking for someone to come and teach speed reading to a Sheikh. I get short-listed and finally appointed to go to Abu Dhabi in the UAE to teach His Excellency Sheikh Sultan Bin Tahnoon Al Nahyan of the UAE royal family. They send me a business-class ticket to fly from Charlotte via Frankfurt via Bahrain to Abu Dhabi, then check me into the Rotana Beach Hotel and give me a limo and driver for my 7-day stay in Abu Dhabi. It's a rough 30-hour trip, door to door, so next time I hope it's with Etihad Airlines, the official airline of the UAE, and of which Sheikh Sultan is a director — 15 hours direct from New

York to Abu Dhabi - he's booked me to return in November to teach his executives.

The UAE is spectacular and hard to recognize after our last trip in 1997, when we visited the UAE and Oman with Lyn De Lacy Smith as part of our series of travel and diving exploratory excursions that included the Maldives, Malaysia, Egypt, Singapore, the Red Sea and the South China Sea. These people realize that the oil will not last forever, and they're on a mission to build a world-class tourism industry. The architecture is surreal and the new Guggenheim Abu Dhabi, Louvre Abu Dhabi and Performing Arts Center on Saadiyat Island have to be seen to be believed. The recently opened Emirates Palace Hotel includes royal suites at US$12000 per night for double occupancy, but the suite is 600 square meters in size (at 6000 square feet, almost twice the size of our house in Charlotte!). The décor is all gold foil, and because of the amount of gold used in the décor, certain parts of the hotel are only accessible to registered guests. Now that I have a friend in high places, and since Sheikh Sultan is also chairman of the Abu Dhabi Tourism Authority, I shall have to take him up on his offer of a complimentary stay in this over-the-top crib!

The roads in the UAE are state-of-the-art, bordered with lush green lawns through a desert that has not seen rain for the past 7 or 8 years. The speed limit is 160kph (100mph) but they don't stop you unless you are exceeding 180kph, which everyone seems to be doing. Other than the Bentley's, Aston Martins, Porsche Mirages and Ferraris, they also have the 680kph 1001hp Bugatti Veyron, a cute little 9-liter 16-cylinder roadster which sells for a mere US$2-million.

After the course, Sheikh Sultan invites me back to his ranch near Al Ain on the Omani border. As is Arab custom, his wife and 6 children stay in a separate house on the ranch, and do not meet regular folk like me. I am entertained at his "thingiri", some distance away – a palatial mansion with office, gym, squash-court, sauna, Jacuzzi, steam-room, cinema and entertainment center. After a couple of hours dune-bashing, and seeing his efforts at turning the desert into a fauna and flora habitat, and surrounded by lush lawns which are irrigated by his oil-well-powered desalination plant, we enjoy the desert sunset while sitting on a ginormous Persian carpet and leaning against massive Persian cushions, being served fresh dates, Turkish coffee and biltong (jerky) which he makes from his herds of white Oryx (gemsbok) and desert gazelle – I took some of my USA biltong for him to taste and will take some South African biltong spice when I next visit in November.

At the time I was a smoker, and Camel cigarettes was my brand. I have a treasured sunset photograph of Sheikh Sultan and I sitting on a Persian carpet, in the middle of his lawn, in the middle of the Arabian desert, leaning against these very large cushions, puffing away at our cigarettes. And his comment "I am more accustomed to riding these things – this is my first time smoking one of them."

I had recently read Kenneth Timmerman's book "Preachers of Hate – Islam and the War on America". After gently broaching the subject and fully aware of the sensitivities, he is quite willing to discuss the issues of the Middle East and especially the Wahabi fundamentalist teachings which have so perverted the principles of Islam and which have bred so many suicide bombers. In the UAE there is a strong move to give the children a strong international education with English as a core language, and I found the average Arab in Abu Dhabi to have an excellent mastery of English and with a level of general knowledge somewhat superior to what I've experienced over the past 6 years. Reading skills, however, are still critical and Sheikh Sultan plans to put me in touch with the Minister of Education on my next trip, with a view to getting ExecuRead introduced to their schools and universities.

On my return to the USA, I have a near disaster at Charlotte immigration – other than two rather nice Persian rugs in my suitcase, I am entering the USA with an almost expired South African passport, an entry visa which expired 2 years ago, but with an Advance Parole document – a temporary entry permit indicating that I am still "in process" with my permanent residence application. Because the Advance Parole is pretty uncommon and generally not recommended for international travel, the Homeland Security guys detain me for an hour, sans my cell-phone, while they scratch their heads and investigate as to whether I should be admitted to the USA or sent back to Frankfurt. When I start complaining about being a property-owning tax-paying person in the USA, thus paying their salaries, and being highly pissed at being treated so badly while my wife and baby children are outside the airport waiting for me, they relent and admit me back into the USA with much admonishment about getting my status, passport and visa in order – not an experience that I want to repeat too often. However, I see from the US Customs & Immigration Services website that they are now only processing permanent residence applications filed on September 6, 2006 and my application was only filed on March 27, 2007 – so with this 7-month backlog, I am unlikely to get a decision on my permanent residence application much before March or April 2008.

Two days later, Michael and I head off to New York to watch baseball. Michael secured tickets to the Yankee Stadium to watch the NY Yankees trounce the Boston Red Sox and then the NY Yankees get walloped by the Tampa Bay Devil Rays. Wow! What a place this Yankee Stadium. We're staying at a hotel in downtown Manhattan, enjoying New York thin-crust pizza for breakfast, lunch and supper, and then a train from 33rd street in Manhattan up to 161st street in the Bronx to watch the game, try to catch an out-of-bounds baseball and then try to get a ball signed by some of the players. Michael catches two balls but fails to secure any signatures.

On our arrival back at the hotel, late Friday night, the foyer is amply decorated by a gaggle of rather cute ladies with short skirts and long eye-lashes, one of whom is leaning towards a wall-mirror re-doing her make-up (I guess) and flashing an eye-full of scantily-clad (red butt-floss as Sarah calls it!) derrière. Michael, aged 13, blushes and admits that he knows what they are, but feels it is a bit too much information at this time.

On the home-front, he is playing baseball again, with me as an assistant coach, and will soon be trying out for the school football team. We have some medical insurance for the kids, but Michael seems to have a knack for tapping out his medical limits very early in the year, and this is only with back-yard football.

With his neighborhood friends, he's playing football in the back yard. Looking over his shoulder to catch a long pass, he runs into our very large cedar tree and knocks himself out. Much consternation from all concerned. When he regains consciousness, his eyes look really funny and he starts vomiting. Suspecting concussion, we dump him in the car and rush off to the hospital emergency room. A CAT scan reveals that he has cracked his skull and has a small air-bubble on his brain. The doctors suggest he remain overnight for observation. When I arrive the following morning, I find that he has had another CAT scan that reveals no increase in the air-bubble, and he is discharged with a course of antibiotics to counter any possible infection and a bill for $6000 for two CAT scans and $1000 for his emergency room visit and a night in the hospital. I send the bill to his school insurance and they offer to pay $500, the maximum for an out-patient treatment. Because he was hospitalized for less than 24 hours, he was deemed by the hospital to be an out-patient. If he had been classified as an in-patient, the insurance would cover the full amount. I talk to the hospital. Since you treated Michael while he was in hospital "for observation", you either decided to unilaterally admit him as an in-patient and give him the second CAT scan, or you unilaterally decided to administer treatment to a minor out-patient who was there for observation, and this without my consent. Should I be talking to a lawyer about unauthorized medical treatment? Michael is quickly re-classified as an in-patient and the insurance company has no leg to stand on.

October 4, 2007 sees the USCIS in receipt of our response to their request for further evidence and a response that we will get a decision in the next 60 days. However, December 4, 60 days since our submission to the USCIS on October 4th, comes and goes with no decision and no news.

In spite of hopes to the contrary, Christmas 2007 is subdued in the Stewart household. Someone somewhere is making a decision that will seriously impact our lives.

Day 2377. January 9, 2008

Just two weeks after Christmas, we receive an email notification from the Nebraska USCIS office to say that all our applications for Permanent Residence in the United States, have been denied. No reason given. It says that they have mailed us the reasons and we should expect to receive the document in the mail. We are in a state of severe shock. We cannot imagine why this could happen and for what legitimate reason.

After a week of agony and depression, we get the reasons for the denial from the USCIS. In introducing the criteria for his decision to deny our petition, USCIS Director F. Gerard Heinauer concedes that *"the petitioner refers to the previous Form I-129's that have been approved for the same petitioner and the same beneficiary."* But then proceeds to really try our sanity. *"USCIS acknowledges that although both the immigrant and non-immigrant visa classifications rely on the similar regulations, the question of overall eligibility requires a comprehensive review of all of the provisions of the statute. There are significant differences between the non-immigrant visa classification, which allows an alien to enter the US temporarily, and an immigrant visa petition, which permits an alien to apply for permanent residence in the United States and ultimately apply for naturalization."*

Let me understand this. The security apparatus of the United States in the post-9/11 era is more concerned about letting people stay here permanently, than it is about letting people come here temporarily? Forgive any sarcasm here, but I seem to recall that the 9/11 hijackers were here on temporary non-immigrant visas and had no need for permanent resident "green-cards".

Heinauer continues ... *"Furthermore, each petition is a separate record of proceeding and receives an independent review. In making a determination of statutory eligibility, USCIS is limited to the information contained in the record of proceeding.*

"USCIS initially noted that the petitioner had not established the qualifying relationship between itself and the foreign entity, Bruce Stewart & Associates. The petitioner had also failed to establish that any purported qualifying relationship existed at the time of filing of the petition. The petitioner also failed to submit a statement of the beneficiary's position abroad which is to be considered as qualifying as well as sufficient evidence to establish that the position in the US qualifies as executive or managerial in capacity."

Chris is of the opinion that this denial is nothing short of bizarre based on the reasons they have given. The first reason for denial, the assertion that I don't function as an executive or manager, is ridiculous – the USCIS has ruled on my executive/managerial status on numerous occasions. The second reason for denial, that my salary is not commensurate with that of an executive, has never been raised until now. It was fine for the last 7 years and we are happy with it, but suddenly it's no longer OK! And the third reason for denial is that I have apparently spent too much time in South Africa in the last 7 years. Less than 6 weeks in 7 years? Too much time? Someone at the USCIS is clearly not reading the evidence. Or perhaps lack of evidence?

Quite honestly, our standard of living in the US can hardly be considered as living below the poverty line, yet if the USCIS is to be believed, we should be knocking on doors for food stamps and donations sometime soon!

Our new strategy will include appealing this denial as well as going back to all our Senators' and Representatives' offices to bring some kind of sanity to this situation. We send out emails to 500 friends, business associates and politicians, requesting any support they can offer – testimonial letters, letters and calls to elected North Carolina officials, media coverage, whatever.

On January 21, 2008, less than a month before my visa is due to expire on February 15, we FedEx our Notice of Appeal documents to the USCIS in Lincoln, NE to appeal their decision to deny our I-140 Change of Status and I-485 Permanent Residence applications.

The Service decision of January 9, 2008 should be reversed on the following grounds:

(a) fails to properly consider all of the evidence in the record;

(b) is based on numerous erroneous facts, not supported by the record;

(c) relies on improper assumptions and inference not supported by the record of proceeding;

(d) is contrary to the Service's own statutory and regulatory meaning of the phrase "executive capacity";

(e) is arbitrary and capricious; and

(f) deprives the Petitioner of due process of law.

The record of the proceeding, as mentioned in the initial submission, clearly establishes the following:

(a) the corporate entity abroad continues to do business within the meaning of the regulation;

(b) the Petitioner and the foreign entity share a qualifying corporate relationship for purposes of the instant petition;

(c) the Beneficiary was previously employed for at least one year of the three years immediately preceding the filing of the petition by the foreign entity in an executive capacity;

(d) the Beneficiary is coming to the United States to render services to the Petitioner which are executive in nature.

In short, all eligibility requirements for approval of the petition were established by the Petitioner.

In its decision, the Service initially notes that "There are significant differences between the non-immigrant visa classification, which allows an alien to enter the United States temporarily, and an immigrant visa petition, which permits an alien to apply for permanent residence in the United States and ultimately apply for naturalization."

Further, the Service notes that each petition is a separate record, receives an independent review, and is limited to the information contained in the record. Petitioner concedes this final point. However, the principal reason for denial of the petition, according to the Service, is that "the Petitioner has not established that the beneficiary has been, or will be, employed in a managerial or executive capacity." On this point, the Petitioner wishes to note that the definition of executive capacity necessary for qualification as an immigrant multinational manager is the EXACT same as the regulatory definition of executive capacity needed to qualify for the nonimmigrant L-1A classification. Furthermore, the Petitioner also wishes to note that the job description for the position of President was the EXACT same as that submitted on the nonimmigrant petition (Form I-129) submitted on behalf of the same Beneficiary.

While there may be differences in the immigrant and non-immigrant classification, there is not one area where there exists a single difference. This is important because the Service was convinced that the position abroad and the position that the beneficiary occupied in the United States both qualified as executive positions for no less than seven years. The job duties of the beneficiary have not changed over the years. But, now the Service inexplicably declares that the position does not qualify. Clearly, to now determine that the position does not qualify as executive in nature would require a volume of evidence to the contrary given the identical statutory and regulatory definition of the terms coupled with the fact that prior petitions were not challenged on this issue after submission of identical evidence. The Service does not have sufficient basis for this determination. The Petitioner is entitled to have the agency follow its own regulations and engage in a pattern of consistent adjudications. Here, the decision of January 9, 2008 is clearly not consistent with past decisions. This issue will be further explored in Petitioner's brief.

Petitioner's brief will also establish that the Service decision relies on improper assumption and inference not supported by the record. As the Service points out, adjudication of each petition is limited to the facts contained in the record of proceeding. Reliance on evidence not part of the record is not only arbitrary and capricious but also deprives the petitioner of due process of law. Because the record in the instant proceeding is sufficient to establish all issue of eligibility, the decision of the Service should be reversed.

We have no idea when this will be adjudicated and can only hope and pray that support from the two North Carolina Senators, and Representative Sue Myrick, may assist us in getting this resolved before we become illegal overstays on February 15th, 2008!

February 5, 2008. We receive letters from Representative Sue Myrick and Senator Richard Burr to say that they are unable to assist us with our matter any further, and explaining our situation to us, if we stay in the US illegally.

This letter from Sue Myrick is interesting in that we are expected to leave the United States and return to South Africa while our appeal is being considered. In effect, close down our business, terminate our contracts with suppliers and clients, sell our home in Charlotte, ship our furniture and personal belongings back to South Africa, sell our three vehicles, pull our children out of school and then sit in limbo in South Africa for months, possibly years, until our future is determined by the USCIS and then to return to the US and start our lives all over again. It seems to be overlooked that we are self-sufficient human beings with real lives and real children, not just some commodity.

"Dear Dr. Stewart: I have received a telephonic update from the Congressional Relations Unit of Citizenship and Immigration Services in Washington, DC regarding your request to be allowed to remain in the United States during the appeal of the denied I-140 occupational visa petition. Unfortunately, this is not an option under existing immigration law and you must return to your homeland before your current L-1 visa expires or else you will become an overstay.

"An expired stay of less than one year imposes a 3-year bar from being eligible to return to the United States or gain a benefit. An overstay of one year or more imposes a 10-year bar from being eligible to return to the United States or gain a benefit. This is true even if an immigrant occupational visa petition is approved on your behalf. If you are still inside the United States at the time of immigrant visa approval, your eligibility to benefit from the approved immigrant occupational visa petition becomes null and void if your non-immigrant visa has expired. If you are in an expired status, you will lose the benefit that the approved petition would have afforded you. The 3-year/10-year bar will be enforced on expired visa holders.

"It is in your best interest to comply with immigration law and not become an overstay. It is unfortunate that the filing was unsuccessful in being completely adjudicated and approved before your L-1 visa expires."

Day 2437. March 11, 2008

Nebraska sends our appeal to the Administrative Appeals Office in Washington, DC, for review. And we are again living on tenterhooks. It's now coming up for 7 years that we have been living in this fascinating, frustrating, brilliant, ignorant, generous, selfish, arrogant, humble country.

On June 3, 2008 an email arrives from the USCIS. Our matter has been denied and reasons will follow in the mail.

This is beyond our comprehension. We are self-sufficient, we own a home, we own a successful business, Sarah is a rising International Baccalaureate senior at Myers Park High School, Michael is part of the Duke Talent Identification Program, is in the top 95% of math students in the country and has spent more than half his life in America. What do these people want from us? After 7 years in this country, WE ARE AMERICANS! We've committed no crimes, we're financially secure, we're part of our community and we ask for nothing. And yet the USCIS says we're not the sort of people they want in America. The USCIS says I'm not an executive or manager! Well then, who the hell has been running and managing my company since I started it 33 years ago? The USCIS says I don't earn enough to live in this country! Balls! I don't live on Wall Street but I can afford to live in a $400k home, own my SUV free and clear and received finance for Dianne's Pontiac Solstice and Sarah's Scion! But I'm not good enough to live in America, while 50,000 Green Cards are GIVEN away each year, mostly to peasants from "God-Knows-Where-The-Fuck-Is-That-Istan". Yes, I'm angry! Wouldn't you be?

On June 7, 2008, we receive the reasons for the denial. And to our surprise, this is NOT a denial of our appeal. It's a denial of an application to extend our L-1 status, filed by Shante on 21 December 2005! Reason for the denial? Shante filed Form 1-539 instead of Form I-129. It's taken the USCIS 2½ years to tell us that Shante filed the wrong form! The good news is that we have still not received a decision on our appeal. The bad news is that a positive decision on our appeal pre-supposes some degree of sanity, professionalism, intelligence and competency within the USCIS.

Chris has been our attorney of record since August 2006, and yet the USCIS does not appear to know this. While not professing to have all the answers yet, we now have a pretty good take on the USCIS, and it is our considered opinion that the USCIS should be quietly euthanized!

Here are just some of the basic problems : Every time you file an application or petition with the USCIS, you get a new receipt number. This receipt number does not indicate your identity. And all enquiries to and communication with the USCIS is based upon the receipt number for that particular application filed. Over the past 7 years, we have filed dozens and dozens of applications and have dozens and dozens of receipt numbers, none of which have any visible link to ourselves or to one another. In fact, we have a strong suspicion that Shante was collecting money and dishing out the same filing receipt numbers and the same approval receipt numbers to multiple clients.

Then the submitted petitions are sent to various USCIS Service Centers for processing - we've been dealing with Service Centers in Texas, Nebraska and Vermont, so we must have files in at least these 3 centers. Since November 2006 we've been dealing with Vermont for our L-1 reinstatement, with Nebraska for our I-140 Change of Status petition, with Texas for our permanent residence petition and now with Washington DC for our appeal. These service centers obviously have little to no communication with one another, which is possibly why Texas, in 2008, has just denied the application filed in December 2005 to extend our stay, not knowing that in 2006 Vermont granted our application to extend our stay, or that in 2008, Nebraska denied our application for permanent residence, or that DC is presently considering our appeal.

I know that the legacy INS (Immigration & Naturalization Service) was embarrassed when it became public that they had just issued visas to some of the dead 9/11 terrorists, and that it was hoped that the system could be improved by incorporating the INS into Homeland Security and changing its name to (US)CIS, but has anything really changed? 2½ years to tell me my former attorney filed the wrong form??

Day 2557. July 7, 2008

Our L-visas expired in February, but because our permanent residence petition is still being adjudicated, we are "in process" and thus not out of status. We are still waiting. Our appeal was filed in March and we were due to receive a decision by the end of May. Is no news good news? Could this be the end of our American Dream?

Then, ironically, the inefficiency of the USCIS works in our favor. Remember back in the Shante days of 2006 when we tried to get our overstay condoned and our visas reinstated? When the USCIS kept dodging a *pro nunc tunc* reinstatement for February 2006 through February 2008? And first gave us December 2006 through December 2008 visas? And only later, under pressure from Senator Burr, the February 2006 through February 2008 visas? Well, when they finally issued the February 2006 through 2008 visas, they forgot to rescind the December 2006 through 2008 visas which are thus still valid. So, we still have legal status until December 5, 2008.

And then in an act of petty cruelty in August, our daughter Sarah, an International Baccalaureate Senior at Myers Park High School is denied getting her driver's license renewed at the DMV - citing that her license has been flagged, and that Homeland Security and ICE need to be advised if she attempts to renew it, in spite of the fact that we have a valid L-visa until December 2008. She is no longer able to drive herself to school and her many extra mural activities, both for the community and school. A major set-back for a young person's self-esteem and confidence. There is no bus from our neighborhood to the school because we were grand-fathered in after Charlotte Mecklenburg Schools changed their zoning areas. So we are having to drive Sarah around, causing much inconvenience to our lives and business activities. Sarah has an impeccable driving record. Again, it's a campaign of phone-calls and emails to pressurize the DMV and Homeland Security into following the laws of this country. Being a nation of laws goes both ways. Two months later, we prevail and Sarah has her Driver's License renewed at the DMV - expiring December 5th, 2008, coinciding with our family's L-1 Visa expiry date.

My mother, Jennifer Stewart, matriarch of Clan Stewart, turns 80 on April 19, 2009. Dianne's mother Kay Ennis will celebrate her 75th birthday 2 days later. To celebrate Jennifer's birthday at the family home in Hermanus, South Africa, family & friends are gathering from Australia, England, Scandinavia, Canada and the USA. The Stewart family has not been together for over 20 years. If our permanent residence is not granted soon, Jennifer's birthday will be without me, her eldest offspring, her daughter-in-law Dianne and her grand-children Sarah and Michael. If we leave the USA to attend this family reunion, we will not be allowed to return to our home and business in the USA. While "hostages" in the USA, Dianne and I have buried both of our fathers in absentia. We now have a painful and heartbreaking choice - whether to attend the Clan Stewart Reunion and Jennifer's 80th, and thus give up our fight for the privilege of living in America, or to be the only absentees at

Jennifer's birthday. We pray daily for a miracle and for strength and guidance.

We are amazed to hear that some of our friends are doing "write-in's" on their ballots for the Senate race in North Carolina. Instead of voting for either Kay Hagan or Elizabeth Dole they are writing in... "Dianne Stewart!" Not sure how this works, but they are doing it!

On October 29 we receive a letter from the Ombudsman's office saying essentially that there is nothing they can do, as our case is pending in the Administrative Appeals Office in Washington DC, and this could take up to 18 months to process. Once again, we are left hanging in the air, with no resolution or decision. How on earth are we meant to continue our lives under these unbearable circumstances? Our L-1 visas expire on December 5th, 2008. No news from Representative Mel Watts, and our stalwart and tenacious crusader, Martha Rea Calkins, continues her crusade on our behalf and receives a phone call from Alice Torres in US Representative Sue Myrick's Office. She undertakes to request that the USCIS grant us an extension of our visas from December 5, 2008 until our Permanent Residence Appeal has been heard.

November 7, 2008 : My 57th birthday and day 2680 of our immigration journey, is spent with attorney Chris working out a possible strategy to buy us a little more "legal-status-time" after December 5, 2008. Notwithstanding the undertaking from Sue Myrick's office to attempt a visa extension for us, which is highly unlikely as I have reached the end of my L-1-visas's 7-year lifespan, we receive a copy of a great letter from Sue Myrick to the Administrative Appeals Office singing our praises and requesting an expeditious appeal decision. How much effect this will have, we don't know. But at least Martha Rea Calkins has some support from Alice Torres and Sue Myrick in her tireless crusade to find a solution. It's essential that we resolve this now -- Sarah graduates from high school in 6 months and is still precluded from applying to colleges and universities without a valid visa or Social Security number -- destined to remain unemployed and uneducated. Our prayers are that Martha and Sue Myrick can pull off a miracle.

At the same time, I lose teaching assignments for the military in Canada, companies and a university in the UK, a United Nations course in Rome and the Department of Education in the UAE, because of my "hostage" status in the USA.

Day 2703. December 2, 2008

Our appeal is dismissed by Acting Chief John F Grissom at the Administrative Appeals Office. Full of errors of fact and in our opinion, an incorrect interpretation and application of the relevant laws of the USA. The USCIS denied the petition on the basis of four adverse findings :

The petitioner failed to establish that the beneficiary was employed abroad in a qualifying managerial or executive capacity, and

The petitioner failed to establish that it would employ the beneficiary in a qualifying managerial or executive capacity, and

The petitioner failed to establish an ability to pay the beneficiary's proffered wage.

The beneficiary will not be an "employee" of the United States operation.

All this in spite of the fact that various Service Centers have granted L-1 visas and renewals on these very grounds over the period 2000 to 2008. The USCIS AAO allows 33 days to submit an appeal – i.e. January 4, 2009.

Notwithstanding the obvious questions as to who HAD been managing the overseas entity between 1975 and 2001, if not me, and who HAS BEEN managing the local entity since 2001, if not me, and the other obviously irrelevant question about the local entity's ability to pay the proffered wage, there is a far more ominous statement in the USCIS decision – *"The approval of a non-immigrant petition, or even multiple decisions as in the petitioner's case, in no way guarantees that the USCIS will approve an immigrant petition filed on behalf of the same beneficiary. The Service is not required to approve petitions merely because of prior approvals that may have been erroneous."*

Essentially the USCIS is saying that it can make a 'mistake' in granting an L-1 visa, and it can compound this 'mistake' repeatedly by extending the visa status over the ensuing years, and it can further compound its 'mistake' in a very unusual politically and public-opinion motivated request for visa status reinstatement "pro nunc tunc", and based upon these repeated 'mistaken' visa approvals, a beneficiary may be motivated to invest skills, resources, intellectual capital and hard labor to build a business, only to have to give it all up when seven years later, the USCIS decides that it has been making repeated 'mistakes' and so sorry, we erred and you must leave now. Perhaps I might be forgiven for concluding that the L-1 visa is an invitation to companies to bring skills, manpower, resources and intellectual property to the USA, to open new business enterprises, pay taxes, contribute to Social Security and Medicare and then after 5 to 7 years, it's goodbye and, by the way, thanks for your donation to the US Economy and the American Gravy-train! If I sound pissed, you're correct. I am. I've seen far too many other people come to the USA, build and enrich businesses and then get forced to leave 7 years later once the L-1 reaches the end of its 7-year life span. One might argue that the L-1 is a non-immigrant visa and that you should not have immigrant intent and thus cannot complain when your immigrant petition is denied. Not so. While the L-1 is a non-immigrant visa, it is also a "dual-intent" visa, recognizing that the non-immigrant may have a 'change-of-heart' and wish to exercise immigrant intent at some stage.

The fourth basis for denial is simply priceless, and goes to show how dysfunctional the entire immigration system is. God save us from wannabe lawyers who screw up people's lives while squandering the taxpayer Dollar. The USCIS determines that *"the beneficiary will not be an employee of the US operation"* and proceeds to opine that *"when a worker is also a partner, officer, member of a board of directors, or a major shareholder, the worker may only be defined as an "employee" if he or she is subject to the organization's "control".* God help us here.

Firstly, the immigration act says the beneficiary (that's me) must be "employed by" the US operation. The act does not state that the beneficiary must be "an employee" of the US operation. To the layman, the two terms might appear inter-changeable and mean the same thing. But laws use precise terminology and must be interpreted very strictly. So, if you wander off topic and want to know whether I am "an employee", i.e. whether I have a boss who controls my work activities and who can hire and fire me, then no, as the owner of the business I am not an employee. But if you follow the precise terminology of the law, and ask whether I am "employed by" the company, i.e. whether I have an employment contract with the company, perform daily duties for the company and receive a wage for the services I perform, then I am "employed by" the company. And just in case the "lawyers" at the AAO need some legal support on this point, here it is.

First, the Board of Immigration Appeals has stated previously that the sole stockholder of a corporation is able to be employed by that organization, as the corporation has a separate legal entity from its owners or even its sole owner. Also, in the Matter of Allan Gee Inc, the Court ruled that where a petitioner corporation has been duly incorporated under the laws of a State, it is a separate legal entity existing independently of its stockholder. Therefore, that sole stockholder may be the beneficiary of a petition filed by the corporation to accord preference classification under section 203(a)(6) of the Immigration and Nationality Act.

The ruling in that case has not been disturbed and mirrors the basic tenet of corporate law. This further highlights the Administrative Appeals Office's misunderstanding of the terms "employed by" and "employee" in the context of an immigration benefit. Such an arbitrary and obviously incorrect legal conclusion should not be permitted to pass muster. It is an error of law and casts a shadow on the decision of the AAO as a whole.

Secondly, the Board has also ruled, in a similar context, that "if we were to adopt the definition of "employee" we would exclude some of the very people that the statute intends to benefit: executives. Thus, how can Congress create legislation purporting to provide benefits to an executive, but then rule that executives do not qualify because they are not considered employees? The answer must be that this was not Congress's intent.

After extensive research, attorney Chris and I are unaware of a single case where the USCIS denied a similar petition on the assertion that they were not an "employee". Additionally, we are unaware of even one instance where the USCIS, or any court, relied on another agency's definition of relevant terms in denying a petition. It simply does not make sense. Immigration benefits are to be decided by the terms of the Immigration & Nationality Act and the Code of Federal Regulations. It is, quite simply, an axiom of immigration law. To do otherwise would frustrate the intent of Congress and fly in the face of years of precedent to the contrary. The cases which hold that an executive may obtain lawful permanent residence from a qualifying organization as long as he is employed in an executive capacity are far too numerous to mention.

There is, of course, the interesting legal question as to whether I am indeed "under the control of the company"? Since the company enjoys a separate legal persona, with its own identity, it has contractual capacity independent of its owners, managers and executives. It is regulated by statute and it can force its managers, executives and even its stockholders to comply with their fiduciary responsibilities in their dealings with, and on behalf of, the company. So, to answer the question, while as president of the company I may have very wide latitude in the decision-making process, I am still acting within the statutory controls that regulate my fiduciary responsibilities. But considering that the USCIS prefers to define an "employee" as someone in a master/servant relationship, this bit of legal gymnastics might prove to be a hill too high to climb.

We are stunned at this decision from the USCIS which flies in the face of US immigration law, the evidence presented and basic reasoning and common sense. Chris and I burn the midnight oil in an effort to adhere to the laws of the United States and to maintain my legal status. And on December 5, 2008, the date that my L-1 visa expires, we file a petition for an L-1 visa for Dianne. If granted, this should afford us sufficient time to remain in the USA while our Motion to Reopen / Reconsider the dismissal of our appeal is being considered. With support from Charlotte friends Jill Dinwiddie and Catherine Connor we seek to secure an appointment to meet with Senator Kay Hagan.

In the realization that the USCIS clearly requires an unambiguous body of evidence to fully support every aspect of our business activities in South Africa since 1975 and in the USA since 2001, we assimilate every piece of evidence and supporting legal argument and case-law previously submitted to the various USCIS Service Centers, together with additional supporting evidence, legal argument, regulatory and case-law. This document comprises some 900 pages and is scrutinized by two separate immigration attorneys to test the validity of our evidence, legal arguments and supporting regulatory and case-law. At the same time, I bring every bit of my legal training to the table – studying the immigration laws and regulations of the USA and playing "devil's advocate" with every argument raised by our immigration lawyers.

On December 31, 2008, attorney Chris Fedex's an I-290B Notice of Motion to Reopen / Reconsider to the USCIS Administrative Appeals Office, together with an advisory that 900 pages of supporting evidence, legal argument and case-law is to follow under separate cover within 30 days. This notice is received by M. Leslie at the AAO on January 2, 2009, 2 days BEFORE due date. However, due to a clerical error on the part of Chris's office, this submission is addressed to the USCIS Administrative Appeals Office in DC that issued the denial, rather than to USCIS Nebraska which originally sent the case to the AAO. IT SHOULD BE NOTED HERE THAT THE I-290B WAS TIMEOUSLY FILED

WITH THE USCIS, ALBEIT TO AN INCORRECT OFFICE –
THE AAO RATHER THAN NEBRASKA.

On January 5, 2009, the day AFTER the submission deadline date, the AAO returns the Notice of Motion to Reopen / Reconsider to Chris, informing him that the I-290B should have been sent to Nebraska rather than to the AAO. Considering that the Service Centers routinely transfer cases to the AAO for adjudication, and the AAO routinely transfers cases back to the Service Centers, it is thus incomprehensible as to why the AAO did not simply transfer this time-critical Notice of Motion to Reopen / Reconsider to the Nebraska Service Center when it received the timely submission on January 2.

On January 9, 2009, Chris again Fedex's the I-290B Notice of Motion to Reopen / Reconsider to the USCIS Nebraska Service Center, together with an acknowledgement of his clerical error in originally submitting the I-290B to the AAO which issued the December 2 denial. This submission is received by R. Cook at the Nebraska Service Center on Jan 12, 2009, 41 days after the December 2 denial by the AAO, 10 days after the timely, yet erroneously addressed, submission to the AAO on January 2 and just 8 days after the submission deadline date of January 4, 2009.

To cover ourselves, we Fedex a duplicate copy of the 900 pages of evidence and legal argument to USCIS Nebraska. This is received by R. Cook at the Nebraska Service Center on February 2, 2009. This entire submission is ignored and neither considered nor adjudicated, because, unbeknown to us at the time, our case has already been deemed abandoned because of the 8-day late-filing of the original submission. Indeed, we end up with the rather incongruous situation that, notwithstanding the AAO advising that the timely filing of the Notice of Motion to Reopen / Reconsider had been erroneously addressed to the AAO rather than the Nebraska Service Center and then declining to simply transfer the matter to Nebraska, when the Nebraska Service Center received the submission, it simply referred the case back to the AAO which will sit on the case for a full 12 months before issuing a decision.

While all this is taking place, seriously ruining another family Christmas, there is still no word on the success of Dianne's L-1 petition. But at least, being "in process" means we're still in-status.

Day 2748. January 14, 2009

Out of the blue, and rather alarmingly, we receive a request for INITIAL evidence in support of Dianne's L-1 application. The USCIS wants evidence about Dianne's CURRENT job-duties and salary in South Africa and evidence describing her PROSPECTIVE job-duties in the USA. WOW! Apparently the USCIS does not know that Dianne has been legally in the USA since 2001 and has previously been granted an L-1B visa by the very same office that is now requesting this information. We have no choice but to send them a full evidentiary and legal brief ... another 800 pages.

February 24, 2009 : Dianne's L-1B is approved until December 2011, longer than we had hoped for. We're ecstatic! But there's no mention of derivative L-2 visas for Sarah, Michael and myself. The following day the USCIS requests copies of I-94 records for Sarah and myself. No mention of Michael, but in case they don't know that Michael exists, we submit I-94 records for all three of us on March 6 and receive a notice that case-processing resumed on March 9. We expect an answer before the end of the month and, *Deo Volente*, we will still make Jennifer's 80th birthday in South Africa on April 18.

Of concern, is that there has been no acknowledgment from the USCIS in Nebraska or the AAO in DC, that the 900-page permanent residence appeal brief has been received or that the appeal is being considered. We have proof of delivery and receipt, but no confirmation that case-processing has resumed. We assume that our appeal is sitting in someone's pending / to-do file. The 900-page document worries me. It's a scary document to digest. But we had Hobson's Choice – send too little and risk an adverse decision based upon insufficient evidence and with no wriggle-room for an appeal, or send too much and risk no-one giving it full consideration.

After a pretty terrible 2008, both in terms of our immigration to the USA, but also the US Economy itself, 2009 looks promising on the business front. A couple of Lt Colonels from the Pentagon come down to one of my weekend courses in Charlotte. In addition to getting some pretty impressive results, we spend after-class time discussing how the course can be tailored to meeting the specific reading needs of military professionals – from intelligence analysts to special forces. Later in the year I present my first group courses to the Pentagon. A Brigadier General describes the course as "the most important professional training I've had in years." In the same year I receive a teaching assignment in Virginia Beach to train a specialist group of very tough and very smart professionals from the US Naval Special Warfare Development Group aka DevGru aka SEAL Team Six. Georgia Tech and the World Bank join my list of clients as does Lincoln Memorial University's DeBusk College of Osteopathic Medicine.

Day 2821. March 28, 2009

L-2 visas are issued to Sarah, Michael and I. But valid only until October 19, 2010, a shorter period than Dianne's L-1B which is valid until December 5, 2011, but better than nothing. We're not sure why the differing validity periods ... we can only assume that this is because Sarah turns 21 on October 18, 2010 and will "age-out" of any benefits she enjoys from being our minor child. Nevertheless, we can now attempt to find air-tickets to South Africa to make Jennifer's 80th Birthday and should hopefully now have sufficient time to await the decision on our Permanent Residence appeal to the AAO.

April 14, 2009 : We are in South Africa. Sarah is heartbroken and traumatized by the knowledge that she is being left behind in the USA and that she cannot be with her Granny Jennifer – Sarah has to remain in the USA to complete her 12th Grade exams. The US

Consulate in Cape Town grants Dianne, Michael and I, L-1B and L-2 visas, valid until 5 December 2011. WHAT A RELIEF!!!

Sarah's L-2 visa is, however, hugely problematic - it expires in October 2010 when she turns 21 and is not renewable. We can only hope and pray that our family's Permanent Residence appeal is granted before that date, failing which she will become an overstay unless she voluntarily departs the USA and leaves her family.

April 19, 2009 : The matriarch of Clan Stewart turns 80 at a family reunion in the family home, Hoy House, Hermanus, South Africa, accompanied by her 4 children, grand-children, great-grand-children, nieces and friends who travelled from the USA, UK and Australia to be with her. This is the first time that Jennifer and her children, Bruce, Ian, Fiona and Craig, have been together since 1988.

May 3, 2009 : In a brilliant example of verbal obfuscation, the following notice is received from the USCIS :

Application Type: I-290B, NOTICE OF APPEAL TO THE COMMISSIONER. Current Status: This case is now pending at the office to which it was transferred. The I-290B NOTICE OF APPEAL TO THE COMMISSIONER was transferred and is now pending standard processing at a USCIS office. You will be notified by mail when a decision is made, or if the office needs something from you.

We call USCIS Customer Service who are unable to explain exactly what this means. Neither can Chris our immigration attorney. Alice Torres from Sue Myrick's office has offered to look into this to see whether she can obtain clarity.

Day 2951. August 5, 2009

Senator Kay Hagan offers to assist us with an investigation into the status of our appeal -- seven months have now passed since we filed our 900-page Notice of Motion to Reopen / Reconsider our case for Permanent Residence. I submit a Privacy Release Form to

Senator Hagan's office. Although I am the beneficiary of the Permanent Residence petition by Speed Reading International, I am also the president of the company and thus the only officer authorized by the company / petitioner to make such an enquiry. Clearly, this might be a head-scratcher, since few non-legal people understand the legal status of an incorporated entity as being a separate juristic person, independent of its owners or shareholders and thus enjoying its own contractual capacity.

September 14, 2009 : Not unexpectedly, we receive the following response from Senator Hagan's office : *"It appears the person (i.e. Bruce Stewart) in whose behalf you are making this inquiry is the beneficiary of this I-140 petition. Immigration and Naturalization Regulations as well as the Privacy Act prohibit providing information to or acting at the request of anyone other than the "affected party." In the case of I-140 petitions, this is defined as the petitioner (i.e. Speed Reading International) or the petitioner's designated attorney or representative. We are unable to provide more detailed information on the status of the I-140 without the written consent of the petitioner or the petitioner's G-28 attorney. Any further questions Mr Stewart may have regarding the status of the I-140 petition should be directed to the petitioner. (From) Immigration Services Officer - NSC Congressional Unit"*

Accordingly, as you may be expecting, in response to this advisory, the beneficiary, Bruce Stewart, discusses the matter with the petitioner, Bruce Stewart, president of Speed Reading International Inc, who is at a loss for words at this hair-splitting and foot-dragging by the USCIS. The petitioner, Bruce Stewart, president of Speed Reading International Inc, and acting on behalf of Speed Reading International Inc, advises the beneficiary, Bruce Stewart, that in the absence of any other qualified officer within the petitioner company, that Bruce Stewart, the beneficiary, but also in his capacity as president of the petitioner, should request attorney Chris to, in turn, request Senator Hagan's office to investigate the status of the case. One can only hope that the USCIS does not invalidate attorney Chris's request, on the grounds that it is not clear whether his instruction emanated from the petitioner, Bruce Stewart, president of the petitioning company, or the beneficiary, Bruce Stewart himself.

November 19, 2009 : It's now almost 10 months since we filed our 900-page appeal against the decision to deny us permanent residence. And no decision from the USCIS. SURELY THEY CANNOT BE READING <u>THAT</u> SLOWLY!

In the interim I've been teaching my ExecuRead for Military Professionals courses at the Pentagon, Special Operations Command, US Naval Special Warfare Development Group, US Marine Corps and World Bank. And to crown it all, I am honored with the award of a 0205-Tactical Intelligence Officer "Plank" (Challenge Medal) by the Warrant Officers of 1st Intelligence Battalion of the US Marine Corps, 1 Marine Expeditionary Force, at Camp Pendleton, California "for his (my) contribution to the enhancement of the intelligence analysis capabilities of the USMC". Only two hundred 0205-Tactical Intelligence Officer "Planks" have been awarded, and this is the first to a civilian and will most likely be the only award EVER to a 'non-immigrant alien'. AND STILL THE USCIS SEEMS TO FEEL THAT WE DON'T DESERVE THE RIGHT TO CALL AMERICA OUR "HOME"!

As 2009 draws to a close, and we face another miserable Christmas in the United States, with ongoing uncertainty about our future, December 22 brings a communication from Cristina Jacome, Constituent Services Representative for U.S. Senator Kay Hagan : *"I spoke with USCIS Headquarters. They informed me that the Administrative Appeals Office is in the process of moving to a different building in a different area. So, for these couple of weeks all the cases are basically packed up until everything is organized in the new building. About your case: In the system, the last action they can see is that the case had been assigned to an officer and that it is under review. They asked me to contact them at the beginning of February to get another update."*

So, eleven months after submitting our documents, and eight and a half years after arriving in this country, we are still awaiting a decision as to whether we deserve permanent residence or not. And in 10 months' time, the break-up of our family begins - Sarah turns 21 and will have to start her own fight to live in the USA or get condemned to return to a country that she barely knows.

Day 3129. In a notice dated February 1, 2010, the USCIS Nebraska office rejects our appeal on procedural grounds. Specifically, that our initial appeal was rejected on December 2, 2008 and our immigration attorney, Chris had 30 days in which to file an appeal, with an allowance of an extra 3 days for the submission to reach the USCIS. We prepared a 900-page submission, covering EVERY SINGLE ASPECT of the evidentiary and legal components of our case. And after a full year - 365 days - the USCIS has not looked at a single page of our submission! Why? Because they only received the submission on January 12, 2009 instead of January 4, 2009! EIGHT days late! Other than the 12 or so days during December that were weekends and public holidays (when lawyers don't work!), we're interested to know why Chris failed to mention that his filing was late and inexcusably so. Chris filed the submission with the AAO instead of Nebraska. The AAO returned the submission to Chris with a note to file with Nebraska and by the time Nebraska received the filing, it was deemed late. Interestingly enough, we also and simultaneously filed a duplicate of the 900-page submission with Nebraska direct, which was received but has never been ruled upon and never mentioned in rulings since then. Nebraska has simply ruled on the submission which was erroneously filed with the AAO and then re-filed with Nebraska. And without considering a single piece of evidence, the ruling is "late submission – case abandoned".

Adding to the confusion, the AAO treated our submission as an appeal rather than as a Motion to Reopen / Motion to Reconsider, and then ruled that we cannot appeal against a denial of a previous appeal. Apparently, this confusion was caused by another Chris clerical error on the filing cover-page that marked the submission as an appeal rather than a motion. (A lesson to be learned here.) The USCIS thus treated the submission as an improper appeal rather than a motion, notwithstanding case law which rules that the substance of a filing (i.e. a motion to reopen / reconsider) supersedes the marking of the cover-page as an appeal. But that's a point of law which seems to fall outside the 6-week training of USCIS case-adjudicators. Of course, there may be another explanation here – it's called Reverse Legal Reasoning. Rather than study the evidence and come to a conclusion based upon the evidence, you simply decide on what you want the conclusion to be, and then selectively look for evidence, real or construed, to support your preconceived conclusion.

If you're a bit confused by all of this, remember that Chris and I are both legal people and if this is taxing our joint gray-matter, just imagine how the rest of the grunts feel!

On March 1, 2010, we file an I-290B Motion to Reopen / Motion to Reconsider the February 3 denial decision and argue that the submission WAS filed with the USCIS within the deadline due date, albeit to the AAO rather than the Nebraska Service Center, that the error was a clerical error on the part of our immigration attorney, that the late period of 8 days is not excessive and that the USCIS should reasonably condone the clerical error. This motion is received by USCIS Nebraska on March 2, 2010 and since the USCIS failed to consider the 900-page brief originally submitted in January 2009, we have to resubmit all 900 pages of legal argument and evidence. On a lighter note, the volume of paper-work submitted to the USCIS appears to be overburdening the tectonic plates as evidenced by the Icelandic volcano! In another cruel twist of the knife, the Nebraska Service Center will simply transfer this motion back to the AAO which will sit on the case for more than 18 months before issuing a decision.

As if we don't already have enough on our plate, on March 1, 2010, we file an I-129 Change of Status petition to have Dianne's non-immigrant status changed from L-1B to L-1A to pave the way for the filing of her I-140 petition to change her from non-immigrant to immigrant status. Just to make certain that we have covered every evidentiary and legal aspect of her case, we add to the tectonic-plate shift with another voluminous submission. The issue here is that

Dianne has an L-1B visa which has a maximum validity of 5 years. The L-1A has a maximum validity of 7 years. The USCIS has already granted her 7 years of valid stay and we are attempting to bring her visa documentation into line with her *de facto* awards by the USCIS.

In spite of our voluminous I-129 change of status submission, filed on March 1, the USCIS comes back to us on March 12 with a request for further evidence. They don't understand how Dianne can have been in the USA for almost 9 years when neither the L-1B or L-1A visas allow for this. They seem to be overlooking the fact that Dianne is married and has had derivative L-2 status from her husband's L-1 visa. We submit this evidence and argument on April 12. At the same time, we hold thumbs and anticipate a favorable decision on Dianne's I-129 by jumping the gun and taking the next step by filing her I-140 petition to change her status from non-immigrant to immigrant status, a submission comprising some 600 pages of evidence and legal argument. Although we filed this on April 12, the filing form that I downloaded from the USCIS website is an out-of-date form, so this is returned to Chris with instructions to resubmit with the latest form. Ten days lost but finally Dianne's I-140 is in the hands of the USCIS on April 22, 2010. Rather amazing that the USCIS's own website contains out-of-date petitioning forms that are unacceptable to the USCIS. One can only wonder how the USCIS would have treated our re-submission if it had arrived a day late because of an out-of-date form obtained from their own website!

On March 25, Nebraska refers my I-290B Motion to Reopen / Motion to Reconsider to the AAO for review. Follow the logic here – we file a petition with Nebraska which passes the buck to the AAO. In response to a denial by the AAO we file a submission back to the AAO which rejects the submission and tells us to file with Nebraska. So we re-file with Nebraska which promptly sends it to the AAO for a decision! And you wonder how your tax-dollars are being spent and why the Federal Government's budget is so big?

Now we await a decision from the AAO as to whether my application for an I-140 will be approved or not. All this to open the door to my applying for permanent residence. That I include the likes of the Pentagon, NASA, US Marine Corps, Special Operations Command and Defense Logistics Agency as clients does still not seem to qualify me as good enough for permanent residence in this country.

Day 3229. May 5, 2010

Success at last! In the second bit of good news in many years, Dianne's I-129 Change of Status petition is approved, her status is changed from L-1B (Specialized Knowledge) to L-1A (Manager/Executive) and her legal stay in the USA, and the rest of the family through derivative status, is confirmed until December 5, 2011. (The first was getting Dianne's L-1B approved in time to get back to South Africa for Jennifer Stewart's 80th birthday.) Meanwhile, Dianne's I-140 is received by the USCIS on April 22 and the normal processing time is 4 months. D-day is around 22 August. We're holding thumbs and as they used to say at NORAD when young Matthew Broderick was about to get WOMPR to unleash a nuclear deluge on the planet, "Confidence Level is High!"

Day 3390. October 18, 2010

Today is my daughter Sarah's 21st Birthday. Generally, a time for celebration, Sarah's gift is not quite what she wants – she becomes the first victim in our immigration journey - she's just lost her legal status in the USA – until yesterday, she enjoyed derivative L-2 status from her parents. Today she has no legal status in the USA. Since she is a full-time 2nd year sophomore student at Greensboro College, we urgently file a petition to have her status changed from L-2 to F-1, international student visa status. This visa is approved on November 6 and Sarah is authorized to continue her studies at Greensboro College.

But then the next piece of bad news. Greensboro College revokes Sarah's academic grants and scholarships, since they are not available to international F-1 students. It was on the basis of these grants and scholarships, offered to Sarah by the college, that motivated her to attend Greensboro College for her Bachelor's degree. Now without these funds, there is no hope of keeping her in school. The end result is that we cannot afford to keep Sarah in school and if she is not a full-time student, her F-1 visa will lapse and she will lose her legal status in the USA and be forced to leave the country. Desperate measures are called for.

Sarah and I draft a letter to the president of Greensboro College. Sarah has lived in North Carolina for almost 10 years. Her family are property-owning, tax-paying, economically-active residents of North Carolina. Sarah is a 4.0 GPA student at Greensboro College and on the Dean's list. Revoking her grants and scholarships would be unfair and an act of extreme cruelty – denying her the opportunity of completing her education and condemning her to leaving the USA and her family. Attempts at raising private financial aid were unsuccessful – no-one lends study finance to people who are in the USA on temporary visas. We acknowledge our understanding of the reasons for not granting financial support to foreign students, but submit that while Sarah may legally be deemed a foreign student, she is factually as American as apple-pie.

Within days, the president of Greensboro College advises that Sarah's grants and scholarships have been reinstated and she is welcome to continue her studies. But Sarah's status in America is now separated from the rest of her family. She derives no benefit from our visa status. She is on her own. She maintains her 4.0 GPA and Dean's List status and will graduate with a Bachelor's degree, Cum Laude, in December 2012.

Day 3399. October 27, 2010

Disaster! Dianne's I-140 Petition is denied! Just 5 months after the USCIS Vermont Service Center approved Dianne's petition for a change of status from an L-1B Specialized Knowledge visa to an L-1A Multinational Executive / Managerial visa, USCIS Texas Service Center Director David L Roark denies her I-140 petition on a single ground - she is not deemed to be a multinational executive / manager!

Is this for real? The definition of a manager for purposes of L-1A classification is identical to the definition of manager for purposes of I-140 classification. To justify this inconsistency in its decision, the USCIS says it is not bound by any previous decision(s) to the contrary. Of course, the USCIS invites us to appeal this decision! Just goes to prove that all crazies are not institutionalized and that some highway-robbers wear suits!

We file an appeal against this inconsistent adjudication on November 16, 2010. And again, not unexpectedly, rather than address this manifest failure in the US immigration system, the Texas Service Center simply passes the buck and refers the case to the Washington DC Administrative Appeals Office on February 10, 2011. That an appeal takes upwards of 16 months to adjudicate, while we have less than 10 months of legal residence in the USA seems to have escaped the USCIS ... or do they have a hidden agenda here?

May 24, 2011 : Desperate Measures. My last appeal is still awaiting adjudication after 14 months. Dianne's appeal is still awaiting adjudication after 6 months. Our visas expire on 5 December 2011, at which time, to avoid breaking the law by becoming "illegal" overstays in the USA, we will have to close down everything and leave the USA.

Not a good time for the Stewart family. Michael is about to start his junior year at Providence High School and Sarah her junior year at Greensboro College. And I am heavily involved in teaching courses at Robins Air Force Base, the Marine Corps Intelligence School at Virginia Beach and at the Camp Pendleton, Camp Lejeune and Quantico Marine Corps bases.

Our last-ditch effort is to motivate a North Carolina Senator to introduce a Private Bill into Congress to grant Permanent Residence to the Stewart Family - an extraordinary measure never done before in North Carolina, but done in California by Senator Dianne Feinstein on a number of occasions to prevent or remedy major injustices on humanitarian grounds. Understandably, a Private Bill is risky business - the Member of Congress or Senator who introduces the Bill, is linking his or her reputation to the people who will benefit from the Bill, and in this case, if the Stewarts turn out to be seriously big-time 'baddies', the Member of Congress or Senator who championed our case, suffers as well.

Accordingly, a Private Bill for the Stewarts is all about character and reputation, and whether the Senator or Member of Congress is convinced and comfortable with TWO essential requirements :

Are there extraordinary circumstances justifying a Private Bill for the Stewarts?

Are the Stewarts of sound enough character to warrant the Member of Congress or Senator linking his or her reputation and political future to the cause of the Stewarts?

Day 3649. In the worst news possible, on July 6, 2011, the USCIS denies my petition for permanent residence on the grounds of the late filing back in January 2009. So, after 30 months, my I-140 petition fails, not because of evidentiary or legal reasons, but simply because a timely filing to the USCIS was addressed to the AAO rather than Nebraska and thus arrived in Nebraska 8 days later than required – a clerical error on the part of our American immigration attorney Chris who responded to the sender of the December 2 denial notice – the AAO – rather than to Nebraska.

And on September 20, 2011, the USCIS denies Dianne's petition for permanent residence on the grounds that she is no longer deemed a manager or executive and that they had repeatedly erred in granting her an L-1 visa and renewals over the past 10 years.

There are now no further doors open to us, and we either leave the USA by 5 December 2011, or we remain as illegal overstays. The only positive aspect to all of this is that the thousands of hours we have invested in trying to become permanent residents of the USA, and the more than $250,000 we have spent in legal and filing fees and lost business, will finally come to an end.

To recap, very briefly, the chain of events; In December 2008, the USCIS Administrative Appeals Office denied my petition on the grounds of insufficient evidence. Remember, attorney Chris fobbed off the request for further evidence as a boiler-plate request and simply referred to evidence previously submitted. Hence insufficient evidence and hence the denial. Screw-up Number 1. Attempting to fix this, we prepared over 900 pages of evidence, legal argument and regulatory and case-law. In another fatal error, our attorney Chris erroneously sent this submission back to the USCIS AAO in Washington DC (which had issued the denial) rather than to the USCIS Nebraska Service Center. Screw-up Number 2. And instead of simply forwarding the submission to their office in Nebraska, the AAO sent it back to Chris and told him to send it to Nebraska. However, by the time the submission reached Nebraska, it was 8 days late - we had 33 days to prepare and file the documents and they were only received on the 41st day. Thus, because of this 8-day late filing, my case was deemed abandoned and the 900-page submission has never been considered. It took the USCIS until February 2010 (12 months) to tell us that our case had been deemed abandoned because of the late filing.

We immediately appealed this decision in March 2010 and had to wait until July 2011 (16 months) for them to reject our appeal. All it took was missing a 33-day deadline by 8 days. And yet the USCIS can take 365 days to tell us this.

One can only ask WHY? Perhaps no-one wanted to read and consider the merits of a 900-page submission and it was so much easier to use reverse legal reasoning – decide to deny the motion and then look for a reason to deny? If the AAO had simply transferred the timely submission to Nebraska, Nebraska would have had to read the full submission or refer it back to the AAO for adjudication. Instead, by returning the documents to Chris, the day after the submission deadline date, when it was obvious that there was no possibility of a timely re-submission to Nebraska, the USCIS could quite simply bury the whole case - and close the last door available to us to remain legally in the USA to continue providing a valuable service in a country where a lack of intelligence management costs American lives and where American reading skills have dropped to number 14 out of 34 developed nations.

Dianne's case is much simpler, but equally difficult to comprehend. At various times since 2000 she has had an L-1B "specialized knowledge" visa. There was no problem in getting this visa or its renewals. And even when Dianne's executive / managerial duties expanded and warranted a change of status from L-1B "specialized knowledge" to L-1A "multinational executive / manager", the USCIS granted her an L-1A visa in May 2010. However, just 5 months later, in an I-140 petition to change her status from non-immigrant to immigrant status, the prelude to the I-485 petition for permanent residence, the USCIS determined that she was NOT a manager, even though the definition of manager is identical for both the L-1A and the I-140. Indeed, the USCIS even went so far as to opine that it had erred in granting her the L-1A visa in the first place. Now perhaps one erroneous interpretation of the facts may be understood. But repeated identical interpretations of the facts tend to suggest a correct interpretation of the facts. Or is this an exception to the Occam's Razor philosophy?

So, the rules of law get tossed out by the USCIS. The principle of *estoppel* says that if you give me a statement of facts and I act upon that information, you cannot then tell me that you gave me incorrect information and expect me to suffer the consequences of acting to my own detriment based on the facts you gave me. Secondly, according to the principles of *stare decisis*, the precedent rule, subsequent decisions should recognize and be bound by previous decisions unless there is overwhelming evidence justifying a deviation from a previous ruling - which there is NOT - Dianne has been granted numerous L-1 visas and renewals over the past 10 years.

Here's our dilemma - most of our training is to the US Military - the Pentagon, NASA, the SEALs, the Naval Special Warfare Development Group and the intelligence battalions of the US Marine Corps. According to a statement from the US Marine Corps

"Since 2010, the ExecuRead course has been integrated into the Marine Air-Ground Task Force's Intelligence Specialist Career Course as an essential course module" and that "any delay or interruption in the supply of this training would be to the detriment of the analytic capabilities of the United States Marine Corps." The words "to the detriment of the analytic capabilities" quite simply means that people will die.

Of lesser importance, but no less relevant, is the future of our children who have spent the past 10 years in the American educational system. Sarah is now a junior at university and Michael is a junior at high school. They are both 4.0-plus GPA students. At what cost do we drag them to another country and expect them to pick up the pieces of their educational futures?

The alternative? We continue to work towards saving military lives and the future of our children, and in the process we all become overstays and start breaking the immigration laws of this country. It's Hobson's Choice.

The ONLY solution is for a politician to consider the big picture and to answer the only question to be answered - "Is there an overwhelming reason on humanitarian and/or national interest grounds to keep the Stewarts in the United States of America?" And if the answer is positive, to immediately introduce a Private Bill to Congress to grant Permanent Residence to the Stewart Family.

We write to President Barack and First Lady Michelle Obama and they ignore us.

We write to Vice-President Joe and Dr Jill Biden and they ignore us.

We write to the Speaker of the House and the Secretary of State and they ignore us.

We write to the Cabinet Members and every US Senator and every member of Congress. Most ignore us, yet some are kind enough to extend their condolences at our situation and refer us to our North Carolina Senators, Richard Burr and Kay Hagan.

Richard Burr says he cannot help us. That there is nothing he can do. Double-speak for he doesn't know what to do, or we are not important enough for him to invest time and effort on our behalf.

Senator Kay Hagan has been the one shining light in this world of darkness ... so far. She has shown interest in our case and has helped to expedite decisions from the USCIS, albeit unfavorable decisions. Now the moment of stepping up to the plate - Will Senator Kay Hagan be willing to introduce the Private Bill to Congress to gain permanent residence for us?

On Monday 26 September, we formally requested a face-to-face meeting with Senator Kay Hagan in Washington DC and now await her response.

In the hope that a lawmaker will step up to the plate, and in the realization that few lawmakers have ever dealt with a Private Bill, and certainly none in North Carolina, I draft a complete Private Bill with accompanying introductory speech. The heavy-lifting intellectual burden of writing the legislation and motivating its introduction to Congress has been done. All we need is a lawmaker to read the introductory speech and introduce the Private Bill.

In spite of this pressure and uncertainty, we are continually overwhelmed and humbled by the tenacity of the many friends around us who are working tirelessly to get someone to listen and to act. Some really choke us up...

Bruce, I just sent this email to my local Congressman. I hope this conveys my sincere gratitude for what you contributed to combat operations in Afghanistan. Please disseminate as you see fit. You are the type of man I go to bat for. David.

Sir,

My name is Captain David ***(redacted for security reasons), USMC. I am writing on behalf of a friend and teacher Dr Bruce Stewart and his family concerning their expiring visas this December 2011 and denial of permanent residence after living legally in the USA for more than 10 years.

As the training officer for 2nd Intelligence Battalion in Camp Lejeune during late 2010, my Commanding Officer tasked me with developing a rigorous training regimen in support of the Battalion's deployment to Afghanistan in early 2011. One of the individuals I reached out to was Dr Bruce Stewart and his company, Speed Reading International, d/b/a ExecuRead, which focuses on speed reading fundamentals. As an intelligence officer, I know how important it is for my analysts to quickly process the myriad information reports flowing in, from and around theater, to produce accurate and timely intelligence analysis. I can say without a doubt that Bruce and his company provided a crucial training aid and skill to the Marines of 2nd Intel Battalion, which led to Marines lives being saved on the battlefield.

Sir, I do not throw these words around lightly. In my estimation, as a Marine Officer, Bruce Stewart and his family deserve to be in this country and moreover, are exactly the type of citizens we need. He and his family hail from South Africa and will have to return there in December unless someone of your stature and influence steps in. Please take a few moments to look at his website and decide for yourself whether this is the individual who should be the target of our laws.

I should note that I am currently stationed in Quantico VA and that I do not speak for my command, nor do I represent the opinion of the Marine Corps or my previous command. I'm just a concerned citizen and a Marine.

Thank you for your time and Semper Fi,

Captain David ***(redacted for security reasons), USMC

To : Captain David ***(*redacted for security reasons*), USMC

David,

I am humbled by these words, proud to be called your friend and honored to be of service to the Marine Corps. Unlike you, however, I am spared the agony of knowing who has made the ultimate sacrifice from failures in intelligence analysis. But in the realization that there is still more to be done in this arena, my personal predicament pales into insignificance. Faced with Hobson's Choice between curtailing this work for the USMC by leaving the USA, or remaining here after December and contravening the immigration laws of this country, I believe the choice is clear. I still have hopes with a couple of US Senators who have expressed interest in resolving my case and I have advised them that I intend to continue working in the USA for as long as humanly possible, and that any personal sacrifice in this regard is inconsequential by comparison.

My warmest regards and gratitude to you,

Bruce Stewart

Day 3740. October 4, 2011

North Carolina Senator Hagan declines the Stewarts' appeal for a Private Bill. We are told by Senator Kay Hagan's office that she has never done a Private Bill before and that she is too busy to help us. We understand that she is busy helping someone with wedding arrangements, but suspect that this very moderate lawmaker is afraid to touch something as intellectually challenging and as controversial as a Private Bill in the immigration arena.

Interestingly, there are presently some 60 Private Bills to confer Permanent Residence on humanitarian grounds pending before Congress. Even more surprising is that every one we can find, deals with people who came here illegally, and who now want permanent residence. We cannot find a single private bill that is attempting to secure permanent residence for someone who came here legally, who is still here legally and who is now seeking permanent residence on humanitarian and national interest grounds. And we cannot find a single Private Bill that has a W.A.S.P. as the beneficiary.

Adding insult to injury is the fact that in spite of the unemployment prevailing in this country, the US continues to give away 50,000 Green Cards each year in the Green Card Diversity Lottery. Through our social networking and immigrant community website, South Africans in Charlotte, which Dianne manages, we are approached regularly by immigrant families who, having won a Green Card in the Lottery, are in need of food support and housing and employment assistance. And some of these people cannot even speak more than very rudimentary English. So we have the incomprehensible situation of America, on the one hand, importing virtually destitute new people into the country, and on the other hand, doing its best to get rid of property-owning, tax-paying, economically active, graduate business-owners.

However, on the brighter side, we have been commissioned to present our information and intelligence management training courses to the Navy & Marine Corps Intelligence Training Center at Dam Neck Virginia, and also to the 1st Radio Battalion of 1st Marine Expeditionary Force of the US Marine Corps at Camp Pendleton. We are honored to be able to continue our contribution to saving the lives of American military personnel in the theaters of war, albeit until this privilege is terminated.

Also on a positive note, and with just 59 days left to live legally in the USA, the media develops an interest in our case. Morgan Fogarty from Fox Charlotte interviews us on Fox Charlotte "News @ 10". We are blown away by the news item on our case that had all four of us totally choked-up and humbled by this show of support. The news item seems to have gone viral with supporters forwarding it to friends and business contacts and countless postings on Facebook.

Added to this exposure of our case, we appear on the 30-minute TV show "Charlotte Now with Mike Collins" and are radio guests on Charlotte Talks on WFAE 90.7 with Mike Collins on 12 October to talk about our immigration case, interestingly enough almost 10 years to the date since I was last a guest of Mike Collins. (My first interview was scheduled for September 11, 2001 but had to be rescheduled - a prophetic event in view of our present role in working to improve the intelligence management capabilities of the US Military to prevent another 9/11 attack on our country.)

Thanksgiving 2011 is bitter-sweet. More than 10 years of uncertainty about our future. Yet we are humbled daily by the support of friends who have taken us into their hearts and homes, and honored to be able to be of service in the protection of what we like to think of as OUR homeland. We are all traumatized by the ongoing stress, and this manifests itself in various ways which we try to ignore, yet have to acknowledge, in order to face, address and deal with.

I maintain a regular dialogue with my students in the Marine Corps and Special Forces who are serving on the battlefronts of Iraq and Afghanistan and I'm honored to hear about the positive impact that my training courses are having. Some communication is less training-specific.

"Battlefront Musings from a Distant War : From a Friend & US Marine in Harm's Way.

"Since the transfer of authority to 2nd Marine Expeditionary Force in Regional Command Southwest in March, more than 50 US Marines have given their lives. Many others have given their lives during my time here and it is proper to stop and think about them and the ones they left behind on this Thanksgiving Day. In addition to our fallen heroes, I also ask you to remember those maimed and mutilated during these wars, the many single, double and triple amputees who we are shipping back to our shores on a weekly basis. The enemy here is determined, and their pride is founded in the list of notable empires they have repelled throughout the ages. I often wonder if our national will is as strong, if our people feel the pain of this war as much as the local tribes who populate this province of Afghanistan. I wonder if those at home had to pay the price of what this is costing, both physically and fiscally, instead of deferring the cost to our grandchildren, would we still be here. These are not questions I often

concern myself with, because, regardless, I have a mission to meet and these musings are not necessarily productive for me or the Marines I lead.

"Still, I think the most patriotic act we could perform is to think critically about what is happening here, to question ourselves and the ones who lead us. It is not unpatriotic to question whether building a generation of amputees is worth this war on terror; neither is it unpatriotic to question whether the changes now raging across the Middle East are because of, or in spite of, our current foreign policies. The truth is that the fighting has stayed away from our US shores and that violent extremism is held at bay, for whatever reason we want to attribute to it. For me, I hope that I have done my part to build a better world for my family, and appreciate the costs paid by others to do the same.

"However, I do not think that sacrifice starts or stops with those in uniform. It will be the business leaders, the clergy, the teachers and the factory workers that truly ensure the continuation of our way of life. It will be leaders who are not only paid for a position of authority, but actually use that authority responsibly. It will be leaders who recognize that they ARE role models and mentors and act accordingly, whether they be actors, scientists or politicians. It will be more than the less than 1 percent of this country, who wears the uniform of the United States Armed Forces, that decides whether we continue as a nation or not."

Monday 17 October, 2011

Just 49 Days left to live legally in the USA. When President Kennedy asked not what I wanted from the USA, but what I could do for the USA, I was a high school student in South Africa. Could I ever have imagined that almost 5 decades later I would have the opportunity of stepping up to the plate to play some small part in keeping safe, those in harm's way? My only regret is that for so many Americans, this is someone else's war, being fought by someone else's children, being paid for with someone else's blood.

Now, after 10 years living and working in the USA and providing "essential intelligence management training" to the US Military, yet denied permanent residence on administrative grounds, I am reminded of Edmund Burke's declaration that "all that is necessary for the triumph of evil is that good men do nothing." Small consolation to the next American who exchanges a loved one for a folded American flag and the "gratitude of a grateful nation".

With just 40 days left to live in the US, we launch a petition to support a Private Bill which will be presented to lawmakers to motivate them to propose this Bill to keep us in the US. Amazingly enough, within only 3 days of launching the petition, it attracts almost 1000 signatures from concerned US citizens who want the situation addressed.

With time becoming critical, Fox News Channel decides to take our story nationally and internationally. Fox News anchor Heather Childers and Producer Ron Ralston and crew are flown from New York to Charlotte; Tom, their cameraman, drives up with all the gear from Atlanta – a full FNC outside broadcast unit - all for our benefit. And our home is temporarily converted into a film studio with batteries of lights, miles of cables and much repositioning of furniture. The story runs nationally and internationally all day in the 24-hour news cycle on November 3.

We receive a delightfully 'vanilla' letter from Senator Richard Burr, dated October 20 and received November 14 and addressed to me personally. The letter contains various platitudes such as *"we have welcomed generations of legal immigrants ... immigrants who respect the law and contribute to our country. Immigrants should demonstrate their intentions of becoming productive, law-abiding members of our society as a condition for receiving citizenship ..."*

Now I ask you, Senator Burr, with tears in my eyes, WHAT THE HECK HAVE I BEEN DOING FOR THE PAST 10 YEARS??

Then Senator Burr continues to opine ... *"I believe that our immigration system is in need of reform for those trying to gain citizenship legally."* REALLY??? *"I do not believe it is fair to reward those who have broken our laws, particularly at the expense of those who have followed the rules and applied for citizenship through the legal process".*

Clearly, Senator Burr has absolutely no clue as to the facts of our situation. Opining about *"it not being fair to reward those who have broken our laws ..."* precisely at a time when we ARE legal, have broken NO laws and are trying desperately to avoid breaking the immigration laws, makes one wonder who this guy really is.

What makes Senator Burr's letter even more priceless, is that people like myself are NOT applying for citizenship. Simply permanent residence FOR WHICH WE MORE THAN QUALIFY, AND FOR WHICH WE HAVE QUALIFIED FOR YEARS. Citizenship we will have to earn, unlike those in the lucky-sperm-club who were born here.

Senator Burr continues with *"I look forward to working with my colleagues in the Senate to enact common sense legislation that ensures the integrity of our borders while also ensuring that we have a legal immigration process that is understandable, consistent, and followed."*

Okay, Senator. This drivel might sound great in a TV sound-bite, but what EXACTLY are you going to do to bring about immigration reform and WHEN EXACTLY do you intend for this to happen. Or is simply breathing and writing letters like this the sum total of your contribution to our society?

"I understand the importance of this issue to many North Carolinians and I will continue to work toward a solution." OH YEAH? And then the best part ... *"If I can be of further assistance to you, please do not hesitate to let me know."*

Thank you for the offer, Senator Burr. I'd like to take you up on this. Now what are you going to do to help someone who came here legally 10 years ago, who has remained here legally, who has never been out of status, who is an English-speaking, educated, law-abiding, tax-paying, property-owning, community-active and business-owning entrepreneur that is providing an essential service to the US Military that is saving lives on the battlefield? But who is going to become an 'overstay' on 5 December 2011 because YOUR legal immigration system is NOT understandable, NOT consistent and NOT followed by your own immigration authorities?

Dianne and I are heading to Washington DC. Representative Sue Myrick has granted us a meeting on Tuesday November 15, 2011 at 10:30 am to discuss the possibilities of resolving our immigration nightmare. We are deeply grateful to Congresswoman Myrick for letting us tell her our story, in person.

We are taken into the House to listen to some of the proceedings, visit with Speaker John Boehner, do some photographs of this historic meeting and discuss the Private Bill. Sue comes from a long line of military ancestors, and has family currently serving in the military. She is highly sympathetic to our cause, accepts both my Private Bill draft and supporting introductory speech and on 18 November 2011, Congresswoman Sue Myrick introduces Private Bill H.R.3505 to grant Permanent Residence to the Stewart Family.

112th CONGRESS

1st Session

H. R. 3505

IN THE HOUSE OF REPRESENTATIVES

November 18, 2011

Mrs. Myrick introduced the following bill; which was referred to the Committee on the Judiciary

A BILL

For the relief of Bruce William Stewart, Dianne Stewart, Sarah Jane Caitlin Stewart, and Michael Bruce Albert Stewart.

Section 1. Permanent resident status for Bruce William Stewart, Dianne Stewart, Sarah Jane Caitlin Stewart, and Michael Bruce Albert Stewart.

(a) In general

Notwithstanding subsections (a) and (b) of section 201 of the Immigration and Nationality Act, Bruce William Stewart, Dianne Stewart, Sarah Jane Caitlin Stewart, and Michael Bruce Albert Stewart shall each be eligible for issuance of an immigrant visa or for adjustment of status to that of an alien lawfully admitted for permanent residence upon filing an application for issuance of an immigrant visa under section 204 of such Act or for adjustment of status to lawful permanent resident.

(b) Adjustment of status

If Bruce William Stewart, Dianne Stewart, Sarah Jane Caitlin Stewart, or Michael Bruce Albert Stewart enters the United States before the filing deadline specified in subsection (c), he or she shall be considered to have entered and remained lawfully and shall, if otherwise eligible, be eligible for adjustment of status under section 245 of the Immigration and Nationality Act as of the date of the enactment of this Act.

(c) Deadline for application and payment of fees

Subsections (a) and (b) shall apply only if the application for issuance of an immigrant visa or the application for adjustment of status is filed with appropriate fees within 2 years after the date of the enactment of this Act.

(d) Reduction of immigrant visa number

Upon the granting of an immigrant visa or permanent residence to Bruce William Stewart, Dianne Stewart, Sarah Jane Caitlin Stewart, and Michael Bruce Albert Stewart, the Secretary of State shall instruct the proper officer to reduce by 4, during the current or next following fiscal year, the total number of immigrant visas that are made available to natives of the country of the aliens' birth under section 203(a) of the Immigration and Nationality Act or, if applicable, the total number of immigrant visas that are made available to natives of the country of the aliens' birth under section 202(e) of such Act.

(e) Denial of preferential immigration treatment for certain relatives

The natural parents, brothers, and sisters of Bruce William Stewart, Dianne Stewart, Sarah Jane Caitlin Stewart, and Michael Bruce Albert Stewart shall not, by virtue of such relationship, be accorded any right, privilege, or status under the Immigration and Nationality Act.

Day 3803. Monday 5 December 2011

Our last day of legal status in the USA. No news on H.R.3505 - looks like it might have stalled in the House Judiciary Committee which is on Christmas Recess. We have been told, off-the-record, that our Private Bill will most likely not even get considered by the House Judiciary Committee. And a whispered unofficial comment that Chairman Lamar Smith (R-TX) dislikes Private Bills and Immigrants equally and will most likely bury it.

Of more immediate concern is the fact that all our driver's licenses expire at midnight tonight together with our visas. North Carolina Department of Transportation regulations prohibit the Division of Motor Vehicles from granting drivers licenses to people who do not have valid visas. Another regulation designed to make life intolerable for "undocumented/illegal" immigrants - which I suppose, after 10 years of legal stay in the USA, is what we have become. Rather a bitter pill to have paid for all our vehicles and now not allowed to drive them. Oh well. *C'est la vie!* Now we'll see what life is like living in the shadows of the DMV.

When I was a child, I had a friend who would rather destroy his toys than let me play with them. So, I got my own toys, and besides finding that MY toys gave me more pleasure than playing with Willy's toys, I soon found that I didn't really need his friendship either.

The North Carolina Department of Motor Vehicles has stopped me from renewing my North Carolina Driver's License. Not because

I'm a bad driver, not because I've broken any traffic laws, not because my vehicle is a road-hazard and not because I have failed to pay my taxes. Quite the opposite - the DMV has denied me a driving license because after 10 years of living legally in the USA, my visa has expired and I have joined the ranks of undocumented immigrants in this country. And the law says that undocumented immigrants are not allowed to have a driver's licenses. What my legal status has to do with my driving privileges, your guess is as good as mine. And so, while I wait for my Private Bill HR 3505 to grant me permanent residence in the USA, to be voted upon by Congress, my vehicles will remain parked in my garage.

My new status as a disallowed driver initially appears to be a disaster, until I consider the hidden benefits of having "my own toys":

Not having to insure my vehicles is going to save me $1800 a year.

Not having to fill my vehicle's gas tanks is going to save me $4500 a year.

Not being able to drive to the store, for my business and home supplies, means I will now have to shop online, able to select the best prices nationwide, cheaper than buying in Charlotte North Carolina, and I won't have to pay 7.25 percent Sales Tax if I buy from out-of-state vendors.

If I actually sell my fully-paid-for vehicles I should clear about $25000

And to keep me mobile, my $1300 49cc 40mph 120mpg $4 per tank-of-gas scooter does not require to be licensed or registered for road-usage and I do not require a driver's license to legally drive this scooter on public roads.

So, when you are stuck behind me in traffic, bear in mind that 40mph is the best I can do. Just relax. And reflect. And if you think that this old guy is riding a "liquor-cycle" because of a DUI conviction, think again.

Bit silly, isn't it?

Through no fault but its own, America has porous borders, a dysfunctional immigration system and 12 million "illegal / undocumented" immigrants living here - sorry - 12 million and 3 now. Remember, Sarah is now on her own, with her F-1 international student visa. These people are *de facto* permanent residents of the USA. Rather than fixing the border-controls and legalizing and taxing the 12 million *de facto* immigrants, we set out to spite them - denying them bank-accounts, denying them drivers licenses, denying them vehicle finance, denying them vehicle insurance, denying them housing finance, denying them education, denying them pretty much everything - marginalizing them and keeping them in the shadows. Encouraging them to be creative and to find alternative solutions. Yet we don't mind them paying tax, which most of them do, and we certainly don't mind them contributing billions to our Social Security and Medicare, for which they will never receive a single penny in benefits. And we secretly love having so many "illegals" staying hidden in the shadows, earning low wages – cheaper fruit and vegetables at the store, cheaper building costs, cheaper lawn and landscaping services. We howl about illegals stealing jobs from Americans, we complain that illegals drive down wages, and we point fingers every time an illegal commits a crime. Yet the inconvenient truth is that we love having cheap labor and the products of cheap labor. We ignore the fact that per capita, illegal immigrants commit fewer crimes than Americans, and illegal immigrants are hardly stealing jobs from Americans, unless you believe that self-entitled Billy-Bob WOULD have taken the 12-hour-a-day back-breaking fruit-picking job in the Florida Summer IF the job had not been taken by an illegal.

Day 3828. Saturday 31 December 2011

Our Private Bill H.R.3505 is still idling in the House Judiciary Committee. Many have asked "what next", so here's the thumb-nail sketch of the road ahead : The Bill goes through 6 phases - 1. Introduced, 2. Referred to Committee, 3. Reported by Committee, 4. House Vote, 5. Senate Vote, 6. Signed by President.

Our Private Bill, introduced by Sue Myrick, is now at phase 2 - it has been referred to the 37-member House Judiciary Committee chaired by Rep. Lamar Smith, where it is one of thousands of Bills awaiting committee consideration. Unfortunately for us, the vast majority of proposed legislation never goes beyond this committee, and never becomes law. Our Bill should be considered by the 10-member Immigration Sub-Committee, chaired by Representative Elton Gallegly and Member Representatives Steve King, Zoe Lofgren, Louis Gohmert, Trey Gowdy, Sheila Jackson-Lee, Daniel Lungren, Ted Poe, Dennis Ross and Maxine Waters. Unfortunately, we do not know any of these people, so lobbying opportunities are bleak, unless we have supporters who know some of these people well enough to champion our case.

If our Bill gets to phase 3, the immigration sub-committee makes available, to Member offices, information on what documentation it requires, and the kinds of Bills on which it is likely to take favorable action. It usually declines to report a Bill if its records show few precedents for favorable House action in similar cases. This is the crucial stage of our Private Bill.

In phase 4, when reported by the immigration sub-committee, Private Bills go on a special calendar, the Private Calendar. Consideration of Bills on this Calendar is in order on the 1st and, at the discretion of the Speaker, 3rd of each month, though the House often dispenses with the call, by unanimous consent. Each Bill is called up automatically, in the order in which it was reported and placed on the Calendar. The Bills are considered "in the House as in Committee of the Whole," meaning that there is no period of general debate, but debate and amendment may occur under the five-minute rule. Usually, little debate occurs and measures are disposed of by voice vote.

During the call of the Private Calendar, if two Members object to the consideration of any Bill, it is automatically recommitted. Each party appoints official objectors, who are responsible for examining Bills on the Private Calendar and objecting to those they deem inappropriate. Sometimes, a member of a subcommittee dealing with immigration or claims, has served simultaneously as an official objector. In practice, instead of objecting, objectors will often ask that a Bill be passed "over, without prejudice," which gives sponsors an opportunity to discuss concerns with them informally, before the next calendar call. Another crucial step for our Bill.

Phases 5 & 6 follow the general lawmaking process - approval by the Senate and signature by the President.

We are beginning to understand what Sue Myrick meant when she told us that if our Bill does not pass the committee-stage by the end of the 112th Congress in December 2012, it becomes void and will have to be re-introduced to the 113th Congress.

In our research into the legislative process, we came across the VoxPop voting system, where the public can vote for or against a proposed Bill. Reading through some of the new Bills makes fascinating reading and offers a good feel for the "pulse" of Americans. For example, The New Illegal Deduction Elimination Act, H.R. 3720: To amend the Internal Revenue Code of 1986 to clarify that those wages paid to unauthorized aliens may not be deducted from gross income (as a business expense), enjoys an 84% VoxPop support. Another nail in the marginalization coffin of undocumented immigrants, most of whom pay income tax, Social Security and Medicare.

Monday 30 January 2012.

Our Private Bill H.R.3505 appears to have stalled in the House Judiciary Committee. The Chairman, Lamar Smith, has indicated his reluctance to support this Private Bill, for the following reasons. (We have written to Chairman Lamar Smith and very delicately and respectfully attempted to change his understanding of the facts and to correct his understanding of the law) :

"Chairman Lamar Smith is not aware of any precedent in the modern private immigration bill era in which a private bill was enacted to grant

permanent residence to a legal immigrant who has now been denied permanent residence."

We agree - there is no precedent for a Private Bill being enacted to grant permanent residence to someone who came to the USA legally, who has lived here legally for 10 years and who has been denied permanent residence on administrative grounds because the USCIS decided to change its mind. All previous Private Bills granting permanent residence have been enacted to give permanent residence to people who entered the USA illegally and who have lived here illegally for many years. We have suggested that perhaps this is a perfect time to create a precedent to acknowledge someone who made the effort to obey the law, to enter the USA legally and to remain here legally. Right now, only the illegals have benefited from private bills and due process.

"Chairman Lamar Smith contends that the House Judiciary Committee only considers private legislation that lack precedent when an alien presents unique and compelling circumstances."

We have respectfully drawn his attention to circumstances which we believe to be unique and compelling, specifically :

a.) While every other immigration private bill has, to our knowledge, been to afford permanent residence to a law-breaker who entered the USA illegally or fraudulently, our private bill is to afford permanent residence to a law-abider who entered the USA legally, has remained in the USA legally for more than 10 years and who seeks to remain here legally.

b.) While every other immigration private bill has, to our knowledge, been to afford permanent residence on humanitarian grounds, our private bill is essentially based on humanitarian AND national interest grounds. Specifically, in that we provide intelligence training to a number of US Military agencies, training that has been described as "essential training", "training that is saving lives of soldiers on the battlefield" and training which is not available from any other company or American Citizen.

c.) The primary reason that we find ourselves in this predicament is because an American Citizen, posing as an immigration lawyer, with a bogus law degree, defrauded us of thousands of dollars, issued us with bogus permanent residence papers in 2006 and left us thinking that we had permanent residence years ago, evidence of which is the fact that, through our efforts, this charlatan is now in prison.

"Chairman Lamar Smith believes that we have not exhausted the administrative appeals process that is in place in the Department of Homeland Security to hear appeals, in addition to possible judicial review."

We have clarified to Chairman Smith that we have appealed our case to the Administrative Appeals Office, filed Motions to Reconsider, Motions to Reopen and Appeals to Reopen / Reconsider denials to Motions and Appeals, amounting to tens of thousands of pages and tens of thousands of dollars. All of which have been unsuccessful as the USCIS has changed its mind about Dianne being a manager of our business, now feels that Bruce's work is not complex enough to be called managerial, and has changed its mind as to whether we ever had a business in South Africa or even have a business in the USA - something it has been totally satisfied with for the past 10 years when repeatedly renewing our L-1 managerial business visas. We also attempt to draw Chairman Lamar Smith's attention to the fact that the judicial review he is referring to, Section 336.9 of the Immigration & Naturalization Act, applies to denials of citizenship through naturalization and NOT denials of permanent residence, for which there is NO judicial review, something which he should, as a legislator, be amply aware of! We furthermore clarify that we are NOT seeking citizenship at this time - simply to continue living, working and contributing to America on a permanent residence basis. That citizenship is a privilege we have yet to earn.

Unfortunately, since we wrote to Chairman Lamar Smith at the House Judiciary Committee, on 12 January 2012, we have not received a response. But it is only 2 weeks and we appreciate that Washington has other pressing responsibilities.

In the interim, we are adjusting to our new lives as previously-legal-now-illegal-overstays, we quite enjoy driving our 50cc scooters which do not require drivers' licenses, and I continue to teach my courses - to the Marine Corps Intelligence Schools in Virginia Beach, to Coca-Cola in Dallas Texas and to the Marine Aircraft Wing at Miramar in San Diego.

Since I still have a valid passport, I am able to fly around the USA – the TSA airport security folk are only concerned with whether I have a valid picture ID, and not whether I am in the USA legally or not. An interesting contradiction that my lack of legal status denies me the right to drive, but allows me the right to fly. I'm sure I'll get to understand the thinking here, one day. Perhaps allowing me to fly requires me to contribute far more cash to the US Economy than simply allowing me to drive a car that I've already paid for? If so, money trumps law?

To go to teach a course on the other side of the country, I can fly there. Then to rent a car, requiring a driver's license, a bit of imagination is required. I simply went to some of the kids at Michael's high school and asked them how they are able to buy beers and get into age-restricted movies. Enough said.

Monday March 12, 2012.

In an effort to 'starve' us out of the country, US Marines are now being denied the benefits of the intelligence analysis training we provide. Quite understandably, the US Military can hardly be seen to be doing business with an "illegal" overstay, notwithstanding the declared importance of such business to the well-being of American Citizens serving in the various theatres of war. This decision to suspend my training directly affects 60 military intelligence analysts scheduled for training this month alone, as well as thousands of front-line Marines whose lives depend on accurate and timely intelligence analysis.

We can only wonder why House Judiciary Committee chairman, Lamar Smith, has not made the effort to look into our USCIS case and to question the reasoning behind the denial of our permanent residence. Especially since the Private Immigration Bill was so boldly introduced by Congresswoman Sue Myrick, a strong supporter of the Military. After all, should he not be even slightly curious as to why we have been denied permanent residence after having been granted visas and repeated visa renewals for the past 10 years, particularly since the visa requirement criteria are identical to the permanent resident requirement criteria? Perhaps because our congressmen and senators and all of our politicians are not people who experience what the average person experiences. Our political parties are full of mostly white, privileged, 70-plus men who think women should still be in the kitchen, and who have absolutely no understanding of the world in its current phase. In short, they no longer, and likely never will, have a finger on the pulse of America and its needs.

While Lamar Smith idles in his comfortable Washington office, safe from the realities of the war he supports and at no personal risk to himself or his own family, Marines are now denied the benefits of this training which has been described as "essential for the analytic capabilities of the Marine Corps" and which is "saving lives on the battlefield." Right now, ExecuRead iterations scheduled for 60 intelligence analysts at 1st Intelligence Battalion Camp Pendleton, Marine Aircraft Wing Miramar and Marine Corps Intelligence Schools Virginia Beach have been cancelled because I no longer have legal status in the USA and will not have legal status until Private Bill H.R.3505 is passed into law.

Am I angry and outraged by this? Damn right I am! Although I'm a foreign national from South Africa and not yet permitted to pledge allegiance to the United States, I have come to love this country that has become my home. And I have a particularly strong loyalty to the Marine Corps that honored me with a 0205 Tactical Intelligence Officer Challenge Medal for my contribution to the enhancement of the intelligence analysis capabilities of the USMC. Lamar Smith may choose to dislike me because I'm an immigrant, but when he lets his rabidly anti-immigrant emotions stand in the way of his sworn duty to protect and serve this country, and in particular the soldiers he has voted to send into theaters of war, I must seriously question the direction of his moral compass and his patriotism. Quite frankly, to willfully deny essential intelligence training support to front-line combat troops verges on treason.

My greatest fear is the knowledge that the next casualty of war who is returned to loved ones in a flag-draped casket or terribly scarred and maimed, will be the casualty of some avoidable failure or delay in front-line intelligence analysis. But at least, mercifully, those loved ones will be without the knowledge that Lamar Smith could have done something to prevent this tragedy, but allowed his emotions and bigotry to stand in the way of his duty.

Day 3912. Wednesday March 28, 2012

When good men do nothing...

The verdict is in -- the government does NOT want the Stewarts in the USA. Our Private Bill H.R.3505 has been given the coup de grace.

On Tuesday 27 March we met in the Capitol Building and the House of Congress with Congresswoman Sue Myrick, the sponsor of our Private Bill H.R.3505, and with Congressmen Howard Coble and Mel Watt and their legislative aides. Coble and Watt serve on the House Judiciary Committee with Lamar Smith. A somewhat fragmented meeting, as all were coming and going throughout the meeting as they all had heavy voting commitments. Additionally, the meeting was in a public and rather busy lounge just outside the House chamber.

In a frank and brutally honest dialogue, the message was clear, specific and unambiguous -- Lamar Smith does not like private bills and he does not like immigrants.

We attempted to address his two "concerns" about H.R.3505 -- the lack of precedent for passing a Bill to grant permanent residence where permanent residence has already been denied by the USCIS, and the need for unique and compelling circumstances to justify such a Bill. We argued that the precedent principle of *stare decisis* requires that a precedent be followed where a precedent exists, but it does not prevent action in the absence of a precedent. We further argued that there are considerable unique and compelling circumstances -- the fact that my petition for permanent residence was rejected *in toto* on administrative grounds because it arrived 8 days late back in 2007 and has thus never been considered; that Dianne's petition for permanent residence was denied because the USCIS failed to apply the provisions of the Immigration Act of 1990; that the educational and developmental lives of the Stewart children will be harmed if they are forced to leave the USA; and on national interest grounds by virtue of the training provided to military intelligence agencies.

Again, the message was clear -- Lamar Smith is not willing to establish such a precedent under any circumstances because of the "large" number of similar requests for private bills this will most likely trigger. Clearly, he is aware that ours is not the only case that has been botched by the USCIS, and that admitting to this fact in our case will open the flood-gates from other victims of a legal immigration system that doesn't work. Perhaps it's more expedient to ignore the problem and pretend it doesn't exist.

As to the unique and compelling circumstances? Well, they are apparently neither unique nor compelling enough to warrant action. Unfair and an injustice? Yes. An admission that there are serious flaws in the legal immigration system? Yes. Damaging to the Stewart children's lives? Yes. Sacrificing American military lives on the altar of political expediency? True and not unusual. Compelling enough to justify remedial action through a private bill? NO!

Lamar Smith does not like Private Bills and he does not like immigrants. It is his stated intent to do away with one right now.

Sue Myrick and her staffer Taylor Stanford do their best to help us swallow this bitter pill. They take us on a private tour of the Capitol, we sit in the House listening to some debates, probably the closest we will ever get to our goal and not exactly what we were looking forward to, and a somewhat tearful and distraught Dianne is introduced to the 'weeper' of the House, Speaker John Boehner.

As difficult as it is hearing that our lives have just changed irrevocably, that we will not be allowed to stay in the US permanently and with no possibility of one day becoming Americans, it is far more difficult to look at the many military men and women we see on our flight home, knowing that they will never know what impact a political decision made earlier that day may have on their lives.

Now it's back to the drawing board...

Wednesday April 18, 2012. The "Reluctant Activist"

Dianne Stewart, not quite the stereotypical "illegal" immigrant, has, it appears, now become a "reluctant activist" for immigration reform with her new Huffington Post Blog which is published today.

The Huffington Post has created a Huffington Post Immigration Forum, motivated, in part, by Dianne's Blog, and by Jose Vargas of Define American, to raise the debate, discussion awareness and need for immigration reform to new levels.

Day 3967. Friday May 18, 2012

Just over two weeks ago, a couple of smallish issues cropped up. Our Private Bill died in the House Judiciary Committee, the US Marine Corps canceled all our training contracts for front-line Intel analysts because we are "illegal" overstays, and our new immigration attorney advised us that on June 2 we will have been overstays for 180 days and thus subject to civil detention and deportation, coupled with a 3-year bar to re-entering the USA.

He advises us to self-deport and leave the USA.

On April 28, we suspend Dianne's BSA PR & Marketing business activities in the USA, suspend my ExecuRead training activities in the USA, put our home on the market and immediately find a wonderful immigrant family from Honduras to rent our home for a year, rent two large PODS for hundreds of boxes of personal and business goods, retain the services of 6-men-and-two-trucks to move our worldly possessions into storage, and leave Charlotte. And all of this in just over two weeks. Simply not possible without the blood, sweat and occasional tears from some tremendous helpers - Tony Holden, Patricia Williams, Martha Rea Calkins, Dianne Maxwell, Sean Stewart, Mo Daniels, John Luke, Patsy Shelby, Patti Scher, Charlie Fitz-William, Cindy Quinlan, Nuris & Madison Skala, Margaret Mayfield, Margaret Lawrence and many others who popped in for a cuppa and to bitch about the insanity of it all, including Lara Morse Peters, a friend of Patti Scher, who came along to help pack dozens of paintings and mirrors in bubble-wrap, just for the heck of it. And we'd never even met her before she arrived!

We are staying temporarily with Catherine and Wilton Connor in Mooresville, without whose incredible strength and support we would not have had the fortitude to do this alone. We've placed much of our possessions in storage and leave the USA on May 30 for Dublin, Ireland, which will be one of our bases over the next 3 months, since we are Irish Citizens as well as South Africans! We don't know yet where we will live in Ireland, but quite frankly, with what we've been going through, we'll cross that bridge when we get to it or even after we get to it! Sarah has an international student visa and as the only "legal" Stewart, will be staying here and working on the X Factor and a Summer Internship for Davidson College.

While in Ireland, we will attempt to get a new visa through our Irish Citizenship, essentially going back to square one, where we were in 2000. We leave the USA with good lines of credit on our credit cards which, hopefully, will keep us fed and housed for three months or more, and also feed the voracious appetites of immigration attorneys and the USCIS.

It's all a bit of a culture-shock. From a home and two businesses in Charlotte, to unemployment, homeless, refugee-status in Ireland, in less than a month. As to the future, who knows.

In some rushed planning to wrap up our lives and businesses in the USA, and to prepare for getting back into the States, we had to look at the available visa options. A new L-1 was out of the question – upon reaching the statutory 7-year lifespan of the L-1A visa, the beneficiary has to remain outside the USA for a minimum of one year before a new petition is filed.

The only option appears to be the H-1B skilled worker visa. Our new immigration attorney, Tim, advises that there are still some H-1B visas available, if Di or I can find qualifying employment and a firm job offer. I am pretty much excluded – who is going to offer a job to a 60-year-old who has been self-employed and without a boss for more than 30 years? So it looks like it will be up to Dianne, almost 10 years my junior. An accomplished public relations, marketing and social media guru, she is also an excellent instructor in the proprietary Morphogine cloud software.

Hearing that Dianne is on the labor market, a start-up company offers her a job, doing PR, marketing, social media and Morphogine training. The salary package will comprise salary and year-end profit sharing. Just what we need.

As a prelude to filing the H-1B petition, the job-offer to Dianne and the job-description is sent to the Department of Labor for labor-certification – the prospective employer must show that the job position is legitimate and cannot be filled from the local labor force, and secondly, that the proffered wage is competitive with those of similar positions in other organizations. If approved, the door is open to Tim to file an H-1B petition on behalf of Dianne and her new employer. If approved, we can return to the USA on 1 September 2012 for her to take up her employment on 1 October 2012. Tim advises that the 65,000 annual "cap" on H-1B visas has not been reached, so there is a visa available to Dianne if she qualifies at the labor-certification stage.

Author's Note : Each year, 65,000 H-1B skilled worker specialty occupation visas for applicants with the minimally required 4-year Bachelor's degree or equivalent work experience are made available on April 1 for the entire USA. This allocation is generally fully subscribed within days of the allocation opening. Successful beneficiaries may only enter the USA after 1 September of that year and may not start their employment before 1 October that year. Unsuccessful petitioners wanting to fill skilled worker positions have to re-apply the following April or simply ship the job overseas to where the skilled worker is located.

For example, in 2016, there were more than 236,000 H-1B petitions. (The USCIS closed the door at 236,000 so we don't know how many petitions were rejected out of hand.) In addition to the 65,000 H-1B visas, 20,000 more are allotted to skilled workers with advanced degrees in STEM fields (science, technology, engineering and math) from American universities. The visas are allocated by lottery. The math is simple – with an advanced STEM degree from an American university, the odds are slightly better at getting a visa. For the rest, you have some 236,000 petitions chasing 65,000 visas. One chance in 3.6 of being successful. And we wonder why so many skilled American jobs are being sent overseas?

The numbers defy logical understanding. In 2017, 95,885 petitions for the 20,000 H-1B Master's Exemption visas were filed. The 75,885 unsuccessful petitions were bundled together with 94,213 petitions for the 65,000 H-1B Regular Cap visas – in short, 170,098 petitions competing for 65,000 available visas. This means that 105,000 highly-skilled workers, educated with advanced degrees i.e. Masters and Doctorates from US universities, or at least with 4-year Bachelor's degrees from US and foreign universities, and already holding job offers from US employers, are being told to take their skills elsewhere. In my humble opinion, it's an asinine situation.

Even more bizarre, in 2021, the number of H-1B petitions had risen to 308,613, of which only 87,500 were selected in a lottery, 48 percent of which requested consideration under the advanced degree exemption. And these are positions for skilled STEM workers that cannot be found in the USA. If a company needs to fill a STEM skilled job in the USA, but cannot find the required skills in the USA or import the skills from overseas, any guesses as to where the job will go? That's right. Overseas. If we can't import the skills, we'll export the jobs. Now that wasn't so hard, was it? So why can't GovCo also figure this out? Because GovCo wants US companies to make do with lesser-qualified and lesser-skilled people from the local labor workforce! To improve the employment statistics. And we wonder why we cannot remain competitive.

As for the Stewarts, with a firm job-offer in hand, an H-1B visa still available and the job submitted for labor certification, we feel pretty confident that we'll be using the return leg of our Charlotte – Dublin air-tickets on 1 September 2012.

SCARS & STRIPES

PART THREE : RECONSTRUCTION

Day 3980. May 30, 2012

Dianne, Michael and I fly out of the USA en route to Dublin, Ireland. We have been "illegal" overstays for 178 days. Two more days in the USA and we'll be barred from re-entering the USA for 3 years. We've never been to Ireland. It's another new country.

Ironically, we are all Irish Citizens. Back in 1951 when I was born in South Africa, my father registered me as an Irish foreign birth. A very unusual thing to do. South Africa was the darling of the world. A country of exquisite beauty, with a stable Nationalist government and a Rand currency even stronger than the US Dollar. But some premonition of the downfall of South Africa prompted my father to give me a doorway to Irish Citizenship. My paternal grand-father, Reginald Stewart was born in Ireland and came to South Africa as a child in 1902 and this entitled me to a foreign birth registration. In later years, working for Coca-Cola in South Africa, I had the need to travel internationally, sometimes to countries that did not view South Africa's Apartheid government and South African passports too favorably. So I applied for permission to hold dual citizenship and dual passports for both South Africa and Ireland. Through my Irish Citizenship, Dianne and my children were able to acquire Irish Citizenship as well. And faced with the prospect of a short period of exile from the USA, Ireland, "just over the pond", so to speak, seemed to be a more attractive alternative to the 30-hour flight to South Africa.

We check into our hotel in Dublin and wait for Tim to send us the good news that Dianne's H-1B visa has been approved. His email arrives, but with bad news. The Department of Labor rejected the submission because it does not recognize Charlotte Company "A" as an "employer". Basically, the DOL does not talk to the Department of Commerce or the IRS, so although Charlotte Company "A" is a registered international corporation that pays taxes to the IRS, the Department of Labor doesn't recognize it as an employer. So Charlotte Company "A" has to send in loads of paperwork – certificate of incorporation, annual tax returns and evidence of being in business. After this two-week delay, Charlotte Company "A" is accepted by the DOL as being a real employer and we are invited to resubmit Dianne's job-offer and job-description. The DOL approves the job-certification but determines an annual wage for the job that is almost double the wage that has been agreed upon between Dianne and Charlotte Company "A" and which is more than Charlotte Company "A" can afford.

This job falls through – Dianne loses the job she wants and needs, and Charlotte Company "A" is denied the marketing expertise it so desperately needs to grow its business, all because GovCo sets a wage that neither party wants. At the time of writing, Charlotte Company "A" is sub-contracting this job to an overseas worker. Essentially another American job lost to an American, but this time, not "stolen" by an "illegal" immigrant, but forced overseas by GovCo because the government-stipulated wage is not lavish enough.

This is devastating news. No job, no income and no way of seeking another job and being interviewed in the USA.

We start sending out emails to everyone we know, offering Dianne and her skills, "sight-unseen" at a price that we now know will be acceptable to the USCIS. And this is where Dianne's social networking in Charlotte over the past 10 years pays off.

Another company, Charlotte Company "B" offers Dianne a job for which she is uniquely qualified and for which no comparable skills exist in the USA. The job-description and job-offer are sent to the Department of Labor and again the submission is automatically rejected because Charlotte Company "B" is also not recognized by the DOL as an employer. Again, the paperwork is prepared – certificate of incorporation, financial statements and tax returns are submitted and the DOL registers Charlotte Company "B" as an employer. We resubmit Dianne's job-offer and job-description and the DOL approves the job-certification and sets the annual wage for the job, higher that what Dianne and Charlotte Company "B" had agreed upon, but acceptable to both parties. All this takes 6 weeks.

Finally, and with a definite job-offer in hand and with the position having been certified by the Department of Labor, we are ready to petition for an H-1B visa for Dianne to return to the USA in September to take up her new DOL job-certified employment with Charlotte Company "B" and for Michael and I to return with her in H-4 derivative status.

Believe it or not, when dealing with the IRS, the Internal Revenue Service, for individuals, your Social Security number is your tax ID number. For corporations, the tax ID number is an EIN number – an Employer Identification Number. Get it? Employer! But only the IRS recognizes the corporation as an employer. And the Department of Labor? No. It wants a separate employer registration. Go figure why.

Living in a very expensive country and paying for everything in Euros, our financial reserves are being depleted at a prolific rate. A packet of smokes at US$15 soon ends that habit. The prospect of a cheap 1-bedroom hotel for the three of us, at almost $200 a night for three months, is none too appealing either. Knowing that we cannot afford this 3-month "vacation", I re-open discussions to sell and set up a franchise operation in Hanoi, Vietnam and to teach a group of Vietnamese instructors. My intentions do not receive a warm welcome from my US military clients, but I assure them that I will be discrete about what I share with Hanoi. The Vietnamese urge me to travel to Hanoi without delay, and we are desperately in need of money, so leaving Dianne and Michael to fend for themselves in Ireland, I fly across the world to Vietnam for two weeks to set up the franchise, train a group of new instructors and officiate at the official launch of the first speed reading company in Vietnam. My family is now literally spread across the globe – Sarah in the USA, Dianne and Michael in Ireland and me in Vietnam.

With sporadic cell-phone contact and questionable and very slow internet in this part of Vietnam that has not enjoyed the Americanization of Saigon, I am ill-prepared for the news from Dianne – bad news from Tim.

All 65,000 H-1B skilled-worker visas for the 2012 / 2013 year have been allocated and there is no H-1B visa available to Dianne to take up her job with Charlotte Company "B". So, because of delays caused by the Department of Labor not talking to the IRS and not maintaining records of IRS-registered employers, Dianne loses a job for which she is eminently qualified and Charlotte Company "B" loses the expertise of a skilled worker who would contribute to its growth, success and profitability. Bottom line? Until October 2013 no US company will be permitted to employ a foreign skilled worker because there are no H-1B visas available.

It's a little hard to comprehend that two successful tax-paying businesses, ExecuRead and BSA Public Relations and Marketing are now lying dormant in the USA because Dianne and I are stranded in Ireland, and unable to take up employment with either of our own companies in the USA, or with other USA businesses that have made firm offers of employment, simply because GovCo has imposed a 65,000 strangle-hold on the number of foreign skilled workers that US companies may employ, regardless of whether the skills are available in the USA from US workers or not.

We are now effectively locked out of America for at least 18 months, separated from Sarah who is on her own in the USA, barred from working in terms of her F1 international student visa status, yet without the funds to support herself or pay her college fees. And the rest of us are in Ireland, unemployed in a stagnant economy and essentially homeless – Dianne and I and a teenage son, all living together in a single hotel room with a bed and a pull-out couch. We feel that this might very well be the lowest point in our lives.

In Vietnam, I am seriously depressed - the heat and humidity of Vietnam is getting to me, and also having no-one to talk to without speaking pidgin-english or using an interpreter. I so miss the English language, even if spoken badly by an American! And the smells are terrible - the stink of decaying vegetation, out-door cooking, open sewage and garbage. Oh, for the crisp fresh air of Ireland!

Trying to figure out the options weighs heavily now. Hermanus, the home of my child-hood, is beginning to look quite attractive. Only issue is Michael and his ties to the USA with girl-friend Shannan and him finishing school. Coupled with poor educational and employment prospects for Michael in South Africa and questions about how to pay for Sarah's university education in America. I guess we just continue playing this out to see where it goes - do our best to get another employment-based visa, and if that doesn't work, an ESTA (an electronic visitor's visa available to Visa Waiver Program countries) with our Irish passports, to get back into the States temporarily to sell everything, and if that doesn't work, I suppose it's Hermanus, South Africa until September 2013.

Then the urgent call from Sarah in the USA to Dianne in Ireland. She is hemorrhaging and needs to go into hospital for emergency surgery! In a near panic about not being able to be with our daughter, Dianne calls me in Hanoi. We have never felt so helpless and so frustrated in our lives. Sarah is extremely ill in America and we have absolutely no way of getting to her bedside.

Again, we call out to our friends in America, and without question they rally to the call, in droves. Their support is over-whelming. They attend to Sarah every minute of the day during her recovery period and they support her emotionally as she worries about her future without a family in the USA, and about her family stranded outside the USA.

As soon as I can, I fly back to Ireland where Dianne, Michael and I sit together for some serious thinking. First priority is to generate some cash. Second, to keep Sarah in school – if she leaves full-time student status, she will lose her student visa and have to leave the USA. Third, to get Michael back into his senior high school year in whatever country we can. We need to liquidate our assets in the USA. We have our home in Charlotte, a couple of vehicles and our personal possessions that we had shipped from our home in Johannesburg and our vacation home in Hermanus, South Africa.

Since there appears no way of getting back to the States to conduct the sale, we propose appointing a liquidator to sell everything, lock, stock and barrel. When we travelled to America from South Africa back in 2001, we each carried two suitcases onto the plane. When we travelled from America to Ireland, we each carried two suitcases. We will do the same when travelling back to South Africa from Ireland – there, at least, we have friends and family to take us in and give us a start again. The funds from the sale of our assets in America should cover Sarah's college fees and living expenses until she can graduate and find employment in 2016.

This is not an easy family meeting. It's not easy, as a parent, to tell your child that his dreams have been shattered, that he will not finish his schooling in America, or go to university in America to get his engineering degree, that he will not see his friends again, and that he will not see his girlfriend again. Neither is it easy to admit to your wife that you can no longer support her, that all is lost.

And we talk for hours and hours. Sometimes angry and shouting. Sometimes just weeping in frustration. Then peace and acceptance. We talk through our anger, frustration, sadness and hatred for a country that took us in, allowed us to fulfill our dreams and then took it all away and threw us out. We take stock of what we have. A solid family. Intelligence. Health. Love. And Faith. Everything else is clutter. It's almost a liberating feeling. We are free, without ties to any country, any place or any material possessions. Free to do whatever we want, to go wherever we want.

I call my Godson in Charlotte to tell him of our decision. The son of my brother in South Africa, Sean popped in to see us in Johannesburg during a flight layover back in January 2000 and ended up staying with us for 18 months until we moved to the States in July 2001. He has become almost a son to Dianne and I, and a big brother to Sarah and Michael. He was heart-broken when we had to leave him behind in South Africa, but soon decided to expand his IT company into the States and moved a few years after we did.

"Don't pack it in yet," he says. "Go for an O-visa."

"That's crazy," I counter. "The O is for people of extra-ordinary ability. It's the 'genius' visa. For people who are internationally recognized as leaders in their field. Who are published. It's for people who are famous. It's for people like David Beckham and Paul McCartney. Not for people like me."

"Sure," Sean retorts, "but I've looked at the regulations and the immigration laws. There are 8 requirements for classification as a person of extra-ordinary ability. To get an O-visa you need to meet only 3 of the 8 criteria. I figure you already meet 4."

"Okay, I'll look into it and we'll hold off on making any decisions for now. Thanks Sean."

And then out of the blue, a call from a company in Charlotte. They have heard that I closed down ExecuRead and left the States because of visa issues. They would like to re-establish the business as part of their marketing research and data management business and they would like me to run the new division. How soon can I start?

Small problem. I cannot apply for an H-1B visa until April 2013 and can only start work in October 2013. Unacceptable. Any other visa possibility? Just an O-visa, but it might be a stretch. Certainly worth a try. Let's go for it.

O-1A Visa - For Aliens in the sciences, education, business, and athletics. For these fields, the alien must show that he/she is in the top of his respective field. This can be established through evidence of receipt of a major, internationally recognized award such as a Nobel Prize. In absence of such an award one can establish himself as a qualifying alien through at least three of the following types of evidence:

Documentation of receipt of lesser nationally (not necessarily U.S.) or internationally recognized prizes or awards for excellence in the field of endeavor;

Documentation of membership in associations in the field of endeavor which require outstanding achievements of their members, as judged by recognized national or international experts in their fields;

Published material in professional or major trade publication or in the major media about the alien and relating to the alien's work in the field of endeavor;

Evidence of participation as a judge (individually or as a part of a panel) of the work of others in the alien's field;

Evidence of scientific, scholarly, or business-related contributions of major significance in the field of endeavor;

Evidence of authorship of scholarly articles in the field, in professional journals or other major media;

Evidence of performance in a critical or essential capacity for organizations or establishments with distinguished reputations;

Evidence of having commanded a high salary or other significantly high remuneration for services in relation to others; and

Other comparable evidence

The days turn into weeks as we dig up proof of every certificate and degree I've received, every award, trophy and testimonial. Plus, letters of commendation from the Marine Corps. Every article, course manual and booklet that I've ever had published. Every media article on the work I've been doing over the past 30-plus years. We have friends scouring through storage boxes in Johannesburg, South Africa, in our storage facility in Mooresville and in the Connor house on loan to us at Lake Norman.

The O-visa petition arguments and supporting evidence grow more and more persuasive. Attorney Tim becomes a tyrant, accepting some evidence, rejecting others, demanding more, better, faster. Demanding clarification. Substantiation. Always questioning, is it the best evidence we have?

Then out of the blue, a letter from a retired Lt. Col. in the Marine Corps with copies to the Commandant of the Marine Corps and to the Senate Committee on Armed Services :

TO : UNITED STATES CITIZENSHIP AND IMMIGRATION SERVICE

RE : DR. BRUCE W. STEWART AND EXECUREAD

"After honorably serving my country in the US Marine Corps for 35 1/2 years and "4" wars as a Security Manager / Investigator / Intelligence Officer, I am very well qualified to comment on the impact caused by delays in the intelligence cycle between the gathering of intelligence data, the analysis of such intelligence data and the production of risk-assessment reports to front-line combat troops in the various theaters of operations. Delays and failures in the intelligence data management and analysis cycle cost military lives and lowers morale.

"It was accordingly with great interest that I was briefed regarding that the Intelligence Battalion's at I MEF and II MEF had retained the services of Dr. Bruce Stewart to present his training course, "ExecuRead for Military Intelligence Professionals." What made this appointment even more unusual was the fact that Dr. Stewart is neither a Marine nor a US Citizen or even a US permanent resident, plus the fact that after the very first iteration of Dr. Stewart's course to 1st Intel Battalion I MEF Camp Pendleton, the warrant officers presented Dr. Stewart with a 0205-Tactical Intelligence Officer Plank to recognize his contribution to the intelligence data-analysis capabilities of the US Marine Corps. Only about

200, 0205-Tactical Intelligence Officer Planks, have ever been awarded to date and this, I understand, is the first to a civilian. The Plank was awarded to Dr. Stewart by Warrant Officers (four names redacted for security reasons) for his ground-breaking work within the US military intelligence community.

"With this in mind, I decided to undertake Dr. Stewart's course in my personal capacity to see whether the course was as good as reported. I can confidently report that I was pleased on both counts. Firstly, the ExecuRead Methodology and Techniques used by Dr. Stewart, while unusual, are logically sound and deliver measurable results -- an average 5-fold increase in reading productivity with a number of Marines achieving 10-fold increases in reading productivity (i.e. a 10-fold increase in reading speed without ANY loss in comprehension.)

"Additionally, I found Dr. Stewart to be an instructor of extra-ordinary ability and detail to order, with an exceptional knowledge of his subject material and an extra-ordinary ability to communicate with and impart ideas to both senior officers as well as enlisted men. At the Pentagon, USAF Brigadier General (name redacted for security reasons) described Dr. Stewart's training as "the most important professional development of my military career." Indeed, Dr. Stewart's personal involvement is so critical to this program that his appointment to teach the courses to the military has been made dependent on his personal availability to teach the courses. It should be noted that since Dr. Stewart's decision to leave the USA on the expiration of his visa, the US Military has taken the unusual step to suspend further iterations of this training, pending Dr. Stewart's return to the USA. While this is an undesirable situation, the fact remains that Dr. Stewart's course and his teaching skills are not replaceable with any other course or instructor of equivalent caliber.

"I recently learned that Dr. Stewart is now obliged to operate his company out of Europe and that he has recently been approached to present his courses in the Middle East and in Hanoi, Vietnam. I suggest that it is totally unacceptable and deplorable that steps have not been taken to secure Dr. Stewart's loyalty and patriotism to the United States of America and United States Military by granting him citizenship or at the very least some legal status on the pathway to US Citizenship.

Additionally, Dr. Stewart is a man of exceptional character and honesty with very high morals.

"This will be an insurmountable loss to the United States of America and the US Military if this problem is not rectified."

Finally, it is done. The petition is ready for filing with the USCIS Service Center in Vermont. Now we just have to wait. We can do no more. We expect a decision in 15 days, approximately 7 August. Most likely will be a YES, or a NO, or an RFE (request for further evidence). If a YES, we should get an interview at the embassy within a week and the visas a couple of days thereafter. If a NO, an appeal will take 12 to 18 months. An RFE just extends the process by another 15 days. So we just kill time, waiting for the days to go by.

Michael's girl-friend can stand the separation no longer, and persuades her parents to bring her graduation European trip forward a year. Michael flies to England and joins them for an idyllic holiday in France and in England.

Dianne and I experience serious cabin-fever and can stand the hotel room no longer, so we hire a car and decide to go researching the origins of our Irish Citizenship. I know that my grand-father Reginald Stewart was born in Londonderry and that my great-grand-father James Stewart was born in or near Buncrana in County Donegal. The family emigrated to South Africa in 1902. I also knew that my great-great-grand-father John Stewart lived and died in Buncrana at the ripe old age of 95. My father always suspected that John Stewart may have had other children, but he never found records of any of them. After the destruction of the Dublin Customs House in a fire in 1922, few records still exist, so genealogy must rely on church records and grave-stones.

Arriving in Buncrana, we start with church records and find documents about John, his wife Margaret and a son Frederick, which is new to us. So we start visiting the grave-yards. Not much there either, as grave-stones have weathered considerably over the past century and prove very difficult to read.

Spying a frail, elderly lady moving from grave-stone to grave-stone with what appears to be a white powder which she is sprinkling on and then rubbing off the grave-stones, we watch her and then inquisitiveness gets the better of us. She is documenting all the grave-stones in Ireland, she tells us. Because of the weathering, soon they will all be illegible. By rubbing chalk onto the grave-stones, she can reveal the engraving and record the inscriptions for posterity.

I tell her that I am the great-great-grand-son of an old resident of Buncrana and that I am trying to find out about the family.

"And now who would this person be?" she asks in that lovely Irish lilt.

"John Stewart, married to Margaret Longwill, father of James Stewart. They lived at Vine Cottage."

"Oh yes, I know the family well" she replies. "And such a large family t'was."

"Large…?" I start.

"Oh yes, John and Margaret had 11 children. I 'tink your Jamie was number 6. I have records of all of them."

"Records?" I ask surprised. "Just from grave-stones?"

"Oh no! My dear. I started with church records to find births and now I'm working on deaths. Only two here. Baby Jane died at 14 months in 1853. Frances Elizabeth lived with her parents and after her mother Margaret died in 1893 at age 69, Frances Elizabeth stayed with her father John until he died in 1907 at age 95. She was 29 then. But I don't know what happened to all the others. I 'tink most would have emigrated. Probably to America I 'tink."

And here this "Irishman" seems to be swimming upstream, back to Ireland and back to where it all began.

So my exile in Ireland leads me to find out about my Irish ancestry .... And, believe it or not, about some of my neighbors in Charlotte, North Carolina. Some months later, I post this genealogy on my family website, and soon get a rather strange call about where I live, in what neighborhood and on what street in Charlotte. Cautiously I yield to the very charming female voice on the phone.

"Well," she says, "if you walk to the end of your street, turn right and walk one block, the house on the corner belongs to David Rice. He is also a great-great-grand-son of John and Margaret Stewart, and great-grand-son of Frederick Stewart, brother to your great-grand-father James Stewart! I suppose that makes you close neighbors and distant cousins."

Back in Dublin and awaiting a decision on my O-visa petition, Dianne and I spend our days walking the streets of Dublin, sitting for hours watching the street-musicians, the hawkers and peddlers, street-artists, window-shopping, and taking hours to enjoy a pint of Guinness and a plate of Irish fish and chips with loads of salt and vinegar. We stand on the Bridge of Locks over the river Liffey and read the inscriptions on the thousands of padlocks placed there by lovers over the years. For us, time has stood still. We have nowhere to go and nothing to do. We've been married for 24 years, but are closer now than ever before. We have nothing but one another. No country, no home, no jobs, no possessions, no obligations, nothing to do. Just us. From our meager funds we buy a padlock and add one more to the Bridge of Locks over the river Liffey.

August 2. It's Day 4044 of our journey and Day 63 of our exile in Ireland. Lunchtime, and we walk into a pub on the banks of the river Liffey and order lunch and a pint. I'm idly scrolling through my email as our lunch is served by the barman, and Dianne starts eating. I freeze, and without a word, pass my cell-phone to Dianne. She reads *"Pleased to advise that your O-visa has been approved by the USCIS for 3 years. Congratulations, Tim"* and promptly bursts into tears.

Poor barman. He must be thinking that there's something seriously wrong with the food.

With the O-visa approval notice in hand, we set up our interview appointment at the US Embassy in Ballsbridge in Dublin. The earliest appointment date we can get is Friday August 10. Procedurally, after this interview, it should take two days to process and issue the actual visa that will go into our Irish passports, and a further two days to mail our passports to us in Dublin. Then we will be free to return to the USA.

On Friday August 10 we arrive at the embassy with our hopes and dreams and copies of the submission filing which has been approved by the USCIS. At the US Embassy, we go through a series of security checks from the Polish guards tasked with the security of American territory in Ireland. Then into the heavily fortified and rather forbidding visa section where we wait. We are then called to a window in full view of everyone sitting in the room awaiting their processing number. We hand over our passports and visa application documents to our "interviewer". Dianne is terrified. She has witnessed the attitude of US embassy staff and immigration authorities towards non-US-citizens before. I am however bubbling with confidence and enthusiasm. After all, I am a lawyer, I hold a doctorate, I'm a contractor to a number of US Military and Intelligence Agencies and I have just been granted the coveted O-visa which is normally only given to musicians, scientists, entertainers and artists of world-class renown. Should I not be accorded just some degree of professional respect for these accomplishments?

The visa interviewing official is outwardly friendly and affable while he abuses us, interrogates us and accuses us of disrespecting the immigration laws of the United States. He humorously relates how his father had been married to three different women at the same time in different cities, but that his mother was the legal first wife. He berates us for overstaying our visas and argues that the 178-day overstay was planned to fall just 2 days inside the 180-day overstay limit which would trigger the 3-year bar, clear evidence of a total disrespect for American law. He argues that my prospective employer had gone for the O-visa specifically to avoid the H-1B cap and that in his opinion I should never have been granted the O-visa. He does however grudgingly concede that he has not yet read any of the submission evidence. When asked, my son admits to having been arrested for misdemeanor under-age drinking just after his 17th birthday. The interviewer then asks my son whether he has enjoyed a Guinness with his father while in Ireland. Michael confirms that he has. When the interviewer points out that drinking while under the age of 21 is illegal, Michael retorts "not in this country!" The interviewer then boasts of only drinking Diet Coke (perhaps a recovering alcoholic?) and advises that my son will require a blood-screening for alcohol and substance addiction at a cost of 350 Euro ($450), that since this will be done by his personal doctor, there will be no waiting period, that he will let us know when to have the test done, that this might be unlikely because he is inclined to deny our visa and to send our case back to the USCIS with a request for revocation. But we should wait in Dublin as he will call us "within the next couple of days" if he has any questions or requires clarification.

Ironically, the O-visa approval from the USCIS is simply an approval to BE in the USA, not to enter the USA. This permission can only be granted by the US Embassy outside the USA and there is no guarantee that the embassy will grant a visa even after an approval notice has been issued by the USCIS. And then, even with a visa from the embassy, Customs and Border Protection has to give permission for you to cross the border into the USA and again there is no guarantee of success. So essentially, we have only crossed the first of the three hurdles, the visa approval notice. Now we need to cross hurdle number 2 and get the visas recorded in our passports.

We leave the embassy, totally stunned. Did that really happen? Are we actually as unworthy of living in the USA as he made out? Was this treatment official US policy? Or the policy of the US Embassy in Dublin, Ireland? Or just some over-enthusiasm on the part of the interviewer? Who still has our Irish passports. All this, and without having one shred of knowledge about what's contained in the petition or in the accompanying evidence. Who does this man think he is? Whose instructions is he following? Is this the face of America? The first thing a visitor to America gets to see? An automatic presumption of guilt and undesirability?

But at least the interview is over. It's August 10 and we have our return air-tickets to the USA booked for September 1. When we left the USA on May 30, we had the expectation of getting an H-1B for Dianne and this would only allow us to enter the USA on or after 1 September for her to start work on 1 October. Now with an O-visa approval, the time-frame from 10 August to 1 September should be no problem.

We report back to Tim as to what happened at the interview. Tim assures us that there are very specific grounds for denying the issuance of a visa by the embassy, that these all relate to the safety and security of the USA and that since we do not meet any of these restrictions, we have nothing to worry about. And as to his threats about revocation, this can only occur if there is evidence that the visa-approval had been obtained by fraudulent or dishonest means. Again, nothing to worry about. But we are worried and we are waiting. And we check the mail every day – no passports with visas.

Two weeks go by. No call from the embassy. No instructions about Michael's blood test. Our attorney Tim writes to the embassy asking for a status update. Our political representative writes to the embassy asking for a status update. The embassy replies that it is still considering whether to deny the issuance of the visas or whether to apply for revocation of the approval. On what grounds, asks our attorney. Knowing he is now in a corner, without reason or grounds for revocation or further delaying the visa-issuance, the embassy official sends an unofficial note to our attorney asking for some clarification as to exactly what work I will be doing for my new employer. Tim replies, equally informally. Clearly, I have an unusual and specialized occupation that either does not meet cookie-cutter job-definitions, or my job-description proved to be more erudite than the reading education of the official could address.

Then we learn that "apparently" the Kentucky Consular Center, a new job-creation of the Department of State and the Department of Homeland Security, has dropped the ball.

"Apparently", when the USCIS approved our O-visa petition, it should have notified Kentucky, which in turn should have entered the approval into PIMS (the Petition Information Management Service), which in turn should authorize the embassy to issue the visa. And of course, when the required notifications do not occur, the Departments can blame one-another and neither accept responsibility. The USCIS claims it notified Kentucky by fax but concedes that no records of fax transmissions are maintained. SERIOUSLY? NO FAX TRANSMISSION RECORDS? BY THE UNITED STATES GOVERNMENT? Conveniently, Kentucky does not accept enquiries from anyone other than the USCIS, embassies and consular offices, so it's back to Dublin to ask them to contact Kentucky to get them to ask the USCIS so that the USCIS can advise Kentucky that the visas were approved 6 weeks previously.

In the interim, the date of our planned flight back to the USA on 1 September has come and gone and our return tickets on US Airways have little value. We will now have the additional expense of buying three one-way tickets from Dublin to Charlotte. Little do we know that the direct flights between Charlotte and Dublin are very much seasonal flights and that when and if we ever do go back to the States, it will be a multi-stop around-the-neighborhood flight.

As dawn breaks on 11 September 2012, we look for news on the 12th anniversary of the 9/11 attacks on the US, only to find news of the deadly attack on the US Embassy in Benghazi.

"Oh my God!" says Dianne. "I wonder on whose watch THIS happened?"

"Some idiot really dropped the ball on this one," I concur.

"And here we are. Intelligence trainers to the US Military, stuck in Ireland, waiting for another US embassy to try to stick it to us. Ironic, isn't it?" she muses with a sigh.

We are stunned. Clearly American laager mentality will kick in and US borders will shut down, effectively stranding us in Dublin indefinitely. We sit silently. How much more do we have to endure? And into this silence, my phone announces an incoming email. *"You are hereby notified to collect your passports and visas from the US Embassy in Ballsbridge Dublin on Thursday 13 September 2012."* It's a full month after the interview and without any reason, explanation or apology for the delay.

We have been in Ireland for 106 days. Other than some brief sightseeing trips, the enjoyment of which was somewhat marred by the uncertainty of our future, employment prospects and dwindling supply of financial resources, the three of us have lived side-by-side in a single hotel room for 16 weeks. During one of the wettest summers in living memory, we spend our days sleeping and watching TV and movies. Admittedly we enjoy the extensive four weeks of back-to-back coverage of the 2012 London Olympics and the 2012 London Paralympics, the latter totally denied to US viewers, yet arguably far more interesting than the regular Games.

Thursday morning, and Michael and I are at the Embassy as the doors open. Not unexpectedly, our visa-interviewer is conspicuous by his absence. Without a word, our passports are handed to us. No congratulations. No welcome to the USA. Nothing. Just silence. We verify that the visas are present and correct and within minutes we're back on Irish soil.

That night we start looking for US Airways flights back to the USA. We hope to at least recover the remaining value of our September 1 tickets. But there are no US Airways flights available for another ten days. It's a no-brainer. We have to get home. We have to get off this swampy island. Between the perpetual rain, Guinness, and Jameson Whiskey, I'm at risk of getting webbed feet and cirrhosis of the liver! And Michael has to get back to school, already having missed the first few weeks of his senior year. We book the first available flight out of Ireland and back to the USA, at 10.45am the very next morning, our 107th day of exile, and at an out-of-pocket cost of $45,000.

March 2013. Six months ago, my family lived in our own home. We owned two successful companies. We earned a good living, we contributed to our community and we paid our taxes. But we lived in the immigration shadows. Today, we are legal. We are heavily in debt. Someone else lives in our home because we cannot afford to. Now we live as guests of friends. Our companies are dormant. I am earning a quarter of what I was earning a year ago and my wife is not allowed to work at all in the USA.

My wife and I are angry. We feel we have been unnecessarily abused, mentally, emotionally and financially. We did this the legal way. We did what America wanted us to do. What America expected us to do. And now we have shown what happens and how it's done, what it involves, what the dangers, pitfalls and risks are, and what the cost may be, financially, emotionally and spiritually.

And perhaps we have also shown why so few choose this route and why so many choose to remain in the shadows of society.

We are however encouraged by the resilience of youth. Our son, now 18, who has lived in America since the age of 6, remained positive throughout this ordeal. In an essay on the life of an immigrant, he wrote "I don't care what country is printed next to my passport photo, I still put my right hand over my heart and pledge allegiance to the only country I could ever call home, America."

We remain puzzled by the treatment we received from the interviewer at the US Embassy in Dublin. Exactly what was he doing with our Irish passports and my O-visa approval for the weeks between August 10 and September 11, 2012? And who exactly are these people at the US Embassy in Dublin? Was our treatment simply an isolated incident or something more coordinated? More ominous?

We start investigating the US Embassy in Ireland, looking for the names of visa officials. Not an easy task. But then finding media articles about the treatment of Irish citizens. And working backwards, establish that the head of the visa department at the US Embassy at the time was Bradley Gifford Wilde. Was he our "interviewer"? We don't know. But it appears that he was the senior visa official at the time. The head of the Visa Section in the US Embassy in Ballsbridge, Dublin, Ireland.

We start researching Mr Wilde.

Perhaps the media might provide some answers. Perhaps we were unwittingly enmeshed in an alleged scandal involving the stealing of Irish passports by the US Embassy, "phantom" ID's and Mossad "hit-squads" travelling on these "phantom" Irish passports? Is there more to Bradley Wilde, and our "interviewer" whoever he was, at the US Embassy in Dublin, Ireland?

We make no allegations. We are simply reporting what the media is saying. And wanting answers to so many questions.

You decide. You be the judge.

Barring of writer Tim Pat Coogan from U.S. is an absolute disgrace - America's greatest friend in Ireland insulted by the U.S. Embassy. -- by Niall O'Dowd

The barring of Tim Pat Coogan from coming to America for a book tour is disgraceful. He was refused a visa when he applied for one for his new book tour. It is one in a clear pattern of a number of recent clueless decisions at the American Embassy in Dublin at the consular level that defy logic.

The Tim Pat Coogan case is a travesty but senior Irish government officials have told me it is by no means the only strange decision emanating from the embassy in recent times. There seems to be a hardening attitude there to make it as difficult as possible for people to come to the U.S.

Blink and you might think you were back in the McCarthy era.

Put simply, there was no greater defender of America in Ireland for the past few decades than Tim Pat Coogan, especially at times when the anti-American sentiment there was at its highest. His pro-American stances, both in his Irish Press newspaper and his writing about the power of the Irish Diaspora were major factors in keeping the American flag flying in Ireland. He played a key behind the scenes role in the Irish peace process, especially in the early days when his contacts with Father Alex Reid, the unsung hero of the entire process, were vital.

He was deeply trusted by the Kennedy family and it was a famous meal in Dublin he had with Senator Edward Kennedy convincing him of the need for a visa for Gerry Adams that swayed the Massachusetts senator as well as helping bring President Clinton into the loop.

Visiting Irish Americans are always assured of a hearty welcome from Tim Pat and his backing for America and stance against the anti-American rhetoric so often spouted in Ireland made him this country's prime defender.

Yet this is the 77-year-old man who the American Embassy just refused a visa to come to America to and humiliated him in the process? Is there no institutional memory whatever at the embassy that can separate and *remember a friend? No one who was able to realize the deep insult they had just inflicted on America's greatest journalistic ally there?*

There are so many questions but one undeniable fact. It will be a blot forever on the Dublin embassy that it humiliated one of its greatest supporters and Ireland's leading historian by refusing a visa to launch his new book on the Irish famine.

Disgraceful is the word for it.

Source
https://bit.ly/3kZlfkW

Irish Central : November 30, 2012

Diplomats gone wild at U.S. Embassy in Dublin say concerned Irish -- Horror stories about how Irish are treated after famed author Tim Pat Coogan refused. – by Niall O'Dowd

Since the Tim Pat Coogan story broke here, I have heard numerous horror stories about the American Embassy in Dublin and how it is treating Irish applicants for visas to the United States.

As we know, famed author and historian Tim Pat Coogan was treated incredibly poorly and denied a visa for his U.S. book tour until Irish American pressure and New York Senator Chuck Schumer reversed the decision.

It is vital how an embassy treats the citizens of the country they are operating in. It sets a tone. The U.S. Embassy currently is presenting a very hostile face to the Irish. There is no good reason for that. Ireland is not the Soviet Union circa 1955.

That's not just my opinion -- it is that of a broad spectrum of Irish government personnel, lawyers who deal with the visa section of the embassy, and people who went through the process who I have spoken with.

It now appears that Tim Pat was the tip of the iceberg. Several who have had dealings with the embassy have recounted episodes of rudeness, arrogance and most of all incomprehensible decisions by visa officers there. It is spoken openly about in Irish government circles. Many prominent figures in Ireland and here are scratching their heads at the treatment.

Representations have been made but nothing has changed. Visa officers in U.S. Embassies have broad latitude, but the division in Dublin seems deliberately set on keeping applicants out of the U.S. based on the slightest whim.

Ambassador Dan Rooney, while a beloved figure to many, hardly seems to have reacted, despite being told on numerous occasions about the treatment of Irish visa seekers.

Since the arrival of visa head Bradley Wilde in 2010, things have quickly gone downhill in Ballsbridge where the embassy is located. Wilde has instituted a very aggressive regime that treats visa seekers in the main like potential burdens on America. Rules appear to have been arbitrarily applied and changed, leaving deep confusion. Rudeness, failure to explain and downright bloody mindedness when depriving people of visas on the smallest technicalities seems rampant.

Source
https://bit.ly/3yLAu6a

Extract from "Ireland in Crisis" by Sean O'Nuallain, Ph.D.

A diplomat gone Wilde, selling our passports

This introduction has been updated in the wake of events in the US Embassy in Dublin centering around the refusal of a visa to renowned Irish historian Tim Pat Coogan and thousands of others, the theft of Irish passports by the Israeli Mossad, and the otherwise inexplicable resignation in December 2012, as US Ambassador to Ireland, of Pittsburgh Steeler owner Dan Rooney, coupled with the immediate subsequent demission and redeployment to the plum posting in Mexico of erstwhile visa head Bradley Wilde.

We will look briefly at the now famous Tim Pat Coogan incident. It had been known for some time that the US embassy in Dublin was treating Irish applicants for visas in a harsh, abusive and arbitrary fashion. Things came to a head only when the renowned writer Tim Pat Coogan – ironically once a lover of then American Ambassador Jean Kennedy Smith – was refused a visa to undertake a book tour to promote a book whose central thesis was that the Irish "famine" was actually genocide. The Irish department of foreign affairs (FA), headed by the deputy prime minister, did nothing. Coogan was granted a visa after activism by the Irish community in the USA led to an intervention by Senator Schumer of New York.

Shortly thereafter, in an environment dominated by the Benghazi affair, the US ambassador to Ireland, whom Coogan had in vain asked to intercede – Dan Rooney, inheritor of the Pittsburgh Steelers – resigned, apparently unexpectedly, and the controversial visa head, Bradley Wilde, was reassigned first to Iran and then to Mexico (source; Irish diplomatic staff).

There is a priori evidence that the consulate of the US embassy in Dublin was a rogue operation. Yet to protect ourselves, we had to go outside the Irish state; and so it goes for many areas of life, to the point where really all we get from the state are our passports – and, as the use of Irish passports by the Mossad indicates, these too may soon be worth less than toilet paper.

The Coogan Affair

Tim Pat Coogan (TPC) is as celebrated a historian in Ireland, as McCulloch is in the USA. He was also editor of the Irish Press and, as the world turns, lover of the 1990's US ambassador to Ireland – one famously sympathetic to Irish nationalism – Jean Kennedy Smith.

The 2012 US embassy could hardly have chosen a bigger target with which to make their point, nor one like TPC about to embark on a more poignant theme; that of the 1840's famine as deliberate genocide.

TPC had recently criticized Israel for its treatment of the Palestinians, and after the events described below involving Israeli copying of Irish passports, the controversial Bradley Wilde of Diplomatic Security Services (a recently created spook service, famously missing when needed at Benghazi) was appointed visa chief in Ireland. It was Wilde who was ultimately responsible for the refusal of a visa to TPC, and perhaps thousands of other Irish.

Tim Pat Coogan slammed the American Embassy as 'Kafkaesque' after his visa refusal and Ambassador Rooney's statement that rules were followed (… until Schumer's intervention?).

However, there is a much bigger story, which explains why Wilde would behave like this with "America's greatest friend", as Schumer described TPC.

Source
https://bit.ly/2WPeSZJ   Page xxvi

The Guardian, June 15, 2010 : Ireland orders Israeli diplomat out of embassy over forged passports. Move follows alleged Irish passport misuse in killing of Hamas official in Dubai. – by Ian Black, Middle East Editor

Ireland today ordered the removal of an Israeli diplomat from the country's embassy in Dublin in protest at the use of forged passports in the killing of a Hamas official in Dubai.

Micheál Martin, Ireland's foreign minister, said today that an investigation had shown that the eight Irish passports used by suspects in the assassination were forgeries.

There were 8 forged Irish passports and it is clear that their REAL owners had to be briefed that their IDs were stolen in the case of the Brit and Australian ones.

According to Sean O'Nuallain, it is consistent with the facts we have that Wilde was handing passports over to the Israelis and then denying visas to the applicant. That allows the imposters free travel in the USA as the Irish citizen will not be able to get in after a visa denial.

Source
https://bit.ly/3l0w9XR

Going to the US? – Avoid The Dublin Consulate (O'Nuallain's Experience at the Dublin US Embassy)

We now know that what is going on at the Dublin embassy has been the subject of an admonishment from immigration and naturalization in the USA. The most innocent explanation is that there is a rogue element at the Dublin embassy that has taken it on itself to refuse applicants from gifted Irish people, and to do so in an abusive and bizarre fashion.

The more likely explanation is that this abuse is toward a goal; and holding passports of Irish people with impeccable records (which is why they were cleared for O status) fits perfectly with all the data we have, in conjunction with recent events that resulted in the expulsion of an Israeli diplomat from Ireland in 2010 after it was found that the Israelis were attempting to increase their stock of Irish passports after their successful use of several such passports to murder Arab "terrorists' in Saudi Arabia.

Even if the "innocent" explanation is correct, the staff involved should be suspended immediately and disciplined. Many have been greatly inconvenienced, and had already paid more than $200 in fees after $8,000 in legal and immigration fees to get the visas approved only to find the US embassy in Dublin overturning the recommendation of the greater US immigration service and denying them entry. Even when entry is allowed, there exists now a practice – rather than a policy as they do not admit to it – of subjecting holders of passports with Gaelic names to further interrogation at the port of entry.

Yes, the Dublin consulate IS the subject of formal complaints first by the greater US immigration authority and now by a team of immigration lawyers. Secondly, the way out would seem to be to avoid it for the moment and get your visa through the Parisian consulate (if you have baggage, it can be left for the day at the nearby Hotel Sanguine for E5). Thirdly, I do not think I would have made it back to the USA but for the intervention of Congresswoman Barbara Lee, who kept up the pressure, and to whom I am very grateful. Now let's look at a very disturbing set of incidents.

The "O" visa is given to non-immigrants of outstanding ability for three years. I have been a joint holder of such a visa with the Celtic jazz pioneer

Melanie O'Reilly through our US Company Mistletoe Music LLC since 2008. Before that my visa status was as a J-1 holder with Stanford and Berkeley, where I taught and researched. I have a PhD from Trinity College, Dublin. I mention all this because we have found out that the Dublin visa head, Bradley Wilde is not an ordinary diplomat; he is a special agent in the Diplomatic Security Service, and the events related here must be seen in this light.

The consulate of the US embassy in Dublin has been the subject of formal complaint by US immigration lawyers as a result of its illegal vendetta against O-visa applicants in clear violation of immigration guidelines. It does so by making the visa applicants feel that there is something insufficient about them — and indeed about their culture — which has resulted in what otherwise would be unconscionable delays in holding the passports for weeks beyond the single night (at most three) the Irish authorities recommend. It's worth noting that an individual stuck in this situation will become furious, and rightly so.

First of all, the situation obviously is absurd; appraisals carefully made by immigration in the USA are being queried and often overturned on the basis of an aggressive "interview" (really, a selective interrogation) in Dublin.

The "Interview"

Let us look at what an "interview" normally comprises. First of all, the conditions should be equitable; there should be a computer system that works, apparently not the case (or so the interviewer said) on Aug 23 2012. The queuing system should work, instead of my being left there for over 4 hours with no food, drink or recourse to the phone without actually being called up after an abortive earlier attempt in which the computer "crashed".

I note that this is not the first time the Dublin embassy has had problems in these regards. I understand also that the embassy has recently taken it upon itself to refuse pre-approved Irish O visa holders. That should have been of interest to the two 2012 vice-presidential candidates who were both courting the ethnicity we're proud to exemplify in our music.

Even more seriously, there should be some indication as to the latitude allowed the questioner. I was asked questions about my intimate/sex life; when I correctly refused to answer, Bradley Wilde appeared suspiciously quickly to chastise me with a poor John Wayne-like admonition that I was speaking to an officer of the mighty USA, etc. I was aware of that; in fact I have now spent 9 years in the USA and got 10 previous visas to the USA without trouble. In fact, such questions are vetted even in divorce court; even there, the witness has representation. To which I replied again; they in turn are dealing with not just a human being, but with an Irish citizen.

Source
https://bit.ly/2WPeSZJ   Page xxviii

The Irish Times : February 20, 2010

Nice and Neutral : why Irish passports are a spook's best friend -- by Dr Tom Clonan, security analyst.

The use of Irish passports in the execution of a Hamas figure in Dubai may have surprised, but it has always been a popular document.

As travel documents – fake or otherwise – Irish passports are highly prized by a wide and disparate range of groups and individuals. Col Oliver North is believed to have travelled to Iran on a forged Irish passport in 1986, during the Iran-Contra affair.

It is widely acknowledged in intelligence and security circles that fake Irish passports have been used by both CIA and Mossad agents travelling throughout the Middle East and Africa. Exploiting Ireland's reputation as a neutral state with little or no colonial baggage, it is believed that international intelligence agencies have on numerous occasions employed false Irish passports as cover for spies and agents transiting through territories otherwise hostile to powerful nations such as the United States or Britain.

International terrorist organizations are also known to have used forged Irish passports in the past. Members of the Provisional IRA are believed to have used fake passports during the 1970s and 1980s on trips to Libya and elsewhere in the Middle East as part of their endeavors to source weapons and explosives during the Troubles. More recently, as minister for justice, Michael McDowell alleged that members of the Colombia Three had travelled to South America on forged Irish passports.

Genuine or legitimately held Irish passports are also the envy of international journalists operating in hostile environments such as Iraq and Afghanistan. As foreign correspondents, Patrick Cockburn of the London Independent, Maggie O'Kane of the Guardian and Orla Guerin of the BBC have all reported from war zones while travelling on their Irish passports.

Cockburn has cited at least one occasion in Iraq where the possession of an Irish passport probably saved his life. He produced it when taken at gunpoint from his car by Sunni insurgents on the outskirts of Fallujah in 2004, and was released unharmed. Many international journalists operating in war-torn countries where militant Islamism is a feature, regard holders of Irish, Swiss and Swedish passports as fortunate, in that their perceived neutrality confers upon them some measure of protection. Unfortunately, many journalists acknowledge that US and British passports can often provoke hostility in parts of the Middle East and Asia, as a consequence of the US and Britain's participation in the so-called War on Terror.

The current Irish passport is a machine-readable electronic ePassport which contains a biometric chip for security purposes. It also incorporates a range of other security features, including holograms and a greyscale digitally printed photograph of the passport holder.

It is fully consistent with the security requirements of the US visa waiver program. The currently configured Irish passport – while considered highly desirable by legitimate users, terrorists and international security agencies alike – is no easier or more difficult to forge than other EU or US passports.

The sheer volume of forged passports estimated to have been involved in the execution of Hamas's Mahmoud al-Mabhouh in Dubai last month suggests that state assets – rather than criminal or terrorist elements – were employed in their manufacture and forgery.

Whatever the outcome of the investigations into the affair, one unfortunate outcome will be the closer and perhaps hostile scrutiny that Irish citizens travelling abroad on genuine Irish passports may be subjected to at foreign airports and points of entry in the coming weeks.

Source
https://bit.ly/3n4Zva1

Amazon Book Review – January 7, 2015

A Sean O'Nuallain book review of Tim Pat Coogan's book "The Troubles"

In 2012, TPC was twice refused a visa to promote "The Famine Plot" at US universities. It had been clear to many of us for some time that then US visa chief in Ireland, Bradley Wilde was hibernophobe; indeed, Irish passports were going missing while in the care of said embassy. TPC's reaction was to publicize the incident, and – when granted a visa in highly unusual circumstances – to call the US embassy a den of spooks.

So did TPC end up on a no fly list? On the contrary; within 3 months, Hilary Clinton flew to Ireland, and forced the resignation both of Wilde and then ambassador, Dan Rooney. Ireland had no ambassador from the USA for two years as affairs were "rectified". The last tranche of Irish passports stolen in the care of said embassy was Feb 28, 2014.

TPC was the partner of Jean Kennedy Smith, ambassador from the USA to Ireland during the negotiation of the Belfast agreement. He is in a position to say in this book that Taoiseach Reynolds phoned her while she was on holiday to say apropos the British attempt to restrict IRA man Joe Cahill's movement in the USA that he was the leader of a f_g sovereign republic and no 3rd country would interfere in this way with an Irish citizen's passport.

Cahill is from Belfast. We now need more men like Coogan, Cahill and Reynolds. Read this book to understand why.

Source
https://amzn.to/3DOBppU

Heavy stuff this. Yet Dianne, Michael and I have our Irish passports in hand and we are in the USA. We appear to have foiled the US Embassy aka "Gitmo in Ballsbridge" plan to deny us our visas into the USA and to then use our identities to create phantom identities and fake Irish passports for Israeli Mossad hit-squads! Seriously? If this was a totally fictional novel, even in our wildest imaginings we could not make this shit up!

Day 4087. Friday September 14, 2012

The Stewarts are back in the USA, legally, after 16 weeks of exile in Ireland. I have the so-called "genius" O-1A visa for persons of extra-ordinary ability and this is valid for 3 years. On a lighter note, Playboy's Miss November 2010 Playmate, Shera Bechard, also managed to snag an O-visa from the USCIS. But then I guess she was able to offer a couple of really good points to her petition!

But we are home, at last, joyously so. And so thankful to those who supported us and our cause, over the years, and who worked so tirelessly to make this happen. Without that support we may not have had the strength to continue the pursuit of our dreams. We now begin the process of putting our lives back together. Our self-imposed 4-month exile in Ireland in 2012 is behind us. The countless hours spent studying the immigration laws of this country and the preparation of tens of thousands of pages of legal submissions leave an emptiness in our lives. Over the ensuing days and weeks, we wake up each morning wondering what's missing in our lives. Michael is back at school, albeit three weeks late, and Dianne and I get out of vegetative state and back into business mode.

We move out to Mooresville, north of Charlotte, as guests of Wilton and Catherine Connor. Our tenant in our Charlotte house wants the lease for a least a year, possibly two. We gave him that option when we left the USA, not knowing exactly when and if we would come home. But we have the use of one of the houses on the Connor "compound" – seven acres of lake-side real estate on the shores of Lake Norman. My nephew, Sean, is to marry Wilton and Catherine's daughter in 2013 and they want a garden wedding. Some serious landscaping is called for, and Wilton and I figure to spend the next six to nine months turning a wilderness into a garden wedding venue.

The war in Iraq and Afghanistan is winding down and the financial sequesters and military cutbacks are on the increase. I do however secure training assignments for the Marines at Camp Lejeune, Camp Pendleton and Twenty-nine Palms out in the Mojave Desert, and some work with the Defense Threat Reduction Agency and the scientists at USSTRATCOM's Center for Control of Weapons of Mass Destruction.

Sarah has fully recovered from her emergency surgery and has settled down to her studies at Greensboro College where she is an undergraduate student. She makes us proud by getting her Bachelor's Degree, cum laude, in December 2012.

Michael finds himself in a more difficult situation. Now in his senior year, he wants to finish his high schooling at Providence High School. However, although we still own the house in Charlotte, we now live in Mooresville. We have zoning issues. Technically Michael can no longer attend Providence High School. Friends of his solve the problem. Michael moves in with them for the year and is now technically and physically a resident within the Providence High School zone.

But it's not ideal. He has left the family home at too young an age, and he has escaped the beady eyes of his parents. He has an addictive personality, he does pretty much everything with an over-zealous dedication, and he thinks he is smarter than every-one else (arguably he is!) and can get away with everything. A lethal combination for a smart kid who is a dumb teenager.

I get the call. Michael has been caught in Hendersonville, excessive speeding, underage drinking (at 18) and an open container in the car he is driving. He's in the county lockup. Sarah and I head up to see what we can do. I'm seriously pissed. This sort of conduct seriously jeopardizes his visa status and also the visa status of his sister and his parents.

My first step is to get his car out of the police pound so I can take it back to Charlotte. Next is to go and see Michael. He looks miserable, behind bars. He is scheduled for a court appearance in 4 weeks' time. Bail has been set at $1500. It's time for some tough love. I tell Michael to use the next 4 weeks behind bars to reflect on the choices he is making, and I leave him there. It's painful.

Later that night, Michael calls me, begging me to get him out of the county lock-up. He's in tears, begging. My heart tears. God, it's hard being a parent. I hang up on my son. Tough-love.

The next afternoon, Michael walks into our home, full of piss and vinegar. He's out on bond. He charmed a guard into giving him his cell-phone. Texted all his friends to raise the bond money and then drive up to Hendersonville to get him released. I am furious. A blatant disregard for my parental authority.

I give Michael a choice. My way or the highway. House arrest, no phone, no car, no friends, until I decide otherwise. No debate. My rules, or you can have the separation-package - your passport, $100 and a one-way air-ticket out of the USA in full and final settlement of all my parental responsibilities to you.

"But that's so unfair," Michael argues.

"Not unfair," I respond. "You have to earn the separation package by fucking up again."

The smart kid chooses my way.

I reach an agreement with the prosecutor. A fine serves no purpose other than to punish me. Suspend Michael's driver's license for a year, give him a boat-load of community service and I'll take his car permanently.

To his credit, Michael graduates from high school with a 4.0 GPA and wants to do engineering at North Carolina State University.

But will he be ready for university where the temptations are that much greater and where penalties for breaking the law are much more serious? Dianne and I decide that Michael should stay at home for a year. He wants to prove that he can do better. Dianne and I don't trust him, and we tell him so.

It's a tough Summer of 2013. He is registered to start Mechanical Engineering at NC State University, and registration date is drawing closer. Michael elicits the help of his sister, who intercedes on his behalf. Give him one last chance to prove himself, she says.

We capitulate, but with a warning – there is an envelope here, with $100, your passport and a one-way ticket out of the USA. Screw up once and you get the envelope. No if's, and's or but's. It's non-negotiable.

And Michael grows up. He becomes addicted to good grades and is ranked number 1 out of his first-year class of 4500 students. At the end of his second year, he is approached by Oracle to co-op for a semester – he spends a semester each year working for Oracle and then returns to NCSU for a semester. This extends his time at university, but he's augmenting academic study with practical experience and earning some good money. He is a member of Team 5 that wins 1st place in the Mechanical Engineering Capstone Senior Design project, and he graduates with his Mechanical Engineering degree in May 2018. It's this addictive personality thing.

On the other side of the "kids-coin", the "Sarah-Crisis" is looming. Sarah finished her Bachelor's degree in December 2012 and will officially graduate in May 2013, at which time her F-1 international student visa starts coming to a close. She may squeeze in a year of Optional Practical Training (OPT) but she's on the clock to leave the USA and her family.

In April 2013 we meet with Chris Sullivan, constituent outreach director & immigration specialist for our new Congressman in District 9-NC, Representative Robert Pittenger, with a view to re-introducing our Private Bill for the entire family, but more urgently and specifically for Sarah who has no hope of getting a Green Card at this stage.

Sarah is in the invidious position of not being allowed to work after graduating from college in December 2012, because the H-1B visa cap has been reached, and the only option open to her is to attend Graduate School and remain a student. She is offered graduate degree slots at three top US colleges in her field and has decided on the University of Cincinnati for her Master's degree.

In spite of the fact that she was brought to the US as a child, because she came legally, she derives no benefit whatsoever from any possible legislation to grant undocumented immigrant children legal status, and 11 million undocumented immigrants a pathway to citizenship, called DACA (Deferred Action for Childhood Arrivals).

Reaching the one-year anniversary of the granting of our O-visas in August 2012, Dianne, Michael and I are now permitted to file I-140 petitions to have our status converted from non-immigrant to immigrant status, the prelude to filing the I-485 petition for Green Card Permanent Residence, now for the third time. Once again, it's a waiting game. We have two children at university, Michael an undergraduate engineering student and Sarah a graduate student. Without permanent residence status, both Stewart children are struggling to get financial loans or any financial assistance to attend college. Doing things legally has sadly not rewarded this family in any way. Our immigration bill is now running at over $350K since arriving in the US in 2001. Not to mention our huge investment of personal finances, business opportunities for Americans and community volunteerism.

Immigration reform is a hot topic, and yet also a political hot potato. Everyone knows that the immigration system is hopelessly broken, but few Americans know that more than half of the 11 million so-called "illegal" immigrants actually entered the USA quite legally, but were failed by the system. And even fewer Americans know that there is no "line" for "illegals" to become "legal". So it's the kiss of death for any politician to run for election or re-election on an immigration reform ticket.

The harsh reality is this : Most Americans have no understanding at all about the immigration laws. They believe the propaganda about immigrants being criminals, about immigrants stealing jobs from Americans and about immigrants sponging off the US taxpayer dollar. Mmmm. Sure. Like Elon Musk, Albert Einstein, Elizabeth Arden, Audrey Hepburn, Aldous Huxley, Bruce Willis, Helena Rubinstein, Charlize Theron, Nikola Tesla, Mikhail Baryshnikov, Anna Kournikova, Martina Navratilova, Igor Sikorsky, Andrew Carnegie, Anthony Hopkins, Ayn Rand, Sergei Rachmaninov and Joseph Pulitzer. I leave out Steve Jobs only because he was born to immigrant parents. The inconvenient truth is that without immigrants, there would be no America.

We have now been waiting for a decision on our I-140 and I-485 Change-of-Status and Green Card petitions for 10 months. We are invited to participate in a film to tell our story. The film, called "The Stranger", is produced by the Evangelical Immigration Table and directed by Emmy Award winner Linda Midgett. And Dianne appears as a guest speaker on NPR to talk about immigration.

In September 2014 we receive an RFE Request for Further Evidence regarding our application for Permanent Residence that was filed in August 2013. The USCIS requests an extensive list of evidence to prove that we have been in the US legally since 2001. Obviously the USCIS finds it hard to believe that we have been here for more than 13 years without permanent residency. If the USCIS can find even a single day of illegal stay, it can deny our petition. Proving that we did not exceed the 180-day overstay limit, before self-deporting to Ireland, is essential. Problem. How do we prove that we exited the USA on May 30, 2012, 178 days after our last visa expired? No passport stamps, since passports are now scanned electronically and not stamped. An air-ticket purchase receipt is not sufficient proof.

Then it dawns on me – while sitting, bored, in the hotel-room in Ireland, I started scanning expense receipts. Indeed, I scanned everything so as to avoid transporting loads of paper. And in those scans, images of our boarding cards. Who the hell saves boarding cards, you might ask? Bored people do! Problem number one solved. Problem number 2 – the USCIS wants further evidence that the awards I have received are from a renown, prestigious organization. Tim suggests that the US Marine Corps is as renown and prestigious as they come. Questioning this could be bad for one's health! After all, what do they say about not fucking with the Marines?

By early November, we have gathered all the evidence we can. Tim responds to the RFE and submits the evidence as requested in the RFE, and this filing is acknowledged by the USCIS on November 5th, 2014. We understand that our application will now be processed further. We have no idea when we will hear from them about their decision. They have provided no date as to when their decision can be expected. Whatever this decision is, our daughter Sarah, 25, who has been in the US legally since the age of 11, will be excluded from this benefit, if it comes. She will have to leave the US - which has been her only home for the past 14 years - when she graduates with a Master's degree from the University of Cincinnati in May 2016. We continue to pray for a miracle that our family will be allowed to stay in the US and that our daughter will be able to be with us.

Tim feels confident that with regard to our permanent residence, it's a slam dunk.

Our tenant in our Charlotte house finishes building his new house and advises that he will be terminating the lease in November 2014. Our house is tired, shabby and out of date. Built in 1995 and purchased by us in 2003, it needs a serious and total renovation. My realtor tells me that if we try to sell the house in its current condition, we will take a bath. Similarly, with trying to rent out the house in its current condition. We have little choice – the house needs a total renovation.

Knowing that labor costs are the most expensive component in any large project, I need cheap labor and a project manager with great design skills and an inhumane attention to detail. I move into the empty house with a sleeping-bag and an inflatable mattress for some "glamping" aka glamorous camping, and some major work. I paint every inch of the two-story interior, refurbish kitchen cabinets, replace all hardware, gut the kitchen counter-tops and replace with quartz, rip out carpeting, lay new oak hardwood floors, sand and stain the hardwoods, and manage the sub-contractors that handle the tasks that I, and YouTube tutorials, cannot do. Dianne is busy running our businesses and keeping some cash-flow moving, but stops in every couple of days to motivate me, nit-pick on minor imperfections in my workmanship and make design decisions on the renovation of "her" new home!

By May 2015, the project is finished and so am I. I have spent about $25k, all on credit card, but have added about $100k to the value of the property, according to my realtor, who now really wants to put the property on the market. "It will sell in one weekend," she says. But no deal, we have a new home to move back into from Mooresville and now being empty-nesters, we are able to create new office-space in those rooms previously resembling war-zones.

Day 4953. January 28, 2015

After a brief 7.15am interview at the USCIS in Charlotte NC, Dianne, Michael and I have the wonderful news. Our permanent residence in the USA has been granted. The approval is however a bitter-sweet victory. Our daughter Sarah, who came to the USA at age 11 and who is now in graduate-school in Cincinnati, aged out along this journey at age 21 and needed to get an F-1 international student visa in order to remain in the USA to complete her studies. She will graduate with her Master's degree in 2016, at which time her student visa will end. The battle to keep our family together continues.

With her permanent residence, Dianne is at last able to work again. She re-opens the doors to BSA PR & Marketing, a business we started back in 1988 in South Africa, transferred to the USA in 2001, closed in 2012 when we went to Ireland and now re-opened in 2015. Her clients return, and she picks up a French-based package-design company that is opening a US-based office in Charlotte. Dianne is appointed to head up business development for the new US operation. And I add the Office of Naval Intelligence to my client portfolio as well as the Squadron Officers College at Maxwell Air Force Base in Alabama.

The story of our fight for permanent residence in the United States, and the right to call America our home, has become well-known, and we have touched the lives of many Americans and been touched by the love and support of many more Americans. Few truly understand the laws, promulgated in their name, that impact the lives of prospective immigrants to the USA. Over the years, we have attempted to explain how the laws work. With few exceptions, we see the blinds of confusion come down over their eyes. "We don't understand all of this," they say. "We never knew it was this complex." Perhaps a sad indictment of a great nation when its citizens can simply walk away with "I don't understand all of this."

We have done it the hard way, but we have also done it the correct way. We have worked within the laws of America. Others want us to show them the path, but without the pitfalls. We opened a new business, Pathway USA, a consultancy to guide others who seek a life and a future in America. A consultancy that will help others avoid the mistakes we made.

Yes, we made mistakes. Perhaps the biggest mistake was to place our trust in the system and to trust others who used the immigration system for personal gain, regardless of the cost to others. We learned that the US immigration system is dysfunctional. A highly complex set of laws and regulations, administered by people with grossly inadequate training who simply cannot handle the work-load. And we learned that immigration lawyers are sometimes human too. They do screw up.

Sarah has now graduated with her Master's degree from the College-Conservatory of Music at the University of Cincinnati. And in spite of everything, she graduated cum laude, just as she did with her Bachelor's degree. She is now a stage manager, specializing in the stage management of Opera. She is granted a year of OPT, Optional Practical Training, to take up a position as Assistant Stage Manager with Virginia Opera. Her OPT is for one year and will expire in June 2017. Then she faces having to leave the USA to make her home in another country. After spending most of her life in the USA, completing her middle and high schooling in the USA and completing both her Bachelor's and Master's degrees in the USA, she will no longer be welcome to stay in America and to give back some of what she has acquired in this country.

I again sit down with a team of immigration attorneys, this time to consider the possible roads ahead for my daughter.

The H-1B skilled-worker visa is problematic. 85,000 H-1B visas are made available each year in April, of which 20,000 are reserved for graduate-degree-holders in the STEM fields – science, technology, engineering and math – leaving 65,000 visas for all other skilled workers who have firm job-offers. In 2016, there were 236,000 petitions for the H-1B, so each petitioner only has one chance in 3.6 of getting a visa. If companies cannot get H-1B visas for skilled workers, they ship the jobs overseas. That's the first problem. Second problem – opera companies go "dark" for 3 months at the end of each season. The production staff are expected to seek alternative experiential employment. Except for the H-1B visa-holders who have their employment linked to the petitioning employer and who are not permitted to take up any other employment with any other employer. So even if Sarah is fortunate enough to capture the one-in-3.6 chance of getting an H-1B visa, she will lose her income at the end of the opera season when the company goes "dark" for three months. No income, no health insurance and no means of paying her apartment rental, car lease, insurance or living expenses.

The L-1 executive / managerial transfer visa is simply not possible. Sarah does not qualify in any form or manner.

The J-1 visa is being explored. This is a non-immigrant visa issued by the United States to research scholars, professors and exchange visitors participating in programs that promote cultural exchange, especially to obtain medical or business training within the U.S. While Sarah would most likely qualify for this visa, it is questionable as to how she might "promote cultural exchange", having lived and been educated in America for almost two decades.

The O-visa is also being considered. It will be somewhat of a stretch to make a case for someone only a couple of years out of graduate school, but desperate times call for desperate measures. There is something fundamentally wrong with a society that so willingly invests in education and then allows bureaucratic legislation to prevent students from using that education to repay the society that made that education possible.

America is still the benchmark society against which all societies are measured. It is still the dream of so many. Yet it is a society that all too often succors bigotry and fosters ignorance. It is a society that requires every immigrant to take the Oath of Allegiance, yet fails to demand the same from those who are born here. It is a society that remains great, in spite of itself. Yet I fear that the greatest threat to the future of our American way of life, is not the threat from outside our borders, but the threat from within.

PART 4 : WHERE IS SARAH STEWART?

January 2017. What do we do about Sarah? She tells us that her Optional Practical Training period with Virginia Opera expires in June. She needs a visa if she is to stay in the USA. Quite understandably, and to our great joy, she has rejected the notion of a convenience "marriage to a green-card".

The L and J visas are not an option.

The H-1B filing date is 1 April but only permits employment to start on 1 October. She would thus be out of status between June and October, more than 180 days, even if she could find a solid job offer AND be lucky enough to beat the 1 in 4 odds of getting a visa AND have the prospective employer be prepared to wait until October, well into the opera season. Not looking good.

On the spur of the moment, Dianne, places a call to Matthew, an immigration attorney in Buffalo, New York, who specializes in "difficult" cases. She outlines our thoughts about Sarah's options.

"Tough case," agrees Matthew. "I suggest you reach out to Laya. She's good, and she's in Charlotte."

I book an appointment for Sarah and I to go see Laya. Quite a character this one, with a snow-white Japanese Hokkaido that meets you at her office door, and a pug on her desk that stares at you in indecision as to whether to sniff you to death or just nibble you a bit.

Laya and her team look through Sarah's resume, nod and purse lips, then look through her website, nod and purse lips some more, and then "an O will work".

"Done many O visas?" I ask innocently. This can't be that easy!

"Oh yea," she smiles sagely. "We do all the O's for all the big artists coming to the States. Been doing this for years."

"Will you take our case?" I ask.

"Sure, get the paperwork together and we'll file at the end of February with a request for 15-day Premium Processing."

Sarah heads back to Norfolk Virginia and starts putting together the evidence. She's clearly learned a few things over the years watching me put together mountains of paperwork for our petitions.

On March 9, Laya files Sarah's O-visa petition with a request for 15-day Premium Processing. On March 16, just 7 days later, we get the email – *"Dear Sarah: We have just received electronic notification of the approval of the I-129 O-1 Petition of Virginia Opera on your behalf valid from April 15, 2017 to April 14, 2020. The next step is to arrange a visa appointment for you at an American Consulate before your OPT expires."*

On April 24, Sarah flies to Toronto, Canada, to an appointment with the US Embassy to have her visa entered into her Irish passport. Again, kudos to my father who registered me as an Irish foreign birth, thus securing for me and my family that coveted Irish passport.

On May 6, Sarah lands in Charlotte, North Carolina with her first employment-based visa. Just a couple of months short of her 16th year in the USA. It's Day 5781.

We are all home at last!

Or are we?

During the Summer of 2017, Sarah remains unemployed. When the opera season at Virginia Opera ends, and the company goes "dark" for three months, the employees are expected to secure other work, pending the start of the new season. Not Sarah. Because her O-visa is linked to employment with the O-visa petitioner, Virginia Opera, Sarah is not permitted to seek employment elsewhere. However, she has a supportive family in Charlotte NC, her old bedroom in the family home and parents who are willing and able to cover her Norfolk apartment rental, car lease payments and health insurance payments during the three months unemployment "sabbatical" she is forced to take until she can take up her promised new contract with Virginia Opera.

In July 2017, Virginia Opera advises Sarah that contrary to their letter of intent to extend her employment for another year, and their petition for her O-visa, due to financial and budgetary constraints, they are unable to renew her employment contract. This effectively invalidates her O-visa, barely 2 months old and acquired at a cost, to us, of $10,000. She has 60 days to find another job and transfer her O-visa to another employer, at a further cost of $10,000. Failure to do so means that she becomes a visa-overstay and subject to deportation. And failure to exit the USA within 180 days will trigger the 3-year bar to lawful re-entry to the USA. It all sounds so familiar.

Sarah and Dianne launch a massive search for another job. They call upon every contact they have in the opera, stage and musical industry. No-one is offering permanent employment – the new season is about to start and they've already signed up new production crew. Sorry, if only you had contacted us a couple of months ago...

Sure, say other companies. We have positions, but they are short-term contracts for a single production. Hardly worth getting a $10,000 O-visa for a job that will last a few weeks. We look at getting an O-visa through an agent. If we can lock in at least three or four back-to-back contracts for Sarah, we can file an agent's petition for her. Easier said than done. Lots of possible contracts but too few are ready for written contracts.

Then a number of job-offers with a great wage, super prospects and "you can start right away". We bounce these job-offers off Laya. Bad news. The jobs do not fall within Sarah's area of expertise and extra-ordinary ability. She has to find not only a job, but a job within the area of production stage-management. Something that will qualify her for another O-visa.

Before we know it, the 60 days are up. Sarah's O-visa has become void. Now she cannot transfer the O-visa to another employer – she has to re-apply for a new O-visa if she can find a new job. She's now technically an overstay and can be arrested and deported at any time. And even if she escapes the Immigration and Customs Enforcement (ICE) troops, she has 120 days remaining before the 3-year bar kicks in.

Day 5933. October 4, 2017

Sarah boards American Airlines Flight 730 from Charlotte Douglas Airport to London Heathrow. She's on a one-way ticket out of the USA. She's self-deporting to avoid breaking US immigration law. She's lived legally in the USA for 16 years 2 months and 27 days. She completed her middle and high schooling in the USA and earned Bachelor's and Master's degrees from American universities. She will not be returning to America. Because she's an immigrant. She wants a country to call home. And America will not give her this.

The journey to and from Charlotte Douglas Airport that day is not an easy one.

Dianne, Michael and I are eligible for US Citizenship in January 2020. Sarah is not. She's now living and working in London, England. As an Irish Citizen who has never lived in Ireland or

England, she is welcome there and free to pursue her new life and her new future. Without her family. Yet, although traumatized emotionally by the family separation, professionally she rises to the challenge and secures a two-month assistant-stage-management position in Sir George Benjamin's World Premiere of "Lessons in Love and Violence" at the Royal Opera House in London.

It's a sad day for the rest of the Stewart family. We came to America as a family. Believing in the rule of law. Of humanity. Family values. And fairness and decency. Today we're not so sure whether American steak is as good as American sizzle.

And now for the kicker. Sarah is not permitted to re-enter the USA. Not even to visit the rest of her family. Although she voluntarily self-deported from the USA to avoid breaking the law, the law prohibits her from re-entry, not because of the 180-day bar, but now because she has family in the USA.

INA Section 214(b), also found in the United States Code at 8 USC 1184(b), states:

"...every alien . . . shall be presumed to be an immigrant until he establishes to the satisfaction of the consular officer, at the time of application for a visa, and the immigration officers, at the time of application for admission, that he is entitled to a nonimmigrant status under section 101(a)(15)."

This simply means that before you can be approved for a non-immigrant visa, such as an ESTA or B1/B2 tourist visa, you must prove that you will return to your home country. You must show that you have no intention of abandoning your residence there. The law places the burden of proof on you to prove that you have "strong ties" to your home country that would compel you to leave the US at the end of your temporary stay, and return home.

Thus, to avoid a 214B visa denial, applicants must convince the Consular Officer of the following:

1. that they intend to return to their home country after a temporary stay in the United States,
2. that their financial situation is such that they can afford the trip without having to seek unauthorized employment in the U.S., and
3. that the travel is for legitimate purposes permitted by the applicant's visa category.

Examples of evidence to show ties to your home country :

- Your home title deeds and mortgage statement showing that you have equity in your home.
- Evidence of business ownership showing percentage of ownership, your job position and salary.
- A letter from your employer confirming your employment, job position and salary, and that you have been granted leave from date X to date Y and that you are expected back in office by date Z.
- Evidence that you have sufficient funds for the trip to the USA and that you will not need to seek employment in the USA.
- Evidence that you will have sufficient funds in your home country to support you upon your return.
- If you will be coming to the USA without your spouse or minor children, evidence that you have a spouse and minor children that will remain in your home country while you are visiting the USA.
- Evidence of other family ties in your home country such as elderly parents.
- If traveling with children, evidence of school registration and school term dates. If children are traveling during school term, questions will be raised unless there is a good reason for children being absent from school.
- Any other evidence to support your claim that you have more reason to return to your home country than to remain in the USA unlawfully.

Here's Sarah's problem. She has spent most of her life living in the USA. She was educated in the USA. The rest of her family are permanent residents of the USA. The family home is in the USA. On the flip-side, she is a contract stage-manager in the UK. She rents a room in a row-house in the UK. She has no spouse, children or other family in the UK. She owns no property in the UK. Indeed, she has more anchors in the USA than in the UK. All she has is her track-record for obeying the laws of the USA. But that's not enough.

She lives with the daily pain of rejection. The pain that she is not allowed to go home. To her family. Or to her friends. Not even to visit. No Christmas. No Thanksgiving. Effectively banned from the USA. It's a heavy burden for a young woman who has known no other home.

And of course, rationally or irrationally, Dianne and I bear the burden of guilt. Could we have avoided this? Could we have done something different?

Michael carries his own burden. He, Sarah's young brother, is a US Permanent Resident, while his older sister lives in exile. He will become a US Citizen in 2020 or 2021. She will remain in limbo. Survivor's Guilt!

January 2018. In Washington DC, the US Government is considering the future of DACA, Deferred Action for Childhood Arrivals. Introduced in 2012, DACA is targeted at minor children who came to the US illegally – some 800,000 of them. Innocent victims brought here by their parents. According to DACA, if minors came to the USA while under the age of 16, are under the age of 31 as of June 15, 2012, and have lived continuously in the USA from June 15, 2007 to the present time, they enjoy prosecutorial discretion to defer 'removal action' (a polite term for arrest, detention and deportation). Under consideration is whether to offer these children a pathway to lawful permanent residence in America and ultimately American Citizenship.

Sarah qualifies for DACA in every respect. Except one. She came to the USA legally, while DACA is only for those who came here illegally. She has lived continuously in the USA in legal status. And she voluntarily self-deported from the USA to avoid breaking US immigration law.

America, you know where the 800,000 Dreamers are. You're considering plans to give them a home in America.

WHAT ABOUT SARAH STEWART?

Sarah is living in exile in the UK. It's a foreign world to her, but she's rising to the challenge – assistant stage manager for Les Enfants Terribles – "Inside Pussy Riot" at the Saatchi Gallery in London, followed by assistant stage manager for the World Premiere of "Lessons in Love and Violence" by Sir George Benjamin, CBE at the Royal Opera House in London.

Yet in spite of these successes, the pain of separation is exacerbated because she cannot visit her family in the USA. As October 2018 approaches, Sarah is faced with the specter of celebrating another birthday away from her family. It's back to the drawing-board – how to apply for a tourist visa for Sarah without getting a 214(b) denial.

With her Irish passport she can go online to apply for an ESTA (Electronic System for Travel Authorization) which is available to certain countries. However, there's a big danger here. Because of her personal circumstances, having all her 'anchors' IN the USA, she might get an ESTA to travel to the USA, but get barred from ENTERING the USA during the CBP (Customs and Border Protection) interview on arrival – remember the 214 regulation presumes immigrant intent. After the uncertainty of so many years, it would be disastrous if Sarah travelled all the way to the USA, only to be barred from entry, detained and returned to the UK. Preferable, would be to physically apply for a B1/B2 tourist visa at a US Consulate abroad, where your qualifying reasons are adjudicated up-front in a face-to-face interview, and before you get the B1/B2 and start to travel.

Sarah books an appointment at the US Consulate in London, only to be told that the Consulate is being renovated and currently not processing B1/B2 applications – also, since Brits can get an ESTA, there is no urgent need to get a B1/B2 office operational. The closest US Consulate to Sarah is in Belfast, Northern Ireland.

With an appointment booked, and with a letter from me guaranteeing that she will comply with the laws and regulations pertaining to the B1/B2, Sarah flies to Belfast for a few days, where she is interviewed, put through the grinder and finally granted the visa.

Her entry into the USA on 12 October is uneventful. She enjoys a wonderful birthday party with us and gets to see and spend time with many of her school and university friends. All too soon, her leave comes to an end, and as promised, on 27 October, Dianne and I, accompanied by a couple of her friends, bid her au revoir at Charlotte Douglas Airport as she returns to her work and life in the UK. But she will miss my birthday in November and Christmas (again), so is looking to use some of her accumulated leave for another trip in the New Year.

Sarah returns to the USA on January 10, 2019 for a 3-week holiday (it helps that I have so many air-miles to give to her!) It's lovely to have our big girl back with us. So worldly, with so much news about what she is doing in the opera industry and what she is planning to do.

Then a change of plans. I have to travel to South Africa in early February. It will be an extended trip for business, family matters – my mother is 91 - and some long-delayed eye surgery. Dianne will be alone in Charlotte.

Sarah offers to extend her trip and gets permission from her employer in the UK. An ideal time for her to bond, one-on-one, as adults, with Dianne. However, she seems to be spending more and more time with an old flame, Luan. He's a bit cautious of me - years ago I saw a strange car parked outside our home, late at night, with park-lights on. Grabbing a very large and powerful flash-light, I went to investigate, and found my darling daughter being very thoroughly kissed by a strange young man. So, whatever was happening between these two on this trip seems to be a continuation of what had been interrupted years before and kept more or less under wraps in the interim.

27 March - I return to the USA but have a lengthy period of recovery after my eye-surgery, and can spend very little time in the office, so Sarah extends her trip again to help Dianne, and care for my needs. However, her authorized stay in the USA is coming to an end, and so is her leave period. She makes plans to return to the UK.

A grateful client had given Dianne and I a gift-voucher to Ruth's Chris Steak House – an ideal opportunity for a good evening on the town with Sarah and to meet Luan who seems to be a fairly regular caller, and who appears to have overcome the embarrassment of having been caught kissing my daughter some years ago.

Because of a bad hip, I can never sit for lengthy periods of time and need to stretch my legs, so I leave the ladies with Luan and head outside for a break. Luan appears. We chat about this and that. Then the bomb-shell.

"Sir…" he starts rather seriously.

Oh shit, I wonder. What's happened?

"Sir" he starts again. "With your permission of course, I'd like to marry Sarah."

Thank God. Nothing serious.

"Have you asked her?" I inquire.

"Not yet. I'd like your permission first."

No hesitation. My daughter is almost 30. She's independent, willful, determined and at times rather bloody-minded. For years she's done pretty much what she wants to do, and occasionally deigns to inform us about her decisions. She's had to survive everything that the US Government has thrown at us. A husband should be a piece of cake.

"You think you can handle Sarah?" I ask.

"I think so" he answers. "If not, I'll figure it out."

"You love her?"

"Absolutely! For as long as I've known her."

"Then let's go ask her."

As we finish our steaks and prepare for dessert, Luan stands up from the table.

"Now where are you going?" demands Sarah.

"Onto a knee" he smiles disarmingly. "To ask you to marry me."

Sarah and Luan are married in a civil ceremony on May 3, 2019. Luan's stepfather, a retired US diplomat, and his mother, a professor at the university of the West-Indies, living in Barbados, fly out to the USA to stay with us and to welcome the new additions to both of our families. Dianne and I adore our new son-in law and having family in sunny Barbados has its perks.

Anthony and Elaine invite us to visit with them in Barbados in March 2020 where the two mothers-in-law become firm friends and the two fathers-in-law find they enjoy the same Whiskey and the same wry sense of humor – essential foundations for a good family.

On our arrival in Barbados on March 11, we are temperature tested for COVID-19 while still on the airport apron and again as we enter the terminal. The same procedure a week later when we depart for our return to the USA. Ominously, and a portent of days to come, absolutely zero screening of any passengers as we enter the USA on March 18 where the US infection rate is already at 2444, up 10-fold from 245 when we left just 7 days previously.

Nevertheless, Dianne and I go into voluntary quarantine for 14 days, as does Sarah and Luan who collected us from the airport.

Luan files a spousal visa petition for his new wife and this is approved, conditionally for two years. (The conditional permanent residence status is to ensure that you do not enter a marriage to circumvent the immigration laws of the United States – hardly the case here - these two kids are inseparable.) In June 2021 Luan can Petition to Remove Conditions on Residence and in June 2022, Sarah can petition for US Citizenship.

After so many years of uncertainty, the stars finally align for our darling daughter and we gain an adoring and adorable son-in-law!

PART 5 : POST SCRIPT

The Ultimate Irony

In January 2020, Dianne, Michael and I have the option of becoming Citizens of the United States of America, having been Legal Permanent Residents for 5 years. If we don't exercise this option, and choose to remain permanent residents, our Green-Cards have to be renewed every 10 years, with no guarantee of renewal and the ever-present risk of having our legal permanent residence revoked.

Should we decide to petition for US Citizenship and should this petition be successful, we will be required to take the United States Oath of Allegiance, something that few American-born persons are required to take. This oath is only for immigrants wishing to become US Citizens, for members of the US Military and for those in public office. Not for the rest of America. (An interesting point of law – having taken the Oath of Allegiance, I could be charged with Treason. But if a born-American has never taken the Oath of Allegiance, could he or she ever be charged with Treason?)

In essence, we will have to swear to uphold the laws of the country that abused us for so many years, and that continues to keep our family, and many other immigrant families, fractured.

At the same time, we need to consider our South African citizenship. While the USA does not mind its citizens from holding multiple passports, South Africa will immediately revoke the South African passport and citizenship of anyone taking foreign citizenship. Many years previously, when working for the Coca-Cola Export Corporation in South Africa, I had to get special permission from the South African Government to hold a foreign passport to travel to countries that would not accept the SA passport.

We still have family in South Africa and want the freedom to travel there. At the same time, we don't want to make decisions for our children who may or may not want to retain their South African Citizenship.

We file petitions to retain our South African passports, notwithstanding an intention to seek US Citizenship. Our petitions and supporting reasons are approved. (I guess we are now getting used to filing winning petitions!)

Dianne and I prepare and file the N-400 petition for US Citizenship through naturalization. In July we receive notification to appear at the USCIS offices in Charlotte for our naturalization interviews on August 6. I am scheduled for an 11am appointment and Dianne for 2pm

August 6, 2020 : Day 6969

I am interviewed for US Citizenship. I am asked loads of questions about whether I have participated in drug-trafficking, child-trafficking, terrorism, genocide, treason, etc etc. Plus, a number of questions about American politics, history and civics – questions that few Americans can answer. Then I'm told to go and stand in front of a large mural depicting the USCIS logo, the Capitol and the US Flag and to take the US Oath of Allegiance. Because of COVID-19, there are no separate group citizenship ceremonies – it's done there and then, one-on-one.

I'm a bit rattled and I pause – I'm being asked to swear to defend a country that kills innocent civilians in drone-strikes, invades sovereign nations without a declaration of war, arrests legitimate asylum-seekers on the border, separates children from parents, holds children in cages, my God, the list of atrocities is endless. For almost 20 years I've had to remain silent – I'm a guest in this country and it's not my place to criticize. Yet I've read the books - Bob Woodward's books Fear and Rage, Michael Cohen's Disloyal, Jean Guerrero's Hatemonger, John Bolton's The Room where it Happened, James Comey's A Higher Loyalty, Mary Trump's Too Much and Never Enough, David Enrich's Dark Towers and Miles Taylor's A Warning. And also, Omar Nasiri's Inside the Jihad and Kenneth Timmerman's Preachers of Hate (recommended to me by my friends in the SpecOps community). But now I'm being offered a voice, and not only the right, but also the responsibility, to speak, to protest and to vote. To end my silence. To decline this responsibility and to remain silent will be nothing less than a condonation of what is wrong and inhumane about this country. I am reminded of John Stuart Mill's admonishment in 1867 that "Bad men need nothing more to compass their ends, than that good men should look on and do nothing." And more recently "When a great democracy is destroyed, it will not be because of enemies from without, but rather because of enemies from within." The truth of this statement is becoming terrifyingly clear as we see this country each day losing on every front …

The official from USCIS stands in front of me. "Dr Stewart, are you ready?" she asks.

I make a decision. After 19 years on this journey, it would be a betrayal of all those who helped us in our quest to become Americans. And of my own values. "Yes, I am ready."

The United States Oath of Allegiance, officially referred to as the "Oath of Allegiance," 8 C.F.R. Part 337 (2008), is an allegiance oath that must be taken by all immigrants who wish to become United States citizens.

I hereby declare, on oath, that I absolutely and entirely renounce and abjure all allegiance and fidelity to any foreign prince, potentate, state, or sovereignty of whom or which I have heretofore been a subject or citizen; that I will support and defend the Constitution and laws of the United States of America against all enemies, foreign and domestic; that I will bear true faith and allegiance to the same; that I will bear arms on behalf of the United States when required by the law; that I will perform noncombatant service in the Armed Forces of the United States when required by the law; that I will perform work of national importance under civilian direction when required by the law; and that I take this obligation freely without any mental reservation or purpose of evasion; so help me God.

A few minutes later I am an American Citizen. It's almost anti-climactic. The journey took 19 years and 29 days. I call Dianne with the news, and head home to fetch her for her appointment at 2pm. She is dressed to kill – she's dreamed of being an American since the age of 10 – Old Glory lapel-badge, Old Glory scarf and a new suit for the occasion.

We arrive back at the USCIS offices, and wait in the car for her scheduled time to enter the building. Above us, on the roof-top of the building, sit two large turkey-buzzards, looking down at us.

"I wonder whose carcass they will soon be picking at?" I wonder.

Dianne enters the building. She will probably be busy for the next few hours, so I head off to do some grocery shopping.

Half an hour later, I get a call from a distraught Dianne. "They sent me away" she says. "They cannot find my application for Citizenship."

We are shattered. How could this happen? But then realize that after what we've gone through over the past 19 years, should we really expect anything different? It's just so unfair that this happened to Dianne and not to me, as I am quite fatalistic about most things.

We refer to the case-status updates on the USCIS website. After my naturalization interview and citizenship swearing-in on August 6, I am now scheduled for my citizenship swearing-in ceremony on November 6 (yet I am already a Citizen - is this a "two-fer" or BOGO?), and after Dianne's naturalization interview, which did not happen, she is also scheduled for her citizenship swearing-in ceremony. Clearly the USCIS has not changed.

Two months later, Dianne has heard nothing from the USCIS. The Presidential Election is looming and she wants to vote – the first time in America and the first time since leaving South Africa almost 20 years ago.

She reaches out to our political representative, Congressman Dan Bishop and is connected with his immigration aide, none other than Chris Sullivan of our earlier days in 2013. Chris obviously knows our case well, is horrified at what has happened, and promises to investigate.

On Monday 19 October, Chris Sullivan calls Dianne. "Can you be at the USCIS offices on Wednesday October 21 at 1.30pm?"

At the front door, Dianne is met personally by USCIS officer Andrew Cox and ushered into the interview room. She is the only person being interviewed. No-one else there. She's treated like royalty. She gets a 100% score on the quiz-questions. Confirms that she's not a terrorist, child-trafficker, drug-smuggler, gun-runner, etc, etc. But the wheels sort of fall off when she's in front of the citizenship mural and has to take the Oath of Allegiance – she bursts into tears – a mix of anger, frustration, relief and happiness. With patience, tissues and a bit of extra time, she completes the oath and is sworn in as a US Citizen, 19 years, 3 months and 13 days after arriving in the USA. It's Day 7045.

Two hours later, with Naturalization Certificate in hand, Dianne reports to our local election office and is registered as a voter in North Carolina and shortly thereafter she votes in the 2020 Presidential Election, as I did, by mail-in ballot, a few weeks earlier.

It is however, quite ironic that after almost 20 years, the United States of America has granted us citizenship and the right to speak, and COVID-19 has basically muzzled us with a mask. Yet on a more humorous side, Dianne has just today, October 29, received a USCIS notification that her naturalization interview is scheduled for October 21!

It will take some time for us to adapt to our new status. Earlier this week, an envelope arrived from the US Department of State. Our hearts sink. For almost 20 years, an envelope from the government invariably means bad news – a negative decision on one of our petitions, appeals, motions. And it's usually close to Christmas when we receive these envelopes. But this time it's not bad news – it's my American Passport. The following day, another Department of State envelope arrives, and again our hearts sink. But it's my US Passport Card. And the following day, another envelope arrives from the Department of State. My God people, put us out of our misery – just draw a smiley-face on the envelope next time if it's good news …. At least to prepare us! It's my naturalization certificate, being returned from the passport office.

The American Eagle has hatched two of its eggs. There are just two more. Sarah is married to a loving husband with 3 cats. She has a great job in the mortgage industry, has a spousal green card and can petition for citizenship in a couple of years. Michael has filed his petition for naturalization and is awaiting his naturalization interview and citizenship swearing-in. After graduating from engineering school, he started his own company designing and manufacturing Mod-Kits for the computer gaming industry. He lives with his girl-friend of 7 years, Elaina, also an engineer.

COVID-19

It is said that every cloud has a silver lining. Perhaps the past 19 years was our silver lining. As the world collapsed under the specter of COVID-19, perhaps our years of adapting to uncertainty prepared us for 2020.

Sarah saw the imminent collapse of the entertainment industry and realized she would need to pursue a new career, at least for a while. Armed with the exceptional organizational skills and the extraordinary attention to detail demanded in staging large-scale operatic performances, she entered the mortgage industry at a time when interest rates were some of the lowest in history, and re-financing at an all-time high. She is doing just fine.

Michael, confined to home isolation because of his allergies and asthma, became a serious FortNite computer-gamer, and designed a gaming-joy-stick, converting their apartment into a factory with a dozen-or-so 3D printers and an assembly line that designs, manufactures, assembles and distributes thousands of his gaming peripherals to all corners of the world.

His longtime girl-friend, Elaina, also confined to a work-from-home environment, saw the potential of Michael's new business, resigned from her civil-engineering job and partnered with Michael in building the new company. After delivering another shipment of GamingJoySticks to the USPS, they stopped off at the local Court-house and got married - somewhat unorthodox, but rather than announce their intentions and then have to deal with family and friends that could not attend a traditional wedding, gave us the news as a *fait accompli*. Two engineers adapting to a changed world and being very successful at it.

Dianne and I are empty-nesters but very busy. My classroom-training has slowed down but my Zoom-training has increased. Dianne's BSA PR & Marketing has adapted to a world of virtual interaction. And PathwayUSA is catering to the demands of global migration prompted by the financial and social impact of the pandemic. We are thankful that all of our businesses are adaptable to a virtual world.

January 6, 2021. In horror we watch the desecration of the US Capitol. We hear the unsubstantiated Republican challenge to the presidential election and the Electoral College votes. We hear a defeated President snub the US Constitution and disgrace the

United States. And for just a minute, we wonder whether our pursuit of the American Dream was worth it. But just for a minute. And then the realization kicks in. This is what the idea of America is all about. The freedom to be misguided and uninformed. The freedom to disagree, justifiably or not. And quite honestly, the freedom to be a total ass-hole. America will invariably rise above the storm because it has the freedom to do so. And if the mob prevails, America will change to reflect what Americans want – the ultimate freedom to determine its future, whatever that might be.

PART 6 : THE ROAD AHEAD

Immigration Act 2021 Proposal

Historically, immigrant entrepreneurs have played a pivotal role in developing the US Economy, particularly in the technology sector. In the years of 1998-2006, 14.76% of all patent applications in the United States had at least one immigrant involved as a lone or co-founder, with the majority of these patents having roots in California and New Jersey. In all American technology and engineering businesses created in the US between 1995-2005, one-quarter of them had an immigrant as a key founder. In 2012, immigrant tech-founded companies employed over 550,000 people and generated close to 70 billion dollars in sales. Over 40% of current Fortune 500 companies were established by immigrants or children of immigrants.

This proposal aims to continue and enhance the critical and essential role of immigrants in the growth of the US Economy, the impact of which will benefit the lives of every American.

1. Levy an annual visa-tax on every visa-holder

Similar to the SEVIS fee levied on international F-1 student and inter-cultural J visas, levy an annual Immigrant Visitor Information System (IVIS) tax of $100 on every visa issued. These funds to be used for :

- maintaining information on immigrant visitors and duration of legal stay in the USA
- enhancing border security
- enhancing USCIS efficiency levels
- development of tuition-free technical training schools to enhance the skills of US workers to make them competitive with immigrant workers

2. Every immigrant visa petitioner to demonstrate English language proficiency or commit to English language proficiency training upon arrival in the USA.

This is not discrimination. It's a practical business and educational consideration.

3. Maintain an unlimited EB-5 investor visa program but implement country limitations.

Investment in the USA is desirable. Every EB-5 investment creates 10 or more permanent full-time jobs. However too much investment from one country is not.

4. International F-1 Students to receive US Permanent Residence upon graduation.

1 million foreign students come to the USA each year to study. They invest $36 Billion in the US Economy. We need to keep these skills in the USA.

If F-1 students graduate with an advanced degree such as Masters or Doctorate they get permanent residence.

For an undergraduate STEM degree, or in a field of study determined by the Department of Labor to be a "priority field", they get an Employment Authorization Document for 5 years, which automatically converts to permanent residence after 5 years if the petitioner has maintained gainful employment and tax-payer status.

Excluded from the above are all students with felony convictions and /or failure to register for income tax or failure to pay all required income taxes.

5. Crime-free tax-paying undocumented immigrants to get US Permanent Residence.

It's an old adage that "possession is nine tenths of the law". Undocumented immigrants are *de facto* residents of the USA. Denying this fact with empty threats of deportation is a disservice to those immigrants and to the people of the USA. Similarly, the argument that granting amnesty is tantamount to rewarding crime, is pointless – doing nothing about crime is little different from condoning crime. If we cannot get rid of all of them NOW, there is something we can do to benefit the USA and the US Economy NOW.

If you are undocumented, have no criminal record, are a registered tax-payer, and have been paying your taxes for at least 10 years, you get a Social Security Card and US Permanent Residence immediately.

If you are undocumented, have no criminal record, are a registered tax-payer, and have been paying your taxes for at least 5 years, you get an Employment Authorization Document and Social Security Card immediately and US Permanent Residence 5 years later.

If you are undocumented, have no criminal record, are a registered tax-payer, and have been paying your taxes for at least 1 year, you get an Employment Authorization Document and Social Security Card immediately and US Permanent Residence 10 years later.

If you are undocumented, have no criminal record, but are NOT a registered tax-payer, but register as a tax-payer within an amnesty period, you get an Employment Authorization Document and Social Security Card immediately and US Permanent Residence 10 years later.

If you are undocumented and do not register as a tax-payer within the amnesty period, you are subject to immediate deportation together with any U-21 children you have, whether they are US citizens or not.

6. Grant unlimited H-1B skilled worker visas.

If companies cannot find the skills they need IN the USA, they will send the jobs overseas to countries that HAVE the skills. And if skilled labor is cheaper to buy overseas, that's where the jobs will go. Trying to force companies to use more expensive and less-skilled US workers will not work. If companies can demonstrate that they cannot find the skilled labor IN the USA, they must be allowed to import that labor without annual caps. Protectionist policies to protect US citizens from work-force competition will further degrade the US economy.

7. Unlimited H-2 visas for unskilled workers.

Every country needs a pool of unskilled labor. Without it, agriculture and construction cannot survive. Allegations that foreign unskilled workers are stealing jobs from Americans is asinine – competition is not stealing. If Americans cannot compete, so be it. If you were to ask every American to make a donation on every agricultural product they purchase, to cover the higher cost of employing Americans to pick crops versus the lower cost of employing foreign workers to do the same work, there is no doubt what the answer would be.

8. Change of Status I-140 petitions to be adjudicated in conformity with adjudication of non-immigrant visa petitions.

The USCIS has a history of granting non-immigrant visa petitions, repeatedly extending such visas and then denying I-140 change of status petitions. The argument by the USCIS that it has to be stricter in granting permanent residence than in granting non-immigrant visas is incomprehensible. From a security perspective this is an asinine argument. If a non-immigrant visa has been granted and if it has been successfully extended with more than two renewal petitions, then the USCIS is obliged to issue consistent rulings in an I-140 petition for change of status, unless there is clear and incontrovertible evidence that the initial petition was obtained fraudulently or illegally.

9. USCIS processing times to be added to validity of stay.

Delays in USCIS processing times are a major contributor to visa-holders becoming overstays. Processing times in excess of 30 days to be added to the visa duration period.

10. Undocumented, tax-paying, crime-free parents of US Citizen children born before 01/01/2021 to be granted legal status.

America is a land of values. If we grant citizenship to the children of immigrants, we should *ipso facto* grant rights to the parents of such citizens. Such parents to be accorded such rights as per clause 5 above. Children born after 01/01/2021 are deemed to have the citizenship of the biological mother and are not granted US citizenship simply because they were born in the USA.

11. Legal "Dreamers" who entered the USA legally with their parents, but who aged-out before their parents were granted

legal permanent residence or US Citizenship, to be granted legal permanent residence.

It is immoral to separate children from their parents and siblings simply because they turned 21 and aged out before their parents acquired legal permanent residence or US Citizenship.

WHAT CAN WE DO?

All too often, Americans, who know our story, have asked "what can we do to make this better?"

Here's my answer. "Stop being afraid of immigrants. And start being informed."

HINDSIGHT IS ALWAYS 20/20

With the clarity of hindsight, here's where I went wrong with our US Immigration – hopefully others will learn from my mistakes :

I left too much in the hands of my immigration attorney. I abrogated my responsibility to educate myself about the visa he was suggesting, and other visa routes that may have been available to me.

Attorneys ask for client instructions. But they need informed instructions. And because I was ignorant about what was needed, I left much of the decision-making in the hands of my attorney. He made mistakes, and I paid the price.

Don't be passive with your attorney. Make him earn his fees. Question, discuss and debate everything he's doing for you. It's your right. But know what you're talking about, before you start questioning your attorney, or he could fire you as a pain-in-the-ass.

Demand that you have final approval of every document being filed on your behalf, and check everything carefully, as if your life depends on it. And if you find something that doesn't make sense, be obstinate. I know that my I-140 RFE asked for everything. I should never have let Chris downplay the importance of this.

You will hardly ever get the USCIS to change a decision. To admit it is wrong. Or that it made a mistake. Only an appeal court can do this, and appeals take time and cost money. You cannot afford to get an adverse decision. You have to be right the first time. And if you do lose, don't appeal. You won't win. Start again with a new petition.

Read the environment. What do the numbers tell you? What is the government telling you? If the government is anti-immigration, your case becomes harder. And if there's also high US unemployment, your case becomes even harder. Admittedly, I could never have foreseen the impact of 9/11 – there could never have been a worse time to immigrate to the USA. Or a worse time to be uninformed about the immigration process.

Plan for the end-game. Your ultimate objective. Don't just think about how you're going to get INTO the USA. Plan for how you're going to STAY in the USA. My mistake is that I never knew about, or even considered, the risks in starting with a non-immigrant visa.

Be aware of the old adage : You will never see what you are not looking for!

THE MISTAKE WE DID NOT MAKE – COMING TO THE USA!

ACKNOWLEDGEMENTS

How does one acknowledge the friendship, encouragement and support of so many who played pivotal roles in a 20-year journey? Supporters in the US Military and SpecOps community cannot be revealed for security reasons. The database of friends who signed our petitions, visited our KeepTheStewartsinCharlotte website, and voted on VoxPop in favor of our Private Bill, runs to many thousands. Also, the testimonials, some sent to us for use in our petitions and some sent direct to the authorities in support of our cause. To all of you, thank you.

Bruce Stewart & Dianne Stewart
Charlotte, North Carolina
September 2021

ABOUT THE AUTHORS

Bruce and Dianne Stewart are South Africans who started their emigration to the USA in 2001 with two small children. Their journey through the United States Citizenship & Immigration Service lasted 20 years. Bruce provides advanced reading skills and intelligence training to corporate executives, business schools and various branches of the US Military. Dianne runs a successful Public Relations and Social Media Consultancy. Together, Bruce and Dianne offer a concierge relocation educational and advisory service to prospective immigrants to the USA through PathwayUSA.

For more information about US Relocation,
please see our websites at
www.PathwayUSA.co.za
www.PathwayUSA.co.uk
www.PathwayUSA.biz.tr

For availability of this book, please see
www.ScarsAndStripesBook.com